MENTAL TRAINING

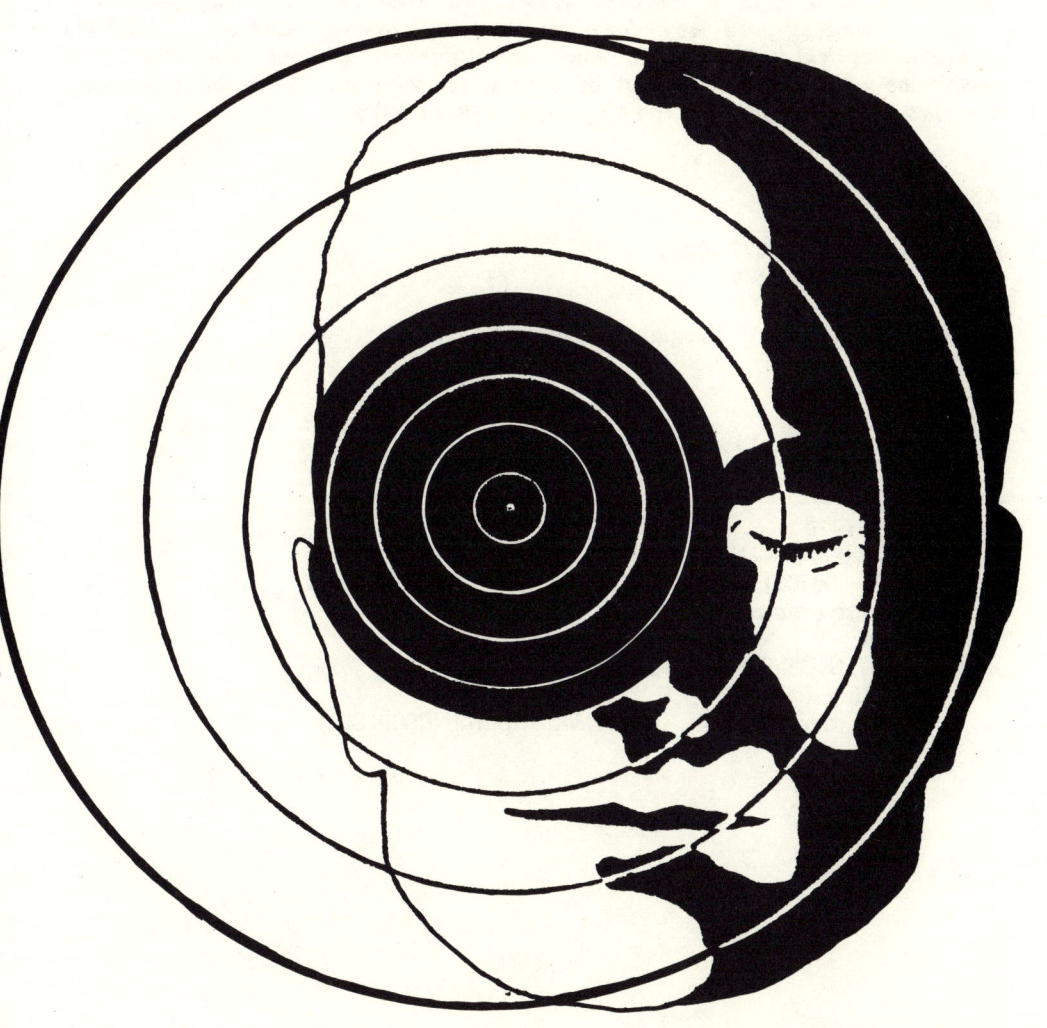

Bob Hickey

Copyright© by Bob Hickey
Copyrights 1979 and 1985

Printed in the United States of America

All rights reserved. No portion of this book may be reproduced, transmitted, transcribed, stored in a retrieval system, or translated into any language or computer language, in any form or by any means, electronic, mechanical, magnetic, optical, chemical, manual or otherwise, without the prior written permission of the author, except by a reviewer who may quote brief passages in a review or as provided in the Copyright Act of 1976.

ASCII
P.O. Box 770222
Eagle River, AK 99577-0222
Phone: (907) 688-9485

Library of Congress Cataloging in Publication Data

  Hickey, Bob
  Mental Training
  Includes bibliographical references
  Indexed
  Orig. Ed.
  Ascii 02/1979
  ISBN: 0-9603432-2-9
  LCCN: 79-067021
  Status: Active entry
  Illustrated
  PBIP SUBJECT HEADINGS:
      Shooting (00428619)
      Health and Physical Education—Sports (00001302)

Dedicated to:

You, who desire the Gold Medal
    In the Olympiad of Tomorrow.
    The future knows your name.
    I know your drudgery,
        dedication and sacrifice.
I have supplied this Modus Operandi
    That your goal may be
    Tomorrow's history.
You, who are alone, now
    Have a starting place.

                Bob Hickey

Thank you!!!

Marie Alkire, Executive Director, United States Women's International Rifle Organization, for seeing merit in this project and for editing it with welcome suggestions.

Sue Ann Sandusky, 1978 Ladies Standard Rifle Prone *World Champion*, for reading the manuscript and offering advice.

Karen Rudolph, Coach of the University of Alaska Anchorage Varsity Rifle Team, who read several drafts of the manuscript and pared the contents to the essentials.

Sharon Hickey 1976 United States Sub—Junior Champion, for considerable time spent typing the drafts and for her dedication to the *Selective Awareness Training*.

Diane Smith, 1976 Junior Rifle Champion of Scotland, whose grasp and application of *Alpha State*, made the technique meaningful.

Especially, I am indebted to *Jack Writer, 1972 Olympic Small—Bore Position Rifle Champion*, for introducing me to the concept of *mental training*.

Mike Hickey, whose financial help got the 1985 edition to the printers.

Donald L. Mellish, Chairman of the Board of the National Bank of Alaska, whose help at a key juncture in the author's life made it possible for this book to be completed. His son, Bob Mellish, (Figure 2—2 on page 32) in 1970, as a member of my junior club's shooting tour of Europe, became the first American junior to win a major class trophy in the British Small—Bore Nationals at Bisley, England.

Mary Jane Hickey, whose nearly a quarter of a century of solid support has made this whole project possible.

Bob Hickey

Contents

One	What Is Mental Training?	7
Two	Basic Mental Training	21
Three	Selective Awareness Training	40
Four	Training Plans	95
Five	Shooter's Training Diary	105
Six	Alpha State Training	144
Seven	Coach's Corner	165
Eight	Computerize Your Shooting Data Records	196
Nine	The Roots Of Mental Training	201
	Appendices	
	A. Sources Of Works Cited	252
	B. Coaching Method: Gun Holding	254
	C. Mike's Diary	255
	Index	263

Special Note to the Reader

This book is written to the beginning shooter. To me, a beginning shooter is one who has advanced beyond the introduction to marksmanship. That person will probably be someone who has had a year, to a year and a half or more, of shooting experience on a high school rifle team. It is also the person who joins a rifle club, intending to take up the sport of competitive shooting, but then finds that he wants something more than the club can offer him in the way of learning the finer points of winning in competition. In some cases, the rifle coach may not be very experience in competitive rifle shooting. This book is especially directed toward those newcomers to competitive shooting who have to "*Go it alone.*" It might be that you have just finished shooting in the JC's BB Gun Championships and now want to get more deeply involved in the shooting sports. If so, this book is designed to put you on the right path.

The mind is the *First Frontier* we should explore as we seek ways to improve our level of shooting skill. Come to know it, understand it, and cultivate it and you will know often, the "*Thrill of Victory.*" This book is your map into that *First Frontier*. Use it to develop your own mental trails. In order to do so effectively, follow the book's advise and record all observations of what you discover about yourself as you train for personal victory.

<u>Mental Training</u> will be of value to the recreational shooter, opening up new vistas of improved self performance. Often the recreational shooter travels in a world which does not include the "super master" or the *World Champion* shooter. In this book, I have tried to translate some of the techniques used by *World Champions* into concrete training programs which will assist the uninitiated in traveling paths leading to mental toughness and a positive self image.

CHAPTER 1
What Is *Mental Training?*

This book is my effort to make available to the beginning shooter and the more established recreational or club shooter, those "mental secrets" of world class American shooters.

If there is one secret to *Mental Training*, it is that to win consistently, you must truly know yourself. As Leonardo da Vinci (1451–1519), pointed out:

if you wish thoroughly to know the parts of man, anatomically, you — or your eye — require to see it from different aspects, considering it from below and from above and from it's sides, turning it about and seeking the origin of each member.

This book offers coaches a different method of presenting marksmanship training to beginning shooters. The training methods currently in use in most American junior shooting clubs are presented in the same way as they have for more than half a century. It is now time for a change! The new NRA shooting program is a big step in the right direction. But, for juniors and coaches to benefit from it, there must be an understanding of how mental preparation can be a positive part of the effort to create good marksmen. This comes about when the junior shooter learns to think positively about himself or herself right from the start of his or her association with a shooting club. This book is not a substitute for the NRA Basic Marksmanship Program. It is, rather, an in depth treatment of the mental training aspect of competitive shooting. This book will provide you with the tools to set up a mental training program for yourself. If you are a coach, this book will provide you with the insight necessary to provide your shooters with a well rounded mental training program.

Many clubs have coaches who are searching for new and better techniques for training their club members. This book offers, in one place, annotated sources of shooting information, not other where available. In addition, there are ideas presented in this book which will allow you coaches to expand your coaching knowledge easily and simply. This is a book for the future. We Americans are fortunate in that a number of events have come together to make it possible for us to take a big leap forward in marksmanship coaching at this time. We live in a country where technology is available in a price range which makes it possible for a great number of Americans to be able to afford inexpensive computers. The intelligent use of computers will enable the club coach to better serve the members of his team. But, more than any thing else, the shooter has to be directed in establishing a firm mental training technique.

Knowledgeable international coaches recognize that, after learning the skills basic to all shooting performance, the further development of the marksman to world class medal winning levels is dependent principally on his acquiring the mental attitude and mental toughness of the champion. Once the basics are learned, about 90% of the individual's shooting preparation time should be devoted to mental training.

The old training methods we coaches are used to employing in our junior club program often hinders our students ever learning or even being exposed to the concepts of *Mental Training*. Why? First of all, our club training, more likely than not, is based on a "Master" lecture. The student then eventually practices what has been told to him in the lecture. Sometimes he may also be shown a demonstration of shooting positions. I know! I was given just such training when I went to my first rifle club meeting in 1950. Curiously, such training still follows the same pattern in clubs today. Hold on there, you say! Isn't that the right way? It is a way, not necessarily the right way! It is the college professor way. On the other hand, many of the most successful coaches of American junior rifle clubs do not do it that way. It is only the most insecure of our coaches and those who are college educated who are found doing it this way. But, unfortunately, these coaches are the biggest majority. This book is provided to this majority so that they may find in one place the help that most seek.

Mental Training — Chapter 1

In my more than thirty years of coaching, I have met and talked with hundreds of such coaches. I was such a college professor type of coach myself. If I can change to a better way, any professorial type coach can change. Most of the coaches I met were just like me. They too, were continually searching and open to new and better coaching ideas. Like me, most were hampered through the lack of a sources of good solid information on coaching at the club level. After teaching the NRA Basic Marksmanship Course, where next did one go for information on the nitty-gritty of club coaching? We coaches of that era read all of the marksmanship articles dealing with shooting. But, the articles never seemed to deal with matters in the depth needed for the club coach. This book remedies that.

The articles on marksmanship never really told us what we were doing wrong. For example, through out student practice, isn't the coach right along side, or in back with a spotting scope, correcting the shooter's mistakes and telling him or her which directions to move the sights on the gun? Yes. That is a coach oriented program. That type of coaching inhibits the development of mental training in shooters subjected to "coaching" of this nature. Shooters trained in these types of local club programs, and they are the vast majority, thus get no training in self-analysis of their shooting progress. Shooters acquire true world class skills only after they have broken from the dependence on someone else which such coaching engenders in them. Mental toughness must be implanted in new shooters right from the start of their training. Having read this paragraph, most of you who coach shooters have probably already started to re-evaluate your coaching. See what a little knowledge will do for you. Can you imagine what will happen when the great majority of American junior shooters are no longer developed as mental pygmies, but are taught to think like champions right from the start of their shooting training in our clubs?

So, just how did I come to develop this program of mental training. It is really more that just a mental training program. It is, more than anything else, a new way to teach marksmanship. It came about as a result of my doing a complete rethinking of the training techniques used in marksmanship training. Being isolated

© Bob Hickey

from the mainstream of American shooting, I have had to rely more on reading reports of shooting research and related matters than my counterparts in the "lower 48," as we Alaskans refer to the continentally contiguous United States. My concept of *Mental Training* was vague and unformed until conversations with Jack Writer in 1971.

At that time, Writer, a silver medalist in the 1968 Olympic Games in 3-position shooting, came to Alaska to put on a series of United States Advanced Marksmanship Unit International Shooting Clinics. Writer went on to win the gold medal at the 1972 Olympics. I first met Jack Writer in the early 1960's when I was a Director of the Illinois State Rifle Association and in charge of junior activities for the State Association. In that capacity, I established the Illinois All-State Junior Rifle Team. The top ten juniors from the State shoulder-to-shoulder Junior Rifle Tournament, were selected to this team and taken to various rifle matches, such as the Ohio State Indoor Team Matches, the Kansas State University Turkey Shoot, the National NRA Open Rifle Sectional Championship at Alton, Illinois and the United States Smallbore Rifle Championships at Camp Perry, Ohio.

In preparing for those Nationals at Camp Perry, Ohio, the team members were gathered together for team training sessions at the Lincoln Sportsmen's Club in Lincoln, Illinois. During Writer's shooting clinics in Alaska, he referred to some of the training he underwent as a member of my Illinois All-State team, when he told our young Alaskan shooters: "We had to shoot one hundred shots in the standing position before we could practice any other position each day." In response to how much he practiced now, Writer pointed out that he may shoot 200 shots standing in a practice session. But, more to the point, he described how he practiced for the 1968 Olympic Games.

Writer told the juniors that he spent hundreds of hours mentally firing the Olympic course of fire. He described doing this mental rehearsal while watching TV and at other times. In this mental practice, Writer would consider the many different situations that might arise as a result of being at a particular place within his ten shots series. Out of this, I developed the Mental Training Cards

© Bob Hickey

Mental Training   Chapter 1

in an attempt to show beginning shooters how to practice this type of mental rehearsal. In other words, new shooters must first learn how to conceptualize their shooting performance. We Americans are essentially a "hands-on" society. We are a people who are games oriented. Working with these cards has proven very helpful for new shooters. I think you will find them valuable as a tool of rehearsing shooting tactics.

I also learned from Writer that he kept track of his shooting performance in a way I had not thought about before. Writer happened to mention that he was in the process of attempting to <u>eliminate</u> the "eights" from his standing position when firing at 50 meters. I later received a postcard from Jack just after he had won the Olympic Gold Medal in the Smallbore Three-Position event at the 1972 Olympics. On that postcard, Jack mentioned that he had fired only nines and tens for a score of 381 standing in Munich. From Writer's concept, I developed the <u>Target Analysis Chart</u> to teach my young shooters to focus their minds on attempting to eliminate "bad" shots.

It was while attending the United States Women's International Rifle Organization's (USWIRO) *Schiessportschule* II, in June of 1978, that I finally became aware of the very important use this chart could be put to for teaching *goal setting*. I am indebted to Dr. William Cole, Ed. D., of the EDGE Institute for this insight.

Shooters, all of the techniques shown in this book are designed with the object of training your mind so that you will be lead naturally to the proper reflexive reactions for each shot you shoot, guided by your subconscious, with an active blocking out of your conscious. That is a long and involved way of saying that these techniques are designed with the <u>idea of training you to enter Alpha State for the time needed to fire each shot</u>.

Just what is Alpha State? Colonel Bill Pullum, in USWIRO's *Schiessportschule Dialogues I*, told us "<u>Alpha is the state in which you are at your maximum concentration</u>. Beta State, like we're in now, conversing, shows up on an oscilloscope as little fast moving jagged lines." Pullum is speaking about the electrical output of the brain as indicated on an instrument used to record alternating current wave forms. These waves are given off by the brain

© Bob Hickey

constantly at a rate of about 8 to 13 cycles per second. These alpha waves are found throughout the brain, and they can be identified by the part of the brain from which they emanate.

How can a learned ability to control Alpha help shooters? In a report of one research investigation into control of Alpha, Dr. Barbara B. Brown, in *Stress And The Art Of Biofeedback* reported:

> *The investigators concluded that alpha training is useless for anxiety, that training to produce alpha simply may assist subjects in learning how to ignore otherwise distracting influences which would account for the reports that increased alpha activity is accompanied by calm, tranquil, and peaceful states. Which, of course, is one chief objective of alpha training. By learning to turn the attention inward, you naturally decrease the visual input of anxiety-related information.*

Each of the techniques and forms to be found in this book has been designed to help lead you to an inner awareness of your inner self. Each has been devised to help you to learn how to produce more Alpha waves. In other words, *Mental Training* is a very comprehensive plan designed to lead you into developing an awareness of your inner-self, that *Little Guy Inside*. This is a prerequisite to establishing inner control of your goals.

Much of the literature about shooting techniques which I've read has been written by professional coaches talking to elite shooters. Both have common reference points. When a coach tells a college All-American to learn to be flexible in modification of a shooter devised training plan, both know what is being talked about and how to go about that modification. Since the new shooter most definitely does not know how to do this, Chapter Five, titled *Training Plans* will help. For example, the Home Time Schedule Plan has a section called "What I Really Did At This Time," which will help you to see how to go about the "modification" of your own training plan. It is that thing we call:

FEEDBACK

© Bob Hickey

Mental Training Chapter 1

You'll be reading that word, *Feedback*, quite a bit in this book. "*Feedback*," according to *Webster's Third New International Dictionary*, means "*the return to the input of a part of the output of a system.*" For example, a premium is paid to you for each time you successfully maintain your rifle sights in harmony with the target. This premium is a "bulls—eye" worth ten points. Your system is the positioning of your body in such a way as to reduce the movement of your rifle so as to attain your desired result time after time. As part of your "system," you need to ascertain whether your desired results are being attained. You do this by glancing through the spotting scope for your *Feedback*. You have to put your body into the same position each time. Inventory and *mentally feel* your muscles. What you learn from their response to your mental stimulation of them will be *feedback*. In the *Selective Awareness Training*, you'll notice a very real inward turning of your mind.

Mental Training is sometimes thought of as a "catch—all" phrase used to refer to the *Basic Feedback Loop*. As with all feedback activity, shooting performance can be precisely measured. The target has a series of measured rings radiating from the center of the bull. Shots fired at such targets are measured to determine their proximity to the center ring of the target. Thus, the shot's location can be precisely determined.

The shooter has a spotting scope which displays the results of his shooting to him.

When the shooter sees that information, he recognizes the result and then puts that information together with information about the nature of the let—off of the shot and the activity of any wind or cloud which may have contributed to the shot placement on the target.

The shooter then reacts to the displayed information. At this point, he is in communication with his *little guy inside*. He reacts by making a determination as to whether or not he has achieved his *individual shot goal*.

© Bob Hickey

Mental Training

MEASUREMENT
OF
ACTIVITY

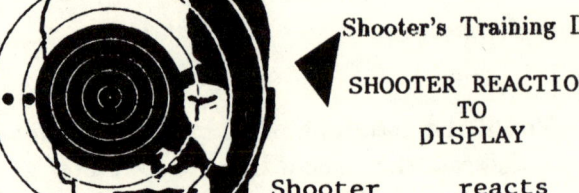

Shooter's Training Diary

SHOOTER REACTION
TO
DISPLAY

The target bull has a measurable series of rings radiating from the center enabling the shot's location to be precisely established.

Shooter reacts by recognizing whether he has achieved his goal for that shot. Then he tells his LITTLE GUY INSIDE:

"That's like me!" for a good shot.
OR
"That's not like me!" for a bad shot.

DISPLAY
OF
INFORMATION

Spotting scope displays that information.

SHOOTER
RECOGNITION
OF THAT
INFORMATION

Shooter sees target with shot placement.

Figure 1-1

BASIC FEEDBACK LOOP

Throughout this book, you will be shown how to set goals. The key idea concerning a goal is MAKE IT MEASURABLE. You have to have some way of determining whether or not you reach your goal. You do this through feedback. Do not set goals which you cannot measure. You need feedback of your efforts to meet your goal. What you want for your *Little Guy Inside* is: *positive feedback*. Remember though, You have to find out where you are, before you can plot a way out of the doldrums of non-directed performance stagnation. Some very fine shooters fire in winter gallery leagues, season after season, with not much difference in their scores from one match to another. But they always anticipate getting "a hot night." Sometimes they experience difficulties with their scores not meeting their vague "wishes." Inside themselves, they experience a dreadful night of inner humiliation. At the same time, they put forth a bold or humorous face to their friends.

You can spare yourself this inner, secret frustration by setting reasonable goals. The goals should be firmly based on your practice

© Bob Hickey

and training feedback, with special emphasis on your duel matches results. You must learn to tell the difference between reality and the fantasy of wishful thinking, not consistent with your level of ability. Used as I show you, in *Mental Training*, your diary becomes your own personal measuring stick.

Because our coaching techniques have not kept up with modern teaching techniques, I offer coaches a different method of presenting marksmanship training to beginning shooters. I had to look at my own training methods, which for years have been as I described above with little deviation! After all, I thought, it had produced Writer, Murdock, Wigger, Bassham, Anderson and a whole multitude of others. Gary Anderson, writing in *Gun Week* in the September 26, 1969 issue, gave me the first clue that there might be a different way of training shooters. He described the training techniques of Armin Klingner, coach of a West German Junior Shooting Club. I have designed training techniques and programs which can be adapted to our American junior rifle clubs. I have accepted and developed three of the four elements of Klingner's method, as described by Anderson:

Dry Firing
Gun Holding
Mental Training

I have been talking about a coaching method which differs from the old fashioned one. I think it is about time to give you an example of just how the new differs from the old. In *Mental Training*, you are shown just how to teach the various parts of marksmanship training. These are the parts which are often given merely lip service in many club programs. However, these same parts are universally acknowledged as being vital to good shooting. For our example we will look at how a coach teaches gun holding practice. the first thing you notice about this method is the first great departure from the old teaching methods. The coach sits facing the guns of the shooters!

The first thing the coach does is to personally remove, or collect, all bolts from rifles. Next, have the shooters assume the shooting position so that all are in a semi—circle facing the wall

© Bob Hickey

where aiming circle will be placed. Aiming circles are place on 3" by 5" note cards. The aiming circles should not be more than half a pencil eraser in diameter. The shooters should be place so that the front sight is between 10 and 15 feet from the aiming circles. Now, put aiming circles on the wall. Then, have a helper or, better still have the shooters paired up, and have the partner adjust the aiming circles so the circle is inside the natural point of aim of the shooter. Now, this is where the biggest change comes for most coaches. Seat yourself on a chair facing the shooters and in front of the aiming circles. Some adjustment of the aiming circles may be necessary. Why sit in front of shooters' guns? Goes against the grain does it? Try it! You will find that you will notice things which might go undetected in the normal behind the shooter coaching you normally do. This is not training to be taken lightly. Remember, you *personally remove or collect the bolt from the rifles and place blocks in the pistols!* Next, allow 30 minutes for the *gun holding practice.* Finally, have the shooters record the sight pattern movement on the Sight Pattern Chart, see Figure 2-2 on page 38. The focus of the shooter's effort here should be to identify the sight pattern which occurs just as the shooter mentally 'fires' the shot.

GUN HOLDING COACHING METHOD

PURPOSE:

    1. To teach shooters how to identify their sight patterns.
    2. To enable the coach to get in front of the shooters and identify and correct position irregularities.
    3. To guide the shooter into accepting the idea of remaining in position for an extended period of time without taking a break.

METHOD:

    1. Place your chair in front of a wall.
    2. Line up the shooting mats of the shooters about 8

to 10 feet in front of your chair, in a semi-circle, facing toward you.
3. Place the rifles on the mats, REMOVING ALL BOLTS.
4. Have each shooter draw a circle about the size of a pencil eraser and blacken it in, on either a 3" x 5" paper card or on the back of a target.
5. Have the shooters assume the shooting position.
6. Put the aiming circles on the wall.
7. Have a helper or a partner adjust the aiming circles so the circle is in the point of natural aim of the shooter.
8. Now have each shooter complete a portion of the *Sight Pattern Chart* as explained in Chapter Two.
9. Allow 30 minutes for this gun holding practice.

WHAT IS THIS MENTAL TRAINING?

Basically, *Mental Training is a formal way of learning to think about performance*, at home as well as on the firing line.

Done properly, that part of the training done at home, can be the most profitable to the shooter. At home, those situations likely, or even unlikely to occur on the firing line, can be thought about and plans or alternative actions for dealing with them, can be made. The home sessions provide a very valuable resource for the shooter, since the stress and concern about a locked-in time frame for completing the match, or practice relay, do not intrude on the shooter's considerations of possible solutions.

Mental Training is day-dreaming in an organized way about how the shooter will act in future tournaments. It is a pre-shooting probe. It is the thought-out rehearsal of various things the shooter considers as likely to happen or occur in the course of his matches. In other words, *Mental Training* is the thinking work done by shooters before they go to the rifle range. You do not expect to learn a long poem assigned in school only during that one hour of class time. You know it must be studied at home.

© Bob Hickey

Mental Training   What Is *Mental Training?*

    It is the purpose of these *Mental Training* techniques to channel the shooter's attitude toward himself and his shooting, into an attitude of alert self-awareness and reflexive analysis of his self-performance. Suggested individual training plans have been included as a special chapter. Each shooter who accepts the idea of mental training, must also accept primary responsibility for his own personal development. If you have a coach who is knowledgeable about *Mental Training*, you may want to share the discoveries, which you will uncover about yourself, with him. But remember, it is you, and not your coach, who must develop your mental discipline. It is you, not your parents or your wife, who must plan your training schedule and then stick to it. Welcome advice, but be guided by your own counsel.

    When people describe their mental insights, there is frequently a communication problem. To say that you should *rehearse the shot*, will mean different things to you at the various levels of your shooting proficiency. The chapter titled *Mental Training Cards* will help you to learn how to rehearse your shots. The *Mental Training Cards* will enable you to learn to verbalize the procedure you go through to fire your shots. Then start to rehearse your record shots in both practice and in your matches. The results will astound you!

    Each of you has a "*Little Guy Inside*" who resides in your mind. He's the one who builds you up when you do something well. He's also the one who really rakes you over the coals when you don't measure up to your expectations. *Mental Training* is a way of helping that *Little Guy* in your mind take over and help you get the kind of shots you want. So, rehearse well, and give him a very definite idea of the kind of shot you want.

    Mental Training is often thought of as a process of developing a positive attitude toward the achievement of your goals. What is a positive attitude? That's when you tell your *Little Guy* inside you: *I'm going to get a really solid score today!* This is all well and good, until you are on the firing line for your first record shot in the Final Try-outs for the U.S. Olympic Rifle Team in Phoenix, Arizona. It is 114 degrees Fahrenheit, on the shady side of your firing point. Then you suddenly become aware that the range flags at the 10 meter line are all standing out in a different direction than the flags at the 40 meter line; the mirage is boiling and the dust from the bullet impact is bellowing straight up and away from you. You can't turn your target back to the sighter, so you shoot that first shot and it's a seven. You make a sight adjustment, check the conditions, still thinking positively; fire the next shot, and it's an eight out the other side. An edge of panic begins to creep into your consciousness. You feel a chink being worn in your positive attitude.

What do you have to fall back on? I suggest, that instead of merely developing a super positive attitude about your shooting, that you, rather, work to acquire an objective attitude about your shooting performance. This way, when you shoot a bad shot, you can be objective about it. You can say to yourself, to your *Little Guy Inside*, "That's not like me." You can develop objectivity through this *Mental Training* program. This book on mental training gives you the foundation of such a program. It will give you the background leading to the control needed to place yourself in alpha state.

This program of *Mental Training* places heavy emphasis on programs of early and continual exposure to, and practice of, internalizing and focusing inward the awareness of the shooter. It is important that the shooter become adept at vocalization of that internalization because research has demonstrated that there is a persistent amount of alpha in the type of attention which is direct to internal stimuli. It is to show the beginning shooter and the recreational club shooter how to take advantage of this, that *Mental Training* was written.

The *Coach's Corner*, Chapter 8, shows coaches how to bring this program of *Mental Training* to the members of their shooting clubs. If you have a coaching record spanning twenty years or more, can you learn anything from *Mental Training*? Yes! First of all, a good coach is a person who never stops learning. When you see a coach who knows it all, you have met a mental pygmy. He'll always wonder how some juniors who shoot for less "knowledgeable" coaches, beat his kids. Such a coach becomes a ready alibier.

Are you such a coach? You do not have to be! Are you a person new to the coaching ranks? Are you still trying to put together a program of marksmanship training for a group of your team members who really want to learn to become good shooters? Then *Mental Training* is for you!

Back to the first idea. As a coach, you must train yourself to be always inquisitive. How do you do this? Attend several matches a year as an OBSERVER! Don't offer to help with the match! When you help at a match, you tend to become task oriented. You miss both the big picture, and the important details. Get yourself a three–ring notebook to record notes of what you observe. It is not a good idea to go to the match without any advance preparation. Know why you are going and then take along something in which to write down what you notice. It is a good blessing to possess a fine retentive memory, but you want to train yourself to become a disciplined observer. You do this by learning to record, in writing, what you notice in a systematic manner. When you do this, you will begin to notice much more. This is your *Reticular Activating System* at work for you. You will find out more about this in Chapter 3, *Selective Awareness Training*. You will hear some junior coaches say "I don't have time to do this! I'm too busy just running my junior program!" If you are one of these, watch out, you are in a dead–end rut!

Training techniques -- any new advances since you learned to shoot? Bound to be some, if you learned to shoot in the 1960's or before. Find yourself a "super master" or maybe even a *World Champion* to observe, if you can. America has many at the present time, and they attend a lot of rifle matches in all parts of the country, so this task should be easy. Ask around and see which match is a 'biggy' and more than likely to attract some of the "big name" shooters.

Motivational techniques -- here you want to learn what other junior coaches use as motivational techniques. Listen to the talk between a coach and his young charges. This will help you gain insight into the ways juniors interact with their coaches. For a coach, this too, is *Mental Training!*

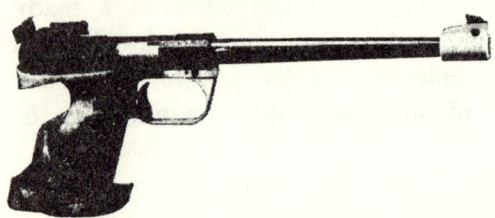

© Bob Hickey

CHAPTER 2

Basic Mental Training

No amount of mental training will help you until both you and your *Little Guy Inside* know what kind of a hold you expect. When you start to learn to shoot, your "hold" may appear to be as formless and uncontrollable as a jumping bean. But, you know others have learned to control their hold. What is the secret of "hold" control? The secret is "hard work."

What is this thing called "hold?" Hold is your ability to hold your rifle so that the sights remain on your target during the act of shooting. The act of holding the rifle sights on the target during a period of time is a "learned" act. It is something which can be practiced. The shooter who practices his "hold" only when he comes to the range will find it hard to see real improvements in his "hold" from one practice to the next. The reason: When you go to the range, it is a very active time for you. There are people who will be watching you and you will be watching and visiting with people. There will be your targets to set up and your equipment to get ready. Then, as you fire your shots, there will be the recoil and disturbance of your "hold" as the shot is fired. All of these are factors which will act against you and your being able to really notice things about your hold. You need to work on just holding your sights on a target. There is very little you can do about the range distractions.

But, you can learn to reduce your hold by working on it as "homework." What is it you want to do in this "homework?" Well, it may seem obvious, but you want to change your "hold" from having that target appear to be a jumping bean, to having it remain located in your front sight when you want it to be there.

Mental Training Basic Mental Training

GUN HOLDING HOMEWORK

1. Suggestion: Combine this homework assignment with the watching of your favorite television program.

2. Prepare a small 3" x 5" piece of paper.

3. Draw a small circle on it, and blacken in the circle. The circle can be about the size of a pencil eraser. If the circle fills too much of the front sight, redraw the circle and make it smaller.

4. Tape the paper in the upper left or right corner of your TV set. The circle should look to you to be the same as a bull on your target when viewed through the sights of your rifle or pistol.

5. Set yourself up so that you are about 5 feet or more, away from the TV set.

6. With the bolt removed from your rifle, or the pistol uncocked, assume the position you want to practice your hold in. Be certain the circle you have drawn really looks the same as it does at 50 feet.

7. The remain in position during your TV program. Try to remain in position all the time, even while you are watching the program or the commercials.

8. While watching the program, try to keep the rifle stock up to your face, or your eye looking over the pistol sights.

9. While in position, select times to go through the process of shooting a shot within your Individual Shot Goal. Try to ignore the program and try to keep the bull in your

© Bob Hickey

Mental Training   Chapter 2

sights.

10. Observe what kind of pattern the front sight makes as it moves across the bull.

11. Record the type of pattern the front sight makes just before you pretend to "fire" the shot. Use the Sight Pattern Chart shown in this chapter.

12. Remember, you are an observer of the sight pattern. Do not make the mistake of trying to "force" your sights into a particular pattern.

You will hear some people speak of "dry-firing." What you are doing in the preceding "homework," is not the same thing. For one thing, you have your rifle bolt removed, or your pistol uncocked, so you cannot do any "dry-firing."

Dry-firing is the act of putting an empty cartridge case in the chamber, closing the bolt on it, and then applying pressure to the trigger in such a manner that the rifle or pistol "fires" on that "empty cartridge."

Gun-holding is the act of holding the gun in shooting position for extended periods of time, attempting to keep the sights and target in perfect alignment.

"Gun Holding" and "Dry-Firing" have different purposes.

GUN HOLDING PURPOSE:

To learn to hold the sights on the target bull.

DRY-FIRING PURPOSE:

To learn to execute a trigger release so that the sights remain on the target bull during and after the trigger "fires."

© Bob Hickey

Dry-firing is also done at home to learn trigger release skills. It is also done on the range to settle the body in position before shooting. As you begin this program of *Mental Training*, try to keep the gun holding and the dry-firing exercises separate. In other words, during the first half hour of your favorite TV show, you could practice your gun holding exercises, plotting your sight patterns on your Sight Pattern Chart. Then, during the second half-hour of the program, practice your dry-firing techniques. Don't be misled into thinking that these should be combined as you begin this *Mental Training* program. Understand the purpose for which you do each exercise.

In the gun holding exercise, you need to learn the type and nature of your hold. There are many shooters who, even after many years of shooting, do not know much about the nature of their "hold" in each of their shooting positions. Learning this is a full-time job at the beginning. So is the skill of learning to release the trigger without disturbing your sight hold pattern. You need to do both gun holding and dry-firing practice, both with full attention but separately.

MENTAL REHEARSAL

In the beginning of your use of *Mental Training*, you will have to mentally work hard to recall to mind the processes by which you shot your "ten." As you proceed through this phase of your *Mental Training* development, you may notice that you will have to spend less time recounting over in your mind the various procedures you used to "get" your "ten." Eventually, you want to work toward the point of non-verbalized rehearsal. What you are seeking is that vague, deeply subconscious, "feeling" of satisfaction, which comes to you when you know that a shot is good "all-the-way," and your spotting scope feeds back the confirmation that indeed it was a good solid "ten," or a shot which was deep within your own personal shot goal aim.

Colonel Bill Pullum, co-author of *Position Shooting* and the premier U.S. Olympic and World Champion rifle coach, described this process in the United States Women's International Rifle

Mental Training Chapter 2

Organization's book titled *Schiessportschule Dialogues* I:

> *Now, I'm going to commit a little heresy here. I'm sure that most of you have been told all through your shooting career that you must do the same thing in training that you do in competition. Right? Wrong! You can't do the same thing in training you do in competition. No way. Now, let's back up. I'm giving you my ideas in order to stimulate your thought. You don't have to accept my ideas. Let me explain why I think you don't do the same thing in training you do in competition. In training you are trying to develop the motor muscles, the techniques, the pattern of hold, and your subconscious to the point that it does the work for you. When you get to a competition, you are not doing these things in the same way. In competition, you have adrenaline running; each shot is for record. Thus it is unlike training in which you may shoot a bad shot over, maybe a number of times, conducting experiments on many things, including your positions. You work out a system for shooting in competition while training for competitions. In competition there is no longer a way to work it out.*
>
> *In training you are training your subconscious and muscle memory groups. The subconscious is what makes your score for you. It is the difference between the good shooter and the mediocre shooter. In your day–in, day–out training program, the repetition you do – the time after time that you bring the rifle up, aim, shoot the shot, be it good, bad or indifferent – shooting it over again if it's a bad one, repeating it, repeating it until you have it right, until the muscle group that controls the exercise learns it thoroughly – is the factor that enables you to learn to shoot well. Every shot you shoot in practice is accompanied by your thoughts on the mechanics, the*

techniques. When you get to a competition, if you have to think about your techniques, your position, you're not a shooter but a mechanic. You better be thinking about outside influences and let your subconscious take over. It will do the job for you.

How often has this happened to you? You're shooting a full course. You are shooting well — you're up to about ten shots and you have the best score going you have ever shot. You've got (Lanny) Bassham (1972 Olympic Gold Medalist) beat, you've got Margaret (Murdock) (1972 Olympic Silver Medalist) beat, all you have to do is get through these next shots. What do you do? You start being over-cautious, over-controlling. You take away the thing that got you there — your subconscious. You take your shooting over, start controlling the **Little Guy Inside** yourself and you blow it. This is known as **choking**. It really isn't. It's poor thinking. The thing that got your there is having trained your motor muscle mechanisms to get you where you wanted to go.

Let's do a simple little motor exercise here. I want you to draw a little square with your finger in the air. Everybody do it. Keep drawing, a square, not a circle. Keep drawing. ----- Okay, stop. When you first started to draw this square you were doing an exercise that was unnatural to you, because you hadn't done it before. When you first started to draw that square, you were concentrating on making that square, on making the corners exact. The longer you went along, the less you had to concentrate, then it became so easy you didn't have to think about it at all and yet you were doing it. It's the same as walking. You don't think how to walk, but once you did have to think about it when you were learning to walk for the first time. I'm trying to illustrate the difference between conscious and subconscious control

Mental Training   Chapter 2

of the muscles to shoot.

What causes all this to take place? Medical science has recognized for a long time that the cerebrum is the most important part of the brain, because this is what gives man the ability to think and to reason, differentiating him from the rest of the animal world. Lower animals don't have this ability, yet they have what we call instinct. A rabbit is uncanny in his ability to weave and run and elude a pack of hounds, yet we know the rabbit cannot think or cannot reason. His subconscious is the part of his brain that takes over his motor movements and gives him the ability to outwit the hounds. Medical science doesn't know how the subconscious works; they only know that it does.

So going back to the square, first you consciously drew it, then your subconscious took over and you were thinking probably verbally of something else. The exact same thing applies to shooting. In your training program, you are training your subconscious as well as your muscles to perform the act of shooting. Your muscles, controlled by your subconscious, perform as a conditioned reflex. Because of training, a conscious thought is not needed to activate the shooting muscles. The trigger finger performs on reflex conditioning by the subconscious. You know that when you think about shooting a shot, it's always a bad one. When you think, "Now is the time to get it," you are behind it. It's gone. You're probably low man on the range with a six. You let it get by because you thought about it. You must train yourself to allow it to operate, keeping your conscious mind on the external influences like the win, sight picture, etc.

Each of us is influenced by factors of our mind. Everything that happens to you is stored in your mind. Dr. Bill Cole, EDGE

Institute, identifies and explains the integration of the areas influencing us as follows:

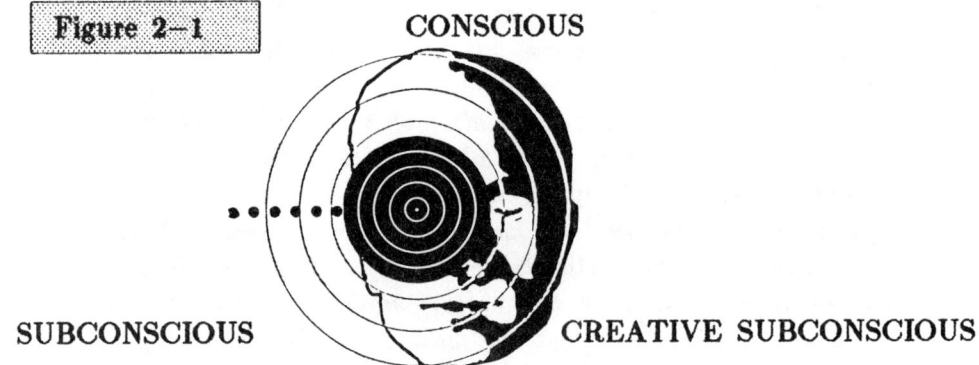

Figure 2-1

CONSCIOUS

SUBCONSCIOUS

CREATIVE SUBCONSCIOUS

In the conscious process, you "perceive" or acquire, much information which is fed into your brain by sensory pathways. Past experiences are integrated with this new information to see if it is redundant or can be related to previously acquired information. This new data provides the basis for new decisions based on our needs and goals. So we can say that the conscious is always "aware," it is the dictator of our actions. When it is alert and acting, it is in very definite control.

We also have a "subconscious." It stores information, sort of like a miniature computer with an unlimited capacity. It "remembers" better and more accurately than the conscious and helps the conscious to recall things. But once the conscious becomes aware or focused on a thing, the subconscious is blocked out. So we need to train our conscious to not interfere with a task which our subconscious can perform much better, such as the learned effort to fire a shot.

You also have what is known as a "creative subconscious." It helps you to maintain the "reality" of "you." Each of us has a perception of the "real me." This "real me" is the way we think of ourselves. That "real me" is the actor brought out for public display. For example, if you think of yourself as "shy," then that is the "real you." But you can change the "truth" of what you are by changing that inner awareness. What you do is let your

Mental Training   Chapter 2

subconscious know that you are outgoing. You go about effecting this change by resolving to say "Hi!" to three people a day for a week, then five people a week. What you are doing is changing the "truth" as perceived by your subconscious. We are going to train our creative subconscious with our Mental Training Cards to accept the idea that we are "good shooters" who think through our shooting tactics. Our creative subconscious knows that we plan and carry out our shooting tactics because he sees us using our *Mental Training* cards. Use your *Mental Training* Cards to help you to learn how to rehearse your shots. As Colonel Pullum pointed out, again in *Schiessportschule Dialogues* I:

> *A very successful training method and a very successful method of overcoming match pressure, is through this visualization of exactly what you want to do. Visualize yourself standing on the firing line with a firearm in your hand, standing outside your body, watching yourself. You have a good position, are squeezing the trigger, watching the recoil, watching the firearm settle back down, seeing the hold come right back into the middle of the target. You'd be surprised how often it does. Don't interfere with anything else, like technique. All you are doing is looking and imagining where you want the shot to go. Somehow, we don't know how, the subconscious, if you train it properly, will take over and produce a ten.*

So start to rehearse your record shots in both practice and in your matches. This is another little secret way of helping that *Little Guy* in your mind take over and get you the kind of shot you want. So rehearse well and give him a very definite idea of the shot you want. This is what we call the tactics of shooting. The *Mental Training* Cards are designed to teach the tactics of shooting. They are especially designed for those shooters who want to tune-up their minds.

These *Mental Training* cards are designed to aid the novice shooter take the first steps at learning how to do that secret of the champions: *Mental Training*. As human beings, we cannot leave our minds at home when we step onto the firing range to practice or shoot a match. Unfortunately, many shooters never use their minds to rehearse their shooting when they are not on the firing line. Some shooters never become more than "trigger pullers" because they never think about their shooting and how they will shoot their practice rounds or rehearse what might occur during a match. With these cards, you can begin to train your mind to explore the possibilities of what might happen during the firing of a match. For example, with these cards, you learn to set a goal. Then you rehearse the mental thoughts you will have as you proceed toward that goal. For example, you set a goal of 99 out of a 100. Somewhere in your course of fire, you turn over a "nine." Consider what your feelings are. How will you get your mind back in order? With enough rehearsals, you will find that a match will no longer hold terrors for you. You will begin to feel confident that you have done your homework.

How To Use These *Mental Training* Cards:

1. Select the course of fire for which you want to mentally train.

   Our Example: International Gallery Rifle Set
   (Suppose you have a problem getting above 98.)

2. Take eleven cards, divided thus: 10 cards with scores of 10 and 1 card with the score of 9.

3. Shuffle the eleven cards so that you do not know where the nine is.

4. Take out one card. Do not look at it.

5. Lay out the cards in the shape of the air rifle target. Be certain that the target without the shot hole in it faces up.

Mental Training   Chapter 2

6. Focus your eyes on the target you intend to "shoot" first.

7. Pretend you are in the standing position. Mentally rehearse everything you will have to do in order to get a "ten," concentrate very hard to try to keep everything else from entering your mind and distracting you.

8. Mentally fire your shot and remember to follow through.

9. Turn the card over and see what your shot is. Think of it as leaning over to glance through your spotting scope.

10. Mentally rehearse the thoughts you would have as you prepare for your next shot.

11. Proceed through the rest of your "string" in the same way.

12. Fill out the Mental Training Cards Feedback Chart.

See Figures 2-4, 2-5, 2-6 and 2-7 at the end of this chapter for the *Mental Training* Cards showing the International Gallery Rifle set. (10 tens and other cards.)

Figure 2-2   Author at Bisley, England, 1970. Left: Bob Mellish, first American junior to win a major class trophy in the British Nationals.

Use your *Mental Training* Cards to prepare for matches. Visualize the complete match process. If your match is outdoors, what will your backstop be like? What effect will the landforms have on the wind patterns? How will your targets get to the target frame? How will they get back? I think you can see that this type of pre-match preparation helps put you in control of the match situations. Instead of the match happening to you, now you are prepared for it. You thought and planned about the match, so you are in control.

Figure 2-3

Think Position In Mind

Mental Training Chapter 2

Figure 2-4

International Air Rifle Set: Tens

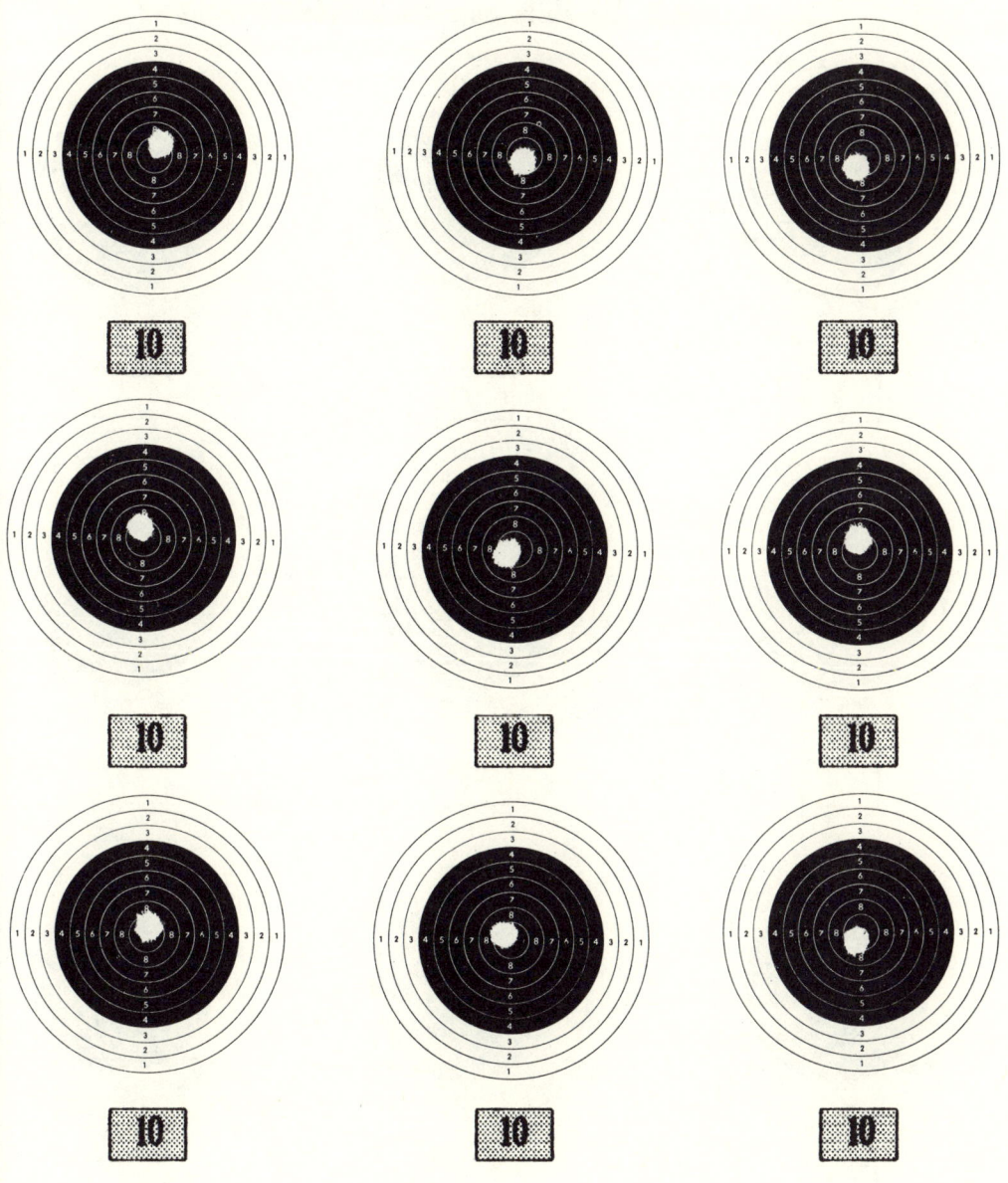

Figure 2–5
International Air Rifle Set: Back Side Of Tens

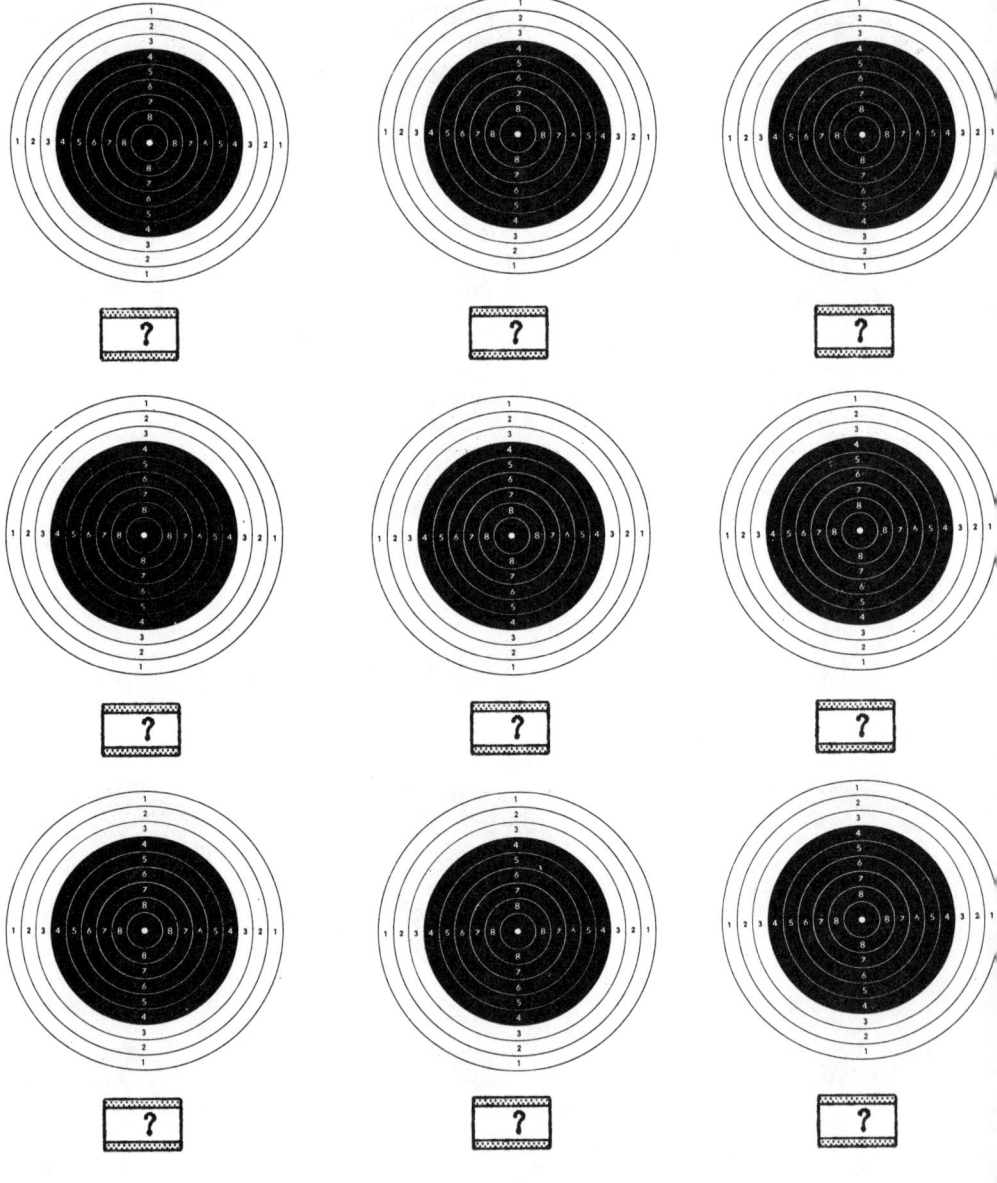

Mental Training Chapter 2

Figure 2-6
International Air Rifle Set: Other Hits

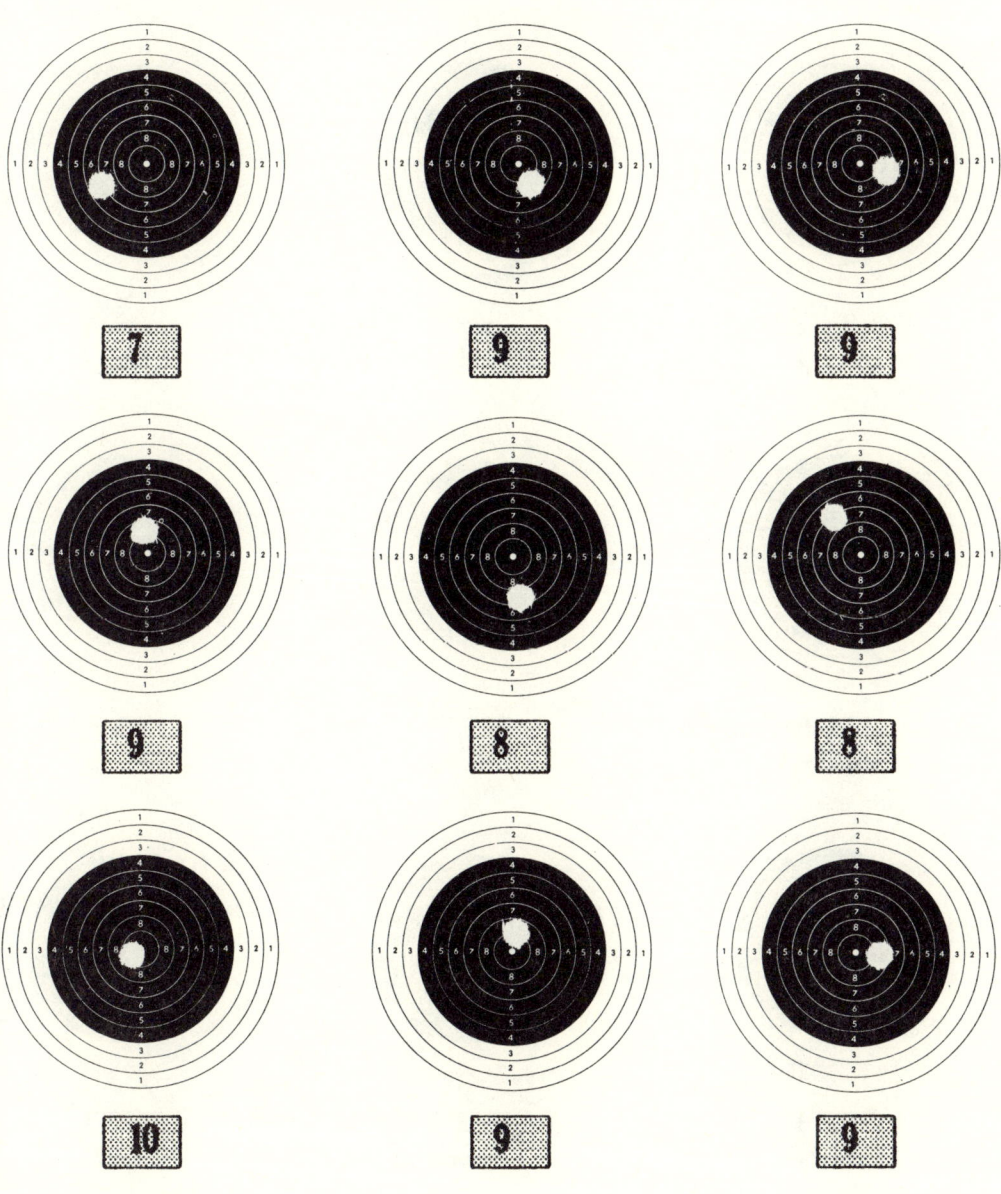

Figure 2-7
International Air Rifle Set: Back Side Other Hits

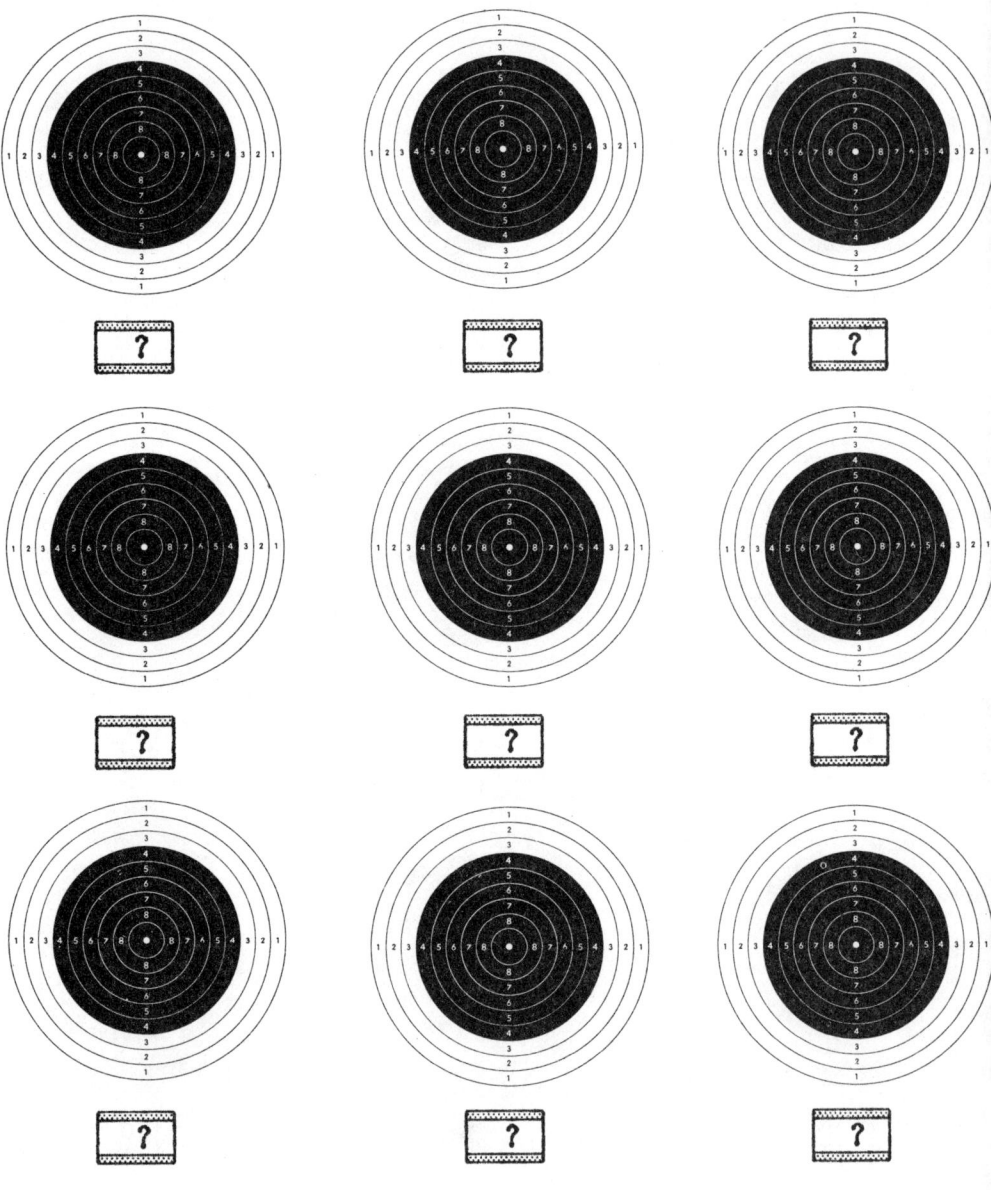

Mental Training Chapter 2

Figure 2-8

MENTAL TRAINING CARDS FEEDBACK CHART

PURPOSE:
    To learn to accurately record your inner-self talk.
    To learn to focus on each individual shot..

METHOD:
1. You need this chart, a pack of *Mental Training* Cards and a pen or pencil.
2. Write your individual shot goal on the chart.
3. Proceed mentally through the Act of Shooting.
4. Record your mentally attained score on this chart.
5. Record your thought just prior to the mental shot let-off.
6. Turn over the shot card.
7. Record your feeling after seeing the result.
8. Write your plan for the next shot.
9. Procede through this process for each shot card.

	Goal	Score	THOUGHTS Just Prior To Shooting	Feeling After Seeing Result	Plan For Next Shot
1.					
2.					
3.					
4.					
5.					
6.					
7.					
8.					
9.					
10.					

© Bob Hickey

Mental Training   Basic Mental Training

Figure 2-9   SIGHT PATTERN CHART

PURPOSE:
To learn the type and nature of your hold. Also, to learn to hold the sights on the target bull over extended periods of time.

METHOD:
1. *Take the bolt out of the gun.*
2. Assume your shooting position.
3. Proceed through the Act of Shooting.
4. Observe and plot the type of hold you have.

EXAMPLE:

O'Clock	Pattern	# 1	# 2	# 3	# 4	# 5	# 6	# 7	# 8
10/4	⊗								
7\1	∞								
9 3	∞								
6/12	8								
8\2	∞								
11/5	⊗								
10/4	◎								
7\1	○								
9 3	○								
6/12	0								
8\2	○								
11/5	○								

© Bob Hickey

Mental Training   Chapter 2

Figure 2-10 DRY FIRING CHART

PURPOSE: DATE: __ __/__ __/__ __

To learn to execute a trigger release so that the sights remain on the target bull during and after the trigger fires.

METHOD:
1. You need this chart, your gun and a pen or pencil.
2. On a sheet of paper, draw a small circle. The circle should not be more than half a pencil eraser in diameter, if you practice aiming across the distance of your bed.
3. Assume your position, with shooting clothing and your equipment, with, of course, your gun.
4. Try to release the trigger so that the sight pattern is not interrupted or destroyed by the release.
5. For each successful sight pattern continuation, put a line in the appropriate circle in the chart below.

EXAMPLE: 1.   ⊘

Shot #	STRING				Comment
	#1	#2	#3	#4	
1.	○	○	○	○	
2.	○	○	○	○	
3.	○	○	○	○	
4.	○	○	○	○	
5.	○	○	○	○	
6.	○	○	○	○	
7.	○	○	○	○	
8.	○	○	○	○	
9.	○	○	○	○	
10.	○	○	○	○	

© Bob Hickey

CHAPTER 3

Selective Awareness Training

We call this part of *Mental Training*, Selective Awareness Training, (SAT), because of what you do in this part of the program. Here, you select certain muscles to investigate. You become your own personal detective, trying to find out what your muscles are doing during the <u>Act of Shooting</u>. But, at the same time, you want to train those muscles to do the same thing, to put forth the same amount of tension each and every time you assume your shooting position. To help you investigate your muscles and what they are doing during the <u>Act of Shooting</u>, this chapter contains a number of Muscle Tenseness Checklists for you to use in organizing your SAT program.

How To Use Check Sheets

These check sheets are designed to help you organize your Selective Awareness Training. When you start this program, you will find these check sheets to be a very valuable guide. They will show you a method of identifying the muscles you must learn to control.

Each check sheet will contain a drawing representing muscle groups important to your shooting. These drawings will be intersected by dotted lines, segmenting the muscles into conceptual units for mental exercising. For shooters, certain muscles are more important in attaining stable positions than others. Many shooters are unaware of how their muscles affect their shooting until, in a match, usually in an important tournament, "Something doesn't feel right." On the firing line, in a match, is not the time to take a mental inventory of your muscles to see if one is too tense, or overly

Mental Training

relaxed, if you have never done so in practice. One purpose of practice, is to eliminate the unexpected from happening in competition. Another purpose, of course, is to train your muscles to accept the degree of tension necessary for you to consistently shoot well. Therefore, it will pay you to learn about your muscles and what you want them to do during your Act of Shooting. One way to do this is to fix yourself a small mirror in which to observe yourself in shooting positions. Big, full length mirrors cost much money. But, you can fix yourself a mirror which will work by purchasing some inexpensive mirror wall panels, which measure 12 inches by 12 inches. They may then be affixed to the door of your bedroom or to a sheet of plywood.

Selective Awareness Training Method

1. Slip into your bathing suit -- or it you're in the privacy of your bedroom, get down to your shorts.
2. Take a look at the muscles you want to focus on while they're at rest.
3. Assume your shooting position.
4. Then look at those same muscles under the normal tension of the shooting position.
5. While still in position, try to exert as much tension on those same muscles as you possible can. This, I call intense.
6. As you go through these exercises, use your Muscle Tenseness Check Sheet, as a means of being sure you go about your training in an organized manner.
7. Use the comments part of the checklist to make a record of your observations. The comment might be merely:

"Muscle looks and feels loose."

Or, "Muscle feels tight."

Or, "I tried to actually 'get' inside my muscle to 'see' what it

© Bob Hickey

Mental Training   Selective Awareness Training

felt like."

8. During these exercises, make an effort to merge your mind into the muscle you are observing. Focus on what it feels like as you give commands for it to tense and untense.

9. Use these Check Sheets to record observations of "pressure" on and in the muscles. For example:

    In kneeling: the pressure on the underside of the left foot.
    In standing: the pressure on the left hand at the place it
                 bears the weight of the rifle.
    In pistol shooting: the pressure in the front shoulder joint
                       of the pistol arm.

This book is addressed to the beginning shooter. You do not need to be an expert shot to start on a training program which will lead to the Olympics. Start this program at the earliest you can, and you will find, that as your technical shooting skill progresses, and progress it will, as you practice, your mental development will allow you to make faster progress than other beginners not using this or a similar program of mental training. To gain the fullest possible benefits from the selective awareness portion of the training, you have to be willing to impose quite a bit of discipline upon yourself. In addition, you must also develop an attitude of patience as you work through these procedures.

As a part of the *Mental Training* of the shooter, Selective Awareness Training is the method by which the shooter teaches himself to control the muscles and circulatory system of his body. This book will show you a method you can use to teach yourself to bring your body under more satisfactory control when you are shooting. By systematically proceeding through the Check Sheets of this chapter, you and your *Little Guy Inside* will learn to do much with your body. Learn what is meant by these Check Sheet terms before going ahead.

Meaning Of Check Sheet Terms

AT REST   This is how the muscles feel and look when they are

© Bob Hickey

Mental Training   Chapter 3

not contorted into a shooting position.

NORMAL

This is the feeling and appearance of the muscles in your normal shooting position.

INTENSE

Here, place your muscles under as much tension, still in the shooting position, as you possibly can.

COMMENTS

Here, make an effort to write something about what you notice about your muscles as you go through your Check Sheet.

MIRROR USE

You will have to use more than one mirror to observe your muscles. Arrange the mirrors so that you do not have to twist around to see your muscles. If you are having to contort yourself to see your muscles, then you will not get a true picture of those muscles in the position from which you will be using them. That's where having several mirror panels comes in very handy. The panels come in various shapes and sizes.

How To Use The Check Sheet

The purpose of the CHECK SHEET is to focus your interest on the relationship between various parts of your body during the act of shooting. You should learn, for example, the effect of what you do with your ankle and leg and what consequently happens in the sole of your foot and toes.

We'll assume, for the purpose of showing you how to begin your own personal SAT program, that you are a right-handed

© Bob Hickey

Mental Training   Selective Awareness Training

shooter. Get into the normal international kneeling position. That is the one in which you sit on your right heel, over a kneeling roll.

AT REST

Sit in a chair and take the shoe and sock off your left foot. Cross your left leg over your right. Put a check in space #1. Do this in order to get used to doing the program in an orderly manner. It also signals the start of your observations. Now, focus your attention on what you feel in various parts of the foot. Record, in the COMMENTS part of the CHECK SHEET, the sensations you feel in the sole of the foot, then the top and the toes.

COMMENTS

example: 1. air tickles sole, toes relaxed.

NORMAL

Now, get into the kneeling position. Take a look at what your left foot "really" looks like in your shooting position. Since this is the first time you've done this exercise, take your time, don't rush things. Also, be certain you use the mirrors mentioned on the previous page. If you do not use mirrors, you will find that there is a shifting of the pressure in the foot each time you shift your head to observe the foot. It is possible to 'feel' the pressure without visual observation, but in the beginning, I believe you need to 'see' what you are focusing on in order to intensify your awareness.

Put your check in Normal space #1. You are now ready to record your observations in the Comments portion of the Check Sheet.

Turn your left foot in toward you, so that is is 30 to 40 angled from the perpendicular to the target. To

© Bob Hickey

do this, keep your heel in place and rotate your foot to the proper angle. Notice what is happening in your foot. Turn the left foot back so it is pointing straight on toward the target. Notice what is happening to the muscles. Angle your foot in again. This time watch the foot very closely and try to feel what is happening as you twist the foot in to your proper shooting position angle. Look at your foot and try to 'get inside' it, to 'feel' what is happening inside that muscle. Do the whole procedure over again, but this time write down under the Comments space on your Check Sheet, just what you 'felt' when you made your foot "twist" in each of the different parts of the TOP of your foot.

| INTENSE |

Record your check mark in space #1 of the intense space of your Check Sheet. Now, make a very intense effort to "tense" the muscles of your left foot. Tighten them and hold them "tense" for a few seconds, then release them. Record what changes you notice under Comments.

You have now gone through your first Selective Awareness Training exercise. But, it is not over yet. In space #1, you identified what was happening in section #1 of the diagram of the TOP of the foot, which include only the first three toes. Just think of what you will learn about your foot as you go through this whole training session.

While these training sessions break up the act of shooting into small parts, you must keep in mind the overall purpose of your Selective Awareness Training. That purpose is to identify what is happening in the muscles and how it varies or is similar in the various shooting positions. You can see for yourself how powerful a shooter you will become by using the training methods you are discovering in *Mental Training*. The shooter on the firing line next to you more than likely has never noted how his toes feel when they are in the proper position for kneeling. Unlike you, he has not studied the difference in muscle tensions between the foot in the kneeling position and the foot in the standing position. Unlike you, he has to "start from scratch" when he encounters a "something doesn't feel right" shooting position in an important tournament. This is the 'edge' which can win a tournament which is important to you.

Here is an example of how one sixteen year old girl shooter responded on her first time to work through a Selective Awareness Training Check Sheet as shown in Figure 3—2.

COMMENTS

(The numbers cited below refer to Check Sheet divisions on Figure 3—2.)

MUSCLE AREA 1.

AT REST

The muscle seemed to melt into the other muscles of the arm.

NORMAL

The muscle tensed and made the muscle be felt away from the other muscles and pull towards the hand.

INTENSE

The pull is felt quite a few times as had and tightened as to when the muscle was in normal position or in At Rest.

SECOND TIME through each stage, my mind seemed more adjusted to readily going to the muscle that I was concentrating on and feeling more accurately where it's located.

© Bob Hickey

MUSCLE AREA 2.

AT REST

The strands of muscle seem to be disassociated.

NORMAL

The strands of muscle join together to form a uniform band of strength which is tightened and as it is one semi—wide strip through the area being concentrated on.

INTENSE

Portion (of concentration) was hardened quicker than before (when was in normal) and seemed to grow quite a bit bigger.

SECOND TIME, was just a little bit more able to move quicker from the changes.

MUSCLE AREA 3.

AT REST

It is easier to tell the difference of where the muscle is.

NORMAL

It feels like a little bubble has popped.

INTENSE

The bubble seems to grow. It is not as distinguishable as the other muscles but there is a difference.

SECOND TIME, felt no different from the first time through. This is a hard muscle to identify.

© Bob Hickey

MUSCLE AREA 4.

AT REST

The muscle feels like it is just one long string of strings flowing along the bottom of my arm.

NORMAL

The string of strings seems to become a solid mass following my arm, but not a part of my bone. It seems to be a separate piece that pulls into a hardened mass, but doesn't exactly pull away.

INTENSE

The muscle begins to feel a little hurt of pain at the closest point; while at the farthest point, it is a little less feeling, but still a stronger feeling that at normal or at rest.

SECOND TIME, I noticed the same differences.

MUSCLE AREA 5.

AT REST

I already mentioned I felt the differences between the lower half and the closest half that you can feel more of a difference in the slightly larger area closer. It tightens harder and seems more compact.

MUSCLE AREA 6.

AT REST

This muscle seems to be the tightest muscle.

NORMAL

The thumb becomes the tightest and I just seem to naturally focus on the tightness that occurs. My mind seems drawn to this side of my hand.

© Bob Hickey

Mental Training   Chapter 3

INTENSE

The muscle feels like a hardened rock. It feels like it will break if I increase it more, but I cannot increase the intensity even when I try.

SECOND TIME, proved similar feelings.

MUSCLE AREA 7.

AT REST

The thumb seems to be a loose object which is segmented.

NORMAL

The muscles of the thumb become a single muscle unit, very tense and no longer segmented into individual little sections. I feel little shoots of tension running through it.

INTENSE

The little shoots become big shoots of tension, but not big enough to hurt; just to be able to be recognized easily. It is not the first place my attention is drawn to, but it is the strongest. The thumb seems to expand and grow as the tension gets bigger (stronger).

SECOND TIME brought the same feelings.

MUSCLE AREA 8.

AT REST

The fingers are like branches of loose thought, with no really central muscle.

INTENSE THEY seem to be flexed, as if waiting.

INTENSE They seem to want to burst out, they are so full of tension. It is the only feeling going through my head and all of my main attention span was directed towards my fingers.

SECOND TIME, the feelings are there, but a little less distinct.

By engaging in this Selective Awareness Training, you will be preparing your mind for competition. When entering a match, you will have already practiced focusing your attention on yourself. This in itself will contribute mightily toward making you a very poised and purposeful shooter. This mind practice will prepare you in a gradual way to control the types of impulses your mind will give off during practices and especially in your competitions. This control is called Alpha State by some rifle coaches.

Go through each Check Sheet two times every time you do it. The second time gives you a chance of observing things you missed the first time through. Remember: this is a methodical arrangement to help you in your program of mental training, not a course in physiology. The drawings are presented only to offer you a plan of focus for your Selective Awareness Training.

Mental Training Chapter 3

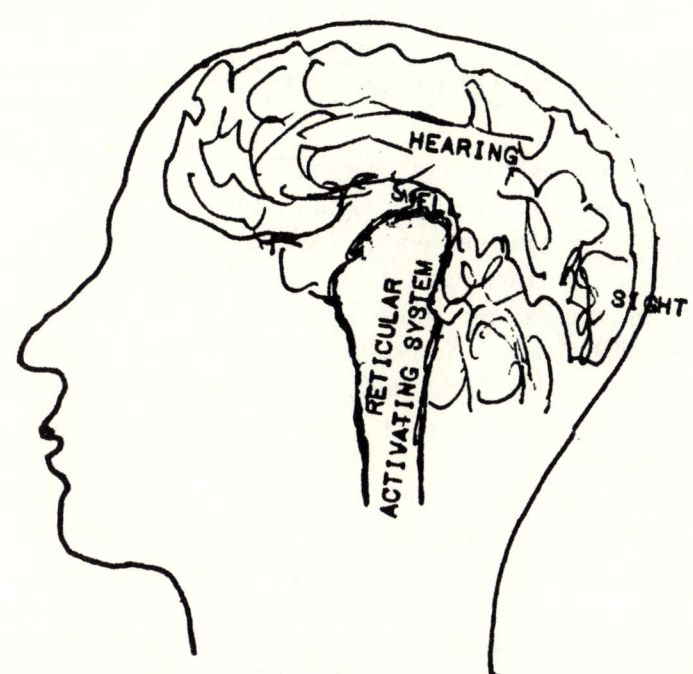

As you begin this program of Selective Awareness Training, you may wish to know something about the theory which stands behind the development of this program.

The "Reticular Activation System" of the brain, in the shortened form, known as "RAS," is the activating mechanism of the cortex of the brain. The RAS gets the attention of the cortex, which receives messages and acts on them directly from the body's senses.

Your work with the muscles in Selective Awareness Training is designed to awaken your RAS to a sense of what the muscles of shooting feel like under the conditions tested. This will then cause an activation of your RAS so you can check your position from self-known reference points.

Mental Training   **Selective Awareness Training**

THE RETICULAR ACTIVATING SYSTEM
AND
YOUR LITTLE GUY INSIDE

The "Reticular Activating System" is a non-articulating area of the brain. It is a bit of nerve tissue about the size of your little finger. It acts as a sentinel whose task is to awaken the cortex so it can respond to the messages it receives directly from your senses. Remember, your senses are those of sight, sound, touch, taste and hearing. The "Reticular Activating System" has the function of stimulating the cortex or "gray matter" of the brain to an awakened awareness of the incoming sensory signals so the cortex can make an appropriate response. In other words, the "Reticular Activating System" is the senses' early-warning station. The sensory messages go by direct pathways to the brain's cortex, but on the way through the brain stem, they pass also through the "Reticular Activating System." The "Reticular Activating System" then sprays alerting signals to the cortex. Without the "Reticular Activating System," we become inactive, non-comprehending creatures, living a vegetable-like existence. The "Reticular Activating System" seems to become programmed to be selective in its sensitivity to certain stimuli. For example, an owner of a new care notices other cars of the same make appearing on the road with greatly increased frequency. However, before the decision was make to acquire the new car, he was probably not aware of noticing them. A mother of a new-born child is readily aroused by the merest whimper of the recently arrived infant. We can use the programability of the "Reticular Activating System" to aid us in our *Mental Training*. In our Selective Awareness Training, we teach our "Reticular Activating System" to give us an "early warning" of a muscle which does not assume the normal tenseness needed for our shooting position. In shooting, muscles often "don't feel right." Sometimes we can identify the muscle and sometimes, "there's just something wrong." That's our "Reticular Activating System" at work. Unknowingly we have programmed it to become aware of an incorrectly functioning muscle. Just look at what you can start to do by just recognizing that you are consciously able to begin to do this type of internal programming! That is what *Mental Training* is designed to do.

Your *Little Guy Inside*, on the other hand, is as you well know, a very articulate presence at times. The inarticulate "Reticular Activating System" brings problems to the awareness of the *Little Guy Inside*. He acts as the translator of the notifications given by the "Reticular Activating System."

Take for example, the *Mental Training* program designed to teach you your sight patterns: by your Gun Holding Program, you train your "Reticular Activating System" to an awareness of what you are expecting when you shoot. When this sight pattern begins to be set up, your "Reticular Activating System" notifies your brain and your *Little Guy Inside*, if permitted, will go ahead and fire the shot for you. However, you can consciously block out your *Little Guy Inside* and either fire the shot deliberately or not fire it at all. The focus of *Mental Training* is to allow that *Little Guy Inside* to fire the shot.

> **Figure 3-1**

> Selective Awareness Training Check Sheet

DIRECTIONS

For Each Numbered Muscle Area, Do The Following:

> **AT REST**

1. Look at and study each of the numbered muscle areas.
2. Try to get "*inside*" and feel the "happening" in each of those areas of your muscles. It's your body, so really try to "feel" what is "happening" when you focus your attention on each area.
3. Write a comment as you do this.

> **NORMAL**

1. Assume your normal shooting position. If you can arrange to view the muscle you're going to focus on in a mirror, you will get more out of this training session.
2. Get "*inside*" your muscle again and try to feel the effort of the tension and pressure in each of the areas.
3. Write a comment in each column as you go through this awareness effort.
4. Make a comment about whatever you discover about yourself.

> **INTENSE**

1. While still in your position, <u>exert</u> <u>an</u> <u>intense</u> <u>amount</u> of tension on each of those areas of the muscle you are focusing on.
2. Get "*inside*" your muscle again and try to feel the effort of the tension and pressure in each of the areas.
3. Write a comment in each column as you do this.
4. Relax and do it again.

Mental Training   Chapter 3

Figure 3-2   SELECTIVE AWARENESS TRAINING

CHECK SHEET 1

DATE: __/__/__   Day Of Week:

Muscle Area #1		Muscle Area #2	
AT REST		AT REST	
NORMAL		NORMAL	
INTENSE		INTENSE	

Muscle Area #3		Muscle Area #4	
AT REST		AT REST	
NORMAL		NORMAL	
INTENSE		INTENSE	

Muscle Area #5		Muscle Area #6	
AT REST		AT REST	
NORMAL		NORMAL	
INTENSE		INTENSE	

Muscle Area #7		Muscle Area #8	
AT REST		AT REST	
NORMAL		NORMAL	
INTENSE		INTENSE	

© Bob Hickey

Mental Training   Selective Awareness Training

Figure 3—3   SELECTIVE AWARENESS TRAINING
SCHEDULING AND TRACKING CHART

For your guidance, I suggest that Check Sheet numbers, 1, 14 and 15, be done in single SAT sessions. Numbers 3, 4, 7, 12, 13, 16, 17 and 18 may work well in dual combination SAT sessions. Numbers 2, 5, 6, 8, 9, 10 and 11 may be joined in triple combinations for a Selective Awareness Session.

NUMBER	SCHEDULED	DATE DONE	COMMENTS
1			
2			
3			
4			
5			
6			
7			
8			
9			
10			
11			
12			
13			
14			
15			
16			
17			
18			

© Bob Hickey

Mental Training Chapter 3

Figure 3-4   SELECTIVE AWARENESS TRAINING

FIGURE INDEX FOR CHECK SHEETS

CHECK SHEET #	MUSCLE FIGURE #	PAGE #	SHOOTING DISCIPLINE
1	3-5	58 & 59	All(Trigger hand)
2	3-6	60 & 61	All(Trigger hand)
3	3-7	62 & 63	All(Trigger hand)
4	3-8	64 & 65	Standing Position
5	3-9	66 & 67	All(Trigger finger)
6	3-10	68 & 69	Kneeling leg
7	3-11	70 & 71	Kneeling leg
8	3-12	72 & 73	Kneeling foot
9	3-13	74 & 75	All(leg back)
10	3-14	76 & 77	All(leg front)
11	3-15	78 & 79	All(side top foot)
12	3-16	80 & 81	All(top foot)
13	3-17	82 & 83	All(top foot)
14	3-18	84 & 85	All(back foot)
15	3-19	86 & 87	All(back torso)
16	3-20	88 & 89	All(lower back)
17	3-21	90 & 91	All(front torso)
18	3-22	92 & 93	All(front chest)

© Bob Hickey

Figure 3–5a SELECTIVE AWARENESS TRAINING

CHECK SHEET 1

PURPOSE

To identify those pathways of the arm and the backside of the hand, which operate during the *Act of Shooting*.

METHOD

This arm is the one which is not supported by the body during the *Act of Shooting*.

AT REST: You may allow it to rest on a table or other artificial support while you observe the muscles. But for NORMAL and INTENSE, you must place the arm in the unsupported shooting position.

FOCUS

On the kind and nature of the tension in the trigger finger, as opposed to the tension of the fingers. Observe the tension of the other muscle areas to the finger tension.

RELATIONSHIPS TO NOTE

Feel what happens as you lift your arm into shooting position. If you your arm is close to your body in kneeling, put it that way now.

© Bob Hickey

Mental Training   Chapter 3

Figure 3-5b   SELECTIVE AWARENESS TRAINING
CHECK SHEET 1

DATE: __/__/__   Day Of Week:

Muscle Area #1
- AT REST
- NORMAL
- INTENSE

Muscle Area #2
- AT REST
- NORMAL
- INTENSE

Muscle Area #3
- AT REST
- NORMAL
- INTENSE

Muscle Area #4
- AT REST
- NORMAL
- INTENSE

Muscle Area #5
- AT REST
- NORMAL
- INTENSE

Muscle Area #6
- AT REST
- NORMAL
- INTENSE

Muscle Area #7
- AT REST
- NORMAL
- INTENSE

Muscle Area #8
- AT REST
- NORMAL
- INTENSE

© Bob Hickey

| Figure 3-6a | SELECTIVE AWARENESS TRAINING |

CHECK SHEET 2

PURPOSE

Here the purpose is to observe the types of tension pathways formed as the hand assumes the *Act of Shooting* position.

METHOD

This arm is the one which is not supported by the body during the *Act of Shooting*. AT REST: You may allow it to rest on a table or other artificial support while you observe the muscles. But for NORMAL and INTENSE, you must place the arm in the unsupported shooting position.

FOCUS

On the interrelationships of the muscles of the hand and arm.

RELATIONSHIPS TO NOTE

Notice particularly the changes in the sections of the hand as you conduct your— self through the numbered muscle areas of this Selective Awareness Check Sheet.

© Bob Hickey

Mental Training Chapter 3

Figure 3—6b   SELECTIVE AWARENESS TRAINING
CHECK SHEET 2

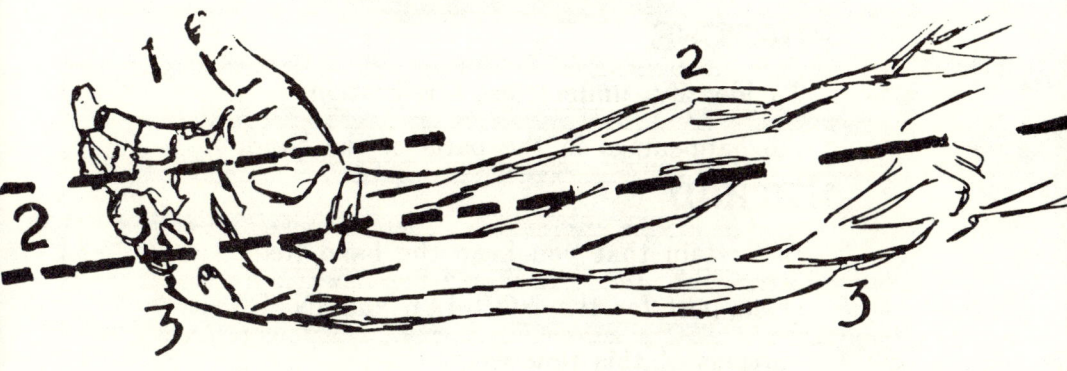

DATE: __ __/__ __/__ __		Day Of Week:	
	Muscle Area #1		**Muscle Area #2**
AT REST			
NORMAL			
INTENSE			
	Muscle Area #3		
AT REST			
NORMAL			
INTENSE			

© Bob Hickey

Figure 3–7a   SELECTIVE AWARENESS TRAINING

CHECK SHEET 3

PURPOSE
To identify, under close observation, the happenings in the parts of the hand.

METHOD
Be certain that you keep the hand free of support for the NORMAL and INTENSE portions of this practice.

FOCUS
On the effort to isolate the tension in each of the numbered muscle areas.

RELATIONSHIPS TO NOTE
Notice the tension which attention to one muscle area produces in other areas. See what repeated practice can do to reduce the associated tension.

Mental Training Chapter 3

Figure 3—7b SELECTIVE AWARENESS TRAINING
CHECK SHEET 3

DATE: ___/___/___
Day Of Week: _____

Muscle Area #1
AT REST
NORMAL
INTENSE

Muscle Area #2
AT REST
NORMAL
INTENSE

Muscle Area #3
AT REST
NORMAL
INTENSE

Muscle Area #4
AT REST
NORMAL
INTENSE

Muscle Area #5
AT REST
NORMAL
INTENSE

© Bob Hickey

| Figure 3–8a | SELECTIVE AWARENESS TRAINING |

CHECK SHEET 4

PURPOSE

To determine the most the most pratical way of joining the fingers and and into a fist as a rest for the rifle in the standing position.

METHOD

Examine your fist during the actual firing in the standing position. Then at home, put the arm in the same position during SAT.

FOCUS

On what you do with the fingers of your hand as you join them into your fist. Determine just how the rifle rests on the top of the fist. Identify the function of the fingers in this support system.

RELATIONSHIPS TO NOTE

Notice the way the fingers are placed when the fist is closed. Be certain they are in the same relative position as if you were wearing a shooting glove.

© Bob Hickey

Mental Training Chapter 3

Figure 3–7b   SELECTIVE AWARENESS TRAINING
CHECK SHEET 4

| DATE: ___/___/___ |
| Day Of Week: |

	Muscle Area #1
AT REST	
NORMAL	
INTENSE	

	Muscle Area #2
AT REST	
NORMAL	
INTENSE	

	Muscle Area #3
AT REST	
NORMAL	
INTENSE	

	Muscle Area #4
AT REST	
NORMAL	
INTENSE	

	Muscle Area #5
AT REST	
NORMAL	
INTENSE	

© Bob Hickey

Figure 3-9a   SELECTIVE AWARENESS TRAINING

CHECK SHEET 5

PURPOSE

To identify the intricate workings of the trigger finger.

METHOD

Simulate the movement of the finger going through the *Act of Shooting* in the firing of a shot.

FOCUS

On the interrelationships of the various numbered muscle areas of the trigger finger.

RELATIONSHIPS TO NOTE

Draw a big circle and then a small circle and with your trigger finger. While drawing, note the amount of attention you have to exert between making a big sweeping movement of the finger and a small tiny movement. Try to make smaller, very tightly controlled movements. Note any sensations you may experience in the rest of the hand during the effort of controlling the trigger squeeze.

© Bob Hickey

Mental Training Chapter 3

Figure 3-9b SELECTIVE AWARENESS TRAINING
CHECK SHEET 5

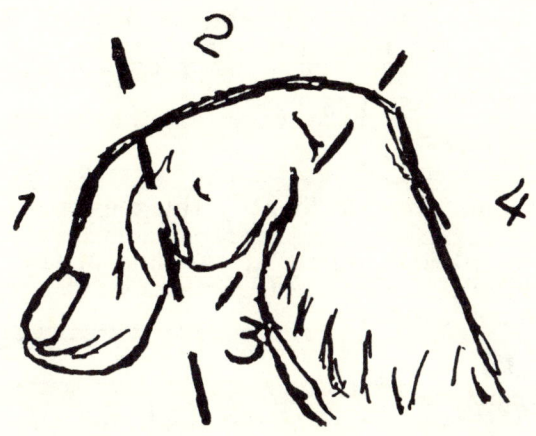

DATE: __/__/__		Day Of Week:	
	Muscle Area #1		**Muscle Area #2**
AT REST			
NORMAL			
INTENSE			
	Muscle Area #3		**Muscle Area #4**
AT REST			
NORMAL			
INTENSE			

© Bob Hickey

Figure 3–10a SELECTIVE AWARENESS TRAINING

CHECK SHEET 6

PURPOSE
To see what tension we have in the left leg in the kneeling position.

METHOD
Make an effort to identify the tension in the numbered muscle areas while in the kneeling position.

FOCUS
On the under area of the thigh and the top calf muscles.

RELATIONSHIPS TO NOTE
Take special note of your left elbow place.

Notice what happens when you turn your left foot inwards while in the kneeling position.

See what happens to your position as you work through the *intense* portion of your Selective Awareness Training practice. Note what happens in these numbered muscle areas if you change the relative position of your torso, such as slumping more forward.

Mental Training Chapter 3

Figure 3—10b   SELECTIVE AWARENESS TRAINING
CHECK SHEET 6

DATE: ___/___/___	Day Of Week:

	Muscle Area #1
AT REST	
NORMAL	
INTENSE	

	Muscle Area #2
AT REST	
NORMAL	
INTENSE	

	Muscle Area #3
AT REST	
NORMAL	
INTENSE	

© Bob Hickey

Figure 3-11a | SELECTIVE AWARENESS TRAINING

CHECK SHEET 7
PURPOSE
To investigate the effect of tension, and the lack of tension, on the muscles of the right leg in the kneeling position.
METHOD
Be sure to place your trunk in your normal kneeling position, so that the muscle numbered area being viewed will be placed under the same pressure as when shooting.
FOCUS
On the degree of normal tension and note the difference when place under *intense* tension in each of the numbered areas.
RELATIONSHIPS TO NOTE
Note what happens in area 1 by placing your fingers in contact with that area. In area 2, note the byplay of tension on the inside top of the leg muscle area. Use your fingers to feel and trace this tension. In 4, let it go to sleep, then begin SAT.

Mental Training   Chapter 3

Figure 3–11b   SELECTIVE AWARENESS TRAINING

CHECK SHEET 7

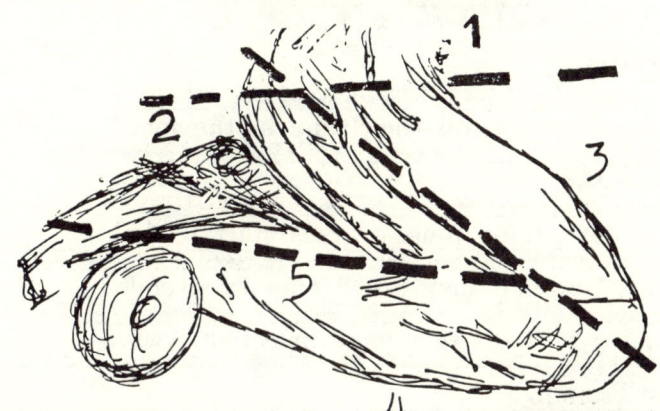

| DATE: ___/___/___ | Day Of Week: |

	Muscle Area #1		Muscle Area #2
AT REST			
NORMAL			
INTENSE			

	Muscle Area #3		Muscle Area #4
AT REST			
NORMAL			
INTENSE			

	Muscle Area #5
AT REST	
NORMAL	
INTENSE	

© Bob Hickey

| Figure 3-12a | SELECTIVE AWARENESS TRAINING |

CHECK SHEET 8
PURPOSE
To learn to control the "ache in the foot."
METHOD
Wait until these muscle areas start to feel "funny" or like they are "going to sleep," or "hurting," then begin your Selective Awareness Training.
FOCUS
On extending the amount of uninterrupted time you can stay in this position.
RELATIONSHIPS TO NOTE
Try different types of kneeling rolls to see if you can get one which you feel is comfortable. Note the amount of body weight you place over your heel. Keep it the same each time. Try to make certain your kneeling roll does not "flatten out," once you start your training or shooting. For consistent shooting results, you need a reliable, unchanging position.

Mental Training   Chapter 3

Figure 3–12b   SELECTIVE AWARENESS TRAINING
CHECK SHEET 8

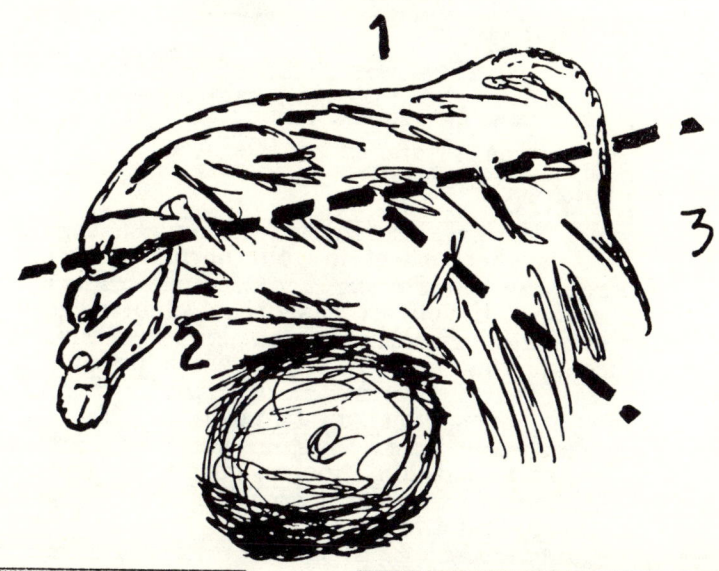

DATE: __/__/__		Day Of Week:	
	Muscle Area #1		**Muscle Area #2**
AT REST			
NORMAL			
INTENSE			

	Muscle Area #3
AT REST	
NORMAL	
INTENSE	

© Bob Hickey

Figure 3–13a SELECTIVE AWARENESS TRAINING

CHECK SHEET 9

PURPOSE
To discover the interrelationships between the various numbered muscle areas.

METHOD
Do this check sheet in your normal shooting position. If you are a shotgun shooter, go through your swing. If you are a pistol shooter, bring you gun to position. If you are a biathlon shooter, go on, do your running, and then start this.

FOCUS
On separating the tension in each muscle area, at least in what you see and feel in your mind.

RELATIONSHIPS TO NOTE
Note upper torso movement effects on these numbered areas. What happens to one area as you pay attention to the tension in one of the others? Assume varying target position heights, what happens as you adjust?

© Bob Hickey

Mental Training   Chapter 3

Figure 3–13b   SELECTIVE AWARENESS TRAINING
CHECK SHEET 9

DATE: ___/___/___

Day Of Week:

	Muscle Area #1
AT REST	
NORMAL	
INTENSE	

	Muscle Area #2
AT REST	
NORMAL	
INTENSE	

	Muscle Area #3
AT REST	
NORMAL	
INTENSE	

© Bob Hickey

Figure 3–14a SELECTIVE AWARENESS TRAINING

CHECK SHEET 10

PURPOSE

To discover the interrelationships between the various numbered muscle areas.

METHOD

Do this check sheet in your normal shooting position. If you are a shotgun shooter, go through your swing. If you are a pistol shooter, bring you gun to position. If you are a biathlon shooter, then do your running, and then start this.

FOCUS

On separating the tension in each muscle area, at least in what you see and feel in your mind.

RELATIONSHIPS TO NOTE

Note upper torso movement effects on these numbered areas. What happens to one area as you pay attention to the tension in one of the others? Assume varying target position heights, what happens as you adjust?

Mental Training Chapter 3

| Figure 3-14b | SELECTIVE AWARENESS TRAINING
CHECK SHEET 10

DATE: ___/___/___

Day Of Week: _____

	Muscle Area #1
AT REST	
NORMAL	
INTENSE	

	Muscle Area #2
AT REST	
NORMAL	
INTENSE	

	Muscle Area #3
AT REST	
NORMAL	
INTENSE	

© Bob Hickey

77

| Figure 3-15a | SELECTIVE AWARENESS TRAINING |

CHECK SHEET 11

PURPOSE

To observe particularly the tension at *normal* and *intense*.

METHOD

Make a very special effort to put your feet and body in the exact postion of shooting. Experiment with the effects of upper torso movement on the grip of the toes and the effect on your shooting balance. If your shooting involves torso swing, practice it.

FOCUS

On the interrelations of tension as you go through each of the numbered muscle areas. Look at the effect of time in position.

RELATIONSHIPS TO NOTE

Note and record the tension changes with respect to the time spent in the position. Position shooters, note the tension re‑quirements of the different shooting posi‑tions.

Mental Training Chapter 3

Figure 3–15b SELECTIVE AWARENESS TRAINING
CHECK SHEET 11

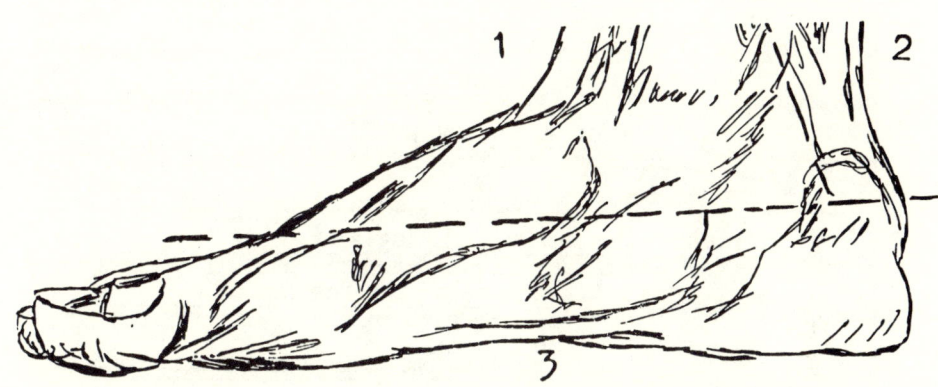

DATE: __/__/__		Day Of Week:	
	Muscle Area #1		**Muscle Area #2**
AT REST			
NORMAL			
INTENSE			

	Muscle Area #3
AT REST	
NORMAL	
INTENSE	

© Bob Hickey

Figure 3-16a SELECTIVE AWARENESS TRAINING

CHECK SHEET 12

PURPOSE

To observe what happens to those marked numbered areas as you extend your time in the position and vary positions.

METHOD

Simulate the loading, aiming and firing sequences. Make note of the tension at each stage of the process.

FOCUS

On the tension during the act of aiming.

RELATIONSHIPS TO NOTE

In pistol shooting, the effect of equilibrium maintainance on the tension in numbered muscle areas. The relationship of time in position to tension control deterioration. The effect of grass firing lines versus concrete firing lines to tension control. Note what happens to attention control and direction as effected by the composition of the firing line.

© Bob Hickey

Mental Training   Chapter 3

Figure 3—16b   SELECTIVE AWARENESS TRAINING
CHECK SHEET 12

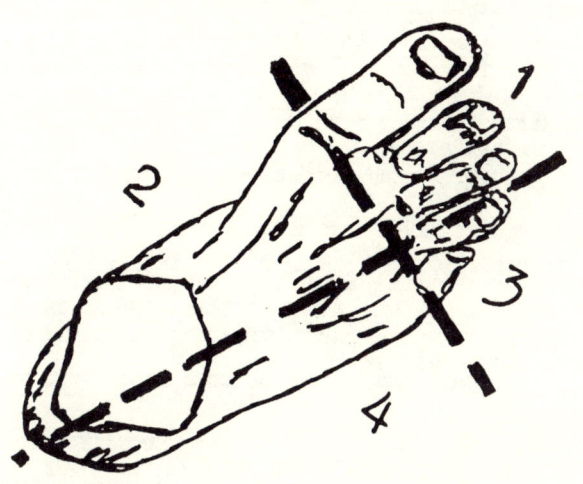

| DATE: __ __ / __ __ / __ __ | Day Of Week: |

	Muscle Area #1		Muscle Area #2
AT REST			
NORMAL			
INTENSE			

	Muscle Area #3		Muscle Area #4
AT REST			
NORMAL			
INTENSE			

© Bob Hickey

Figure 5-17a SELECTIVE AWARENESS TRAINING

CHECK SHEET 13

PURPOSE

To observe how the distribution of your body weight affects the muscles in the numbered areas.

METHOD

Simulate the loading, aiming and firing sequences. Make note of the tension at each stage of the process.

FOCUS

On the types of tension created in your normal shooting position tension as you make very small shifts or changes in your shooting.

RELATIONSHIPS TO NOTE

What happens to the tension in each of the numbered muscle areas as you shift your position very slightly.

Mental Training   Chapter 3

Figure 3–17b   SELECTIVE AWARENESS TRAINING

CHECK SHEET 13

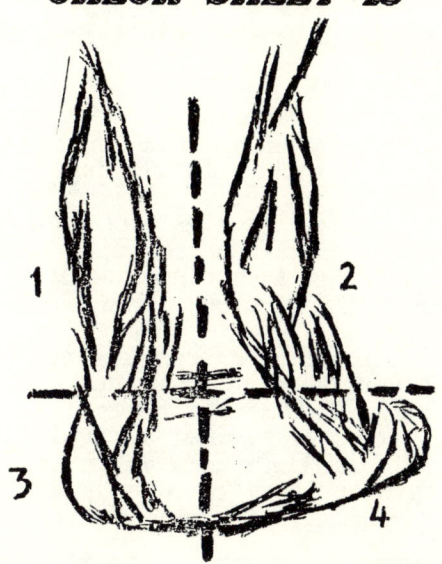

DATE: __ __ / __ __ / __ __		Day Of Week:	
	Muscle Area #1		Muscle Area #2
AT REST			
NORMAL			
INTENSE			
	Muscle Area #3		Muscle Area #4
AT REST			
NORMAL			
INTENSE			

© Bob Hickey

Figure 3–18a — SELECTIVE AWARENESS TRAINING

CHECK SHEET 14

PURPOSE

To observe the response of the numbered muscle areas to the differing degrees of tension. To see the effects of prolonged tension while in a shooting position.

METHOD

Assume your shooting position. Focus on the numbered areas most affected by the position, then on those not overtly affected.

FOCUS

On just what the various numbered muscle arease are doing during this process.

RELATIONSHIPS TO NOTE

Observe how the numbered areas respond when mental commands are being given to one of the other areas. Try to figure out whether this interplay occurs very frequently in the firing of your practice and matches.

See what control is needed over the associated areas as you simulate firing.

© Bob Hickey

Mental Training   Chapter 3

Figure 3—18b   SELECTIVE AWARENESS TRAINING
CHECK SHEET 14

DATE: ___/___/___

Day Of Week:

Muscle Area #1	
AT REST	
NORMAL	
INTENSE	

Muscle Area #2	
AT REST	
NORMAL	
INTENSE	

Muscle Area #3	

Muscle Area #4	
AT REST	
NORMAL	
INTENSE	

Muscle Area #5	

© Bob Hickey

Figure 3-19a SELECTIVE AWARENESS TRAINING

CHECK SHEET 15

PURPOSE

To identify the degree and extent of muscle area involvement in the back, while in the shooting position. To see the effects of upper back tension.

METHOD

Assume your shooting position. Focus on the numbered areas most affected by the position, then on those not overtly affected.

FOCUS

On the relationship of the "pain-in-the-back" to the maintaining of the position over an extended period of time. Notice this in each of the numbered areas.

RELATIONSHIPS TO NOTE

The difference in the areas between the times you do this with your gun and those times you pretend to have it in your position.

© Bob Hickey

Mental Training   Chapter 3

Figure 3–19b   SELECTIVE AWARENESS TRAINING

CHECK SHEET 15

DATE: __ __/__ __/__ __

Day Of Week:

Muscle Area #1	
AT REST	
NORMAL	
INTENSE	

Muscle Area #2	
AT REST	
NORMAL	
INTENSE	

Muscle Area #3	
AT REST	
NORMAL	
INTENSE	

Muscle Area #4	
AT REST	
NORMAL	
INTENSE	

Muscle Area #5	
AT REST	
NORMAL	
INTENSE	

Muscle Area #6	
AT REST	
NORMAL	
INTENSE	

© Bob Hickey

Figure 3-20a   SELECTIVE AWARENESS TRAINING

CHECK SHEET 16

PURPOSE

To identify the degree and extent of muscle area involvement in the lower back, while in the shooting position. To identify inner muscular tension.

METHOD

Assume your shooting position. Focus on the numbered areas most affected by the position, then on those not overtly affected.

FOCUS

On the degree of tension required to maintain the shooting position so the sights are on target. Notice the interplay between frontal muscles and those in the back.

RELATIONSHIPS TO NOTE

Pay attention to the relationship between the tension in area 1 and that in area 2 at the same time. Note especially the job each does in maintaining the position. Note their function in control of body sway.

Mental Training   Chapter 3

Figure 3-20b   SELECTIVE AWARENESS TRAINING
CHECK SHEET 16

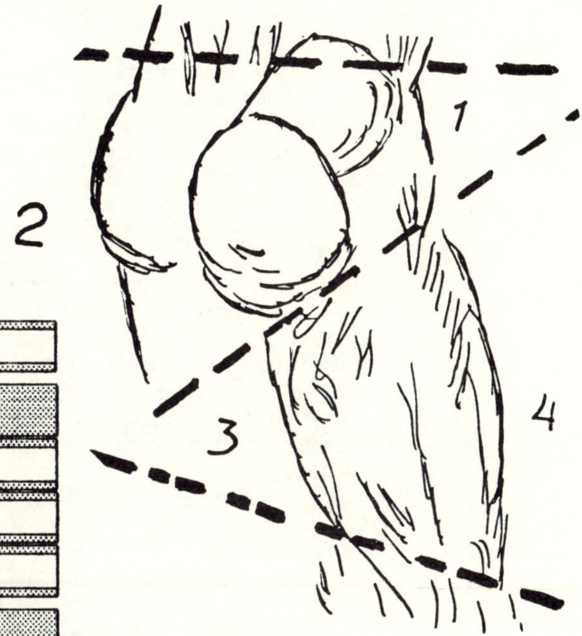

DATE: ___/___/___

Day Of Week: _____

Muscle Area #1
- AT REST
- NORMAL
- INTENSE

Muscle Area #2
- AT REST
- NORMAL
- INTENSE

Muscle Area #3
- AT REST
- NORMAL
- INTENSE

Muscle Area #4

© Bob Hickey

Figure 3–21a SELECTIVE AWARENESS TRAINING

CHECK SHEET 17

PURPOSE

To observe and control the tension reactions of the muscles in the numbered muscle areas.

METHOD

Assume your shooting position. Before beginning this Selective Awareness Session, stay in your shooting position at least 20 minutes.

FOCUS

On the degree of tension required to maintain the shooting position so the sights are on target. Note the tension reactions as the position is sustained.

RELATIONSHIPS TO NOTE

Notice just what the muscles do as the effort to sustain the position wears on. What happens when you try to control this effort to sustain the position?

Mental Training   Chapter 3

Figure 3-21b   SELECTIVE AWARENESS TRAINING

CHECK SHEET 17

DATE: ___/___/___

Day Of Week: _____

	Muscle Area #1
AT REST	
NORMAL	
INTENSE	

	Muscle Area #2
AT REST	
NORMAL	
INTENSE	

	Muscle Area #3
AT REST	
NORMAL	
INTENSE	

Muscle Area #4

© Bob Hickey

Mental Training   Selective Awareness Training

Figure 3-22a   SELECTIVE AWARENESS TRAINING

CHECK SHEET 18

PURPOSE
To investigate the effect of tension, and the lack of tension, on the muscles of the numbered areas with/without gun.

METHOD
See if you can keep the tension of these numbered muscle areas separate as you go through this Check Sheet. For pistol shooters, note the tension during aiming.

FOCUS
On what happens as these muscles react tension.

RELATIONSHIPS TO NOTE
Note the degree of control you have over these muscles, as compared to those in the fooot. Notice what happens as you try to control the tension in these sections.

© Bob Hickey

Mental Training   Chapter 3

Figure 3–22b   SELECTIVE AWARENESS TRAINING
CHECK SHEET 18

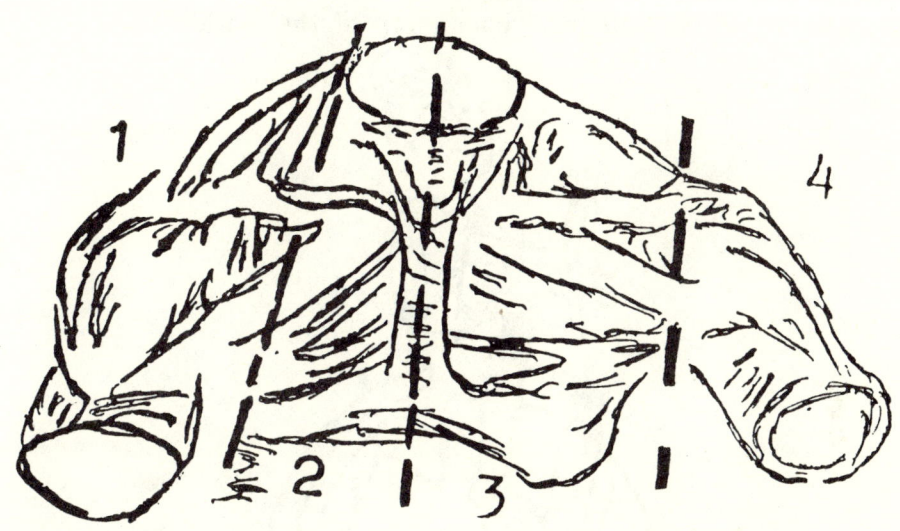

DATE: __/__/__   Day Of Week:

	Muscle Area #1		Muscle Area #2
AT REST			
NORMAL			
INTENSE			

	Muscle Area #3		Muscle Area #4
AT REST			
NORMAL			
INTENSE			

© Bob Hickey

As you go through this program of *Selective Awareness Training*, discuss your observations with your coach.
RECORD YOUR OBSERVATIONS IN YOUR SHOOTING DIARY.
It will put you on top of the world!

Colonel Bill Pullum pointed out in the United States Women's International Rifle Organization's *Schiessportschule Dialogues I*, "Mental Training takes time. In order to be a real help to a shooter, a coach must work with him on the range, and for a long period of time. Just coming to talk for an hour now and then doesn't get it. You must know an individual well to help him think properly, analyze properly and execute properly."

CHAPTER 4

Training Plans

Before going any further you have to organize yourself. You have to become an organized person. Just as an industrial nation organizes itself for a major war effort or a large company correlates all of its departments to market its new product line, so you must shape your living arrangements to make certain you get to your goal. This often requires you to adjust your living arrangements so that your efforts to make yourself a better shooter go from a haphazard hoping for better scores, to a planned, systematic effort to achieve better performance. In other words, you need to make a "training plan." You may have found yourself wondering once in a while just how a champion becomes a champion. One thing many champions have done on their road to world champion status is to set up and follow a training plan. You too can take a big step in becoming a better shooter by getting yourself organized, or as is said in some quarters, "getting your act together."

So what does a training plan look like? Above all else, it is a schedule of what you do with your time. You, as the maker of the plan, are also the enforcer of its provisions. So rule number one in constructing a training plan is:

> 1. *Plan to do only what you want to do!*

Rule number two is:

> 2. *Set your training plan to focus on a single element.*

When looking at the time available to you for home training, you need to be realistic. First of all, you have family duties to perform. Next, homework, that bane of the the student the world over, has to be done. Then you also have friends with whom you want to play or talk with on the telephone. So, where does that leave you? Do you have any time left for shooting training? I don't know! You are the only one who can find time in your busy schedule. So, let's look at a method which can help you to make such time. Remember, you must want to make time for home training to give you an edge over the other members of your team and other competitors. They don't know the secrets of this book, or it they do, they are too busy to find time to work at them. But not you! You're going to make time. I've made up a Home Time Schedule Plan form for you who are still in school. Of course, if you are a working person, just substitute the word, work, where you find the word, school. A carpenter's time plan will differ from a banker's Home Time Schedule Plan. Take a look at it. Notice the morning is completely knocked out. School starts early and so you're probably really pushing it to get to school on time. After 9:30 in the evening, you're probably in bed or in the shower. So that leaves:

RIGHT AFTER SCHOOL TIME

SUPPER TIME

PRIME TIME TV WATCHING TIME

Write down what you expect to do today at the time you expect to do it. Then try to follow that plan at home. Work in the type of training and the amount of time you want to spend on that shooting training. Work this training around what you want to do and what your parents expect you to do. You decide where, when and how much training you want to do.

As with everything else connected with this *Mental Training* program, you will find that you can make time for your home training if you assume a positive attitude about actually wanting to

Mental Training Chapter 4

do it. If your coach schedules a time at the range for you to do this, it will also help you. But to tell it like it is, it would be more effective for you to find the time to do this training at your own home. You will have fewer distractions in your home, and probably more of a chance to set up an efficient practice schedule.

While at home, set your shooting goal. You need a goal for each shot you shoot because of the importance of goals to improved shooting performance. In each position or stage, you need to establish a very down-to-earth, realistic goal for each shot your fire. The reason, you need the immediate feedback on each shot to help you determine if your are meeting your performance expectation. A vague *hope* for a "90" can be translated into an individual shot goal of a "nine" each time your fire. A "90" as a goal allows for too much leeway and promotes, to a degree, a haphazard inconsistency to your shooting. Both you and a competitor may shoot a "90" in a match. The other shooter "tried" for a "90." You "tried" for a "nine" on each shot. You are training yourself to be consistent, the other competitor is settling for inconsistency. The other competitor will often wonder about his inability to improve. You will be able to measure your progress each time your fire.

There is a bit of a trick in setting this goal in the beginning. First, establish in your mind an idea of your present ability to keep all of your shots inside a particular scoring ring. For example, in the kneeling position, can you keep all of your shots inside the 2-ring? 3-ring? Not sure about the 4-ring? But, yes, sure you can keep them inside the 4-ring! So, go ahead, set your goal as keeping all of your shots inside the 4-ring. You have now set for yourself and *individual shot goal* of a 4 or better. Now, just exactly what is meant by the 4-ring goal? With this as your goal, it means that you must try to keep each of your shot holes from having the outer edge of the hole touch the inside of the 4-ring scoring circle. Sort of a different idea isn't it? This is what we call a "concept." It is a mental thing. It is a way of *tightening* your mental attitude toward your shooting efforts. This is where you begin to restructure your mental approach to your shooting. It is clear that your ability to make improvements in your shooting skill

© Bob Hickey

Mental Training — Training Plans

is tied more certainly to your mental attitude than any other single factor, including the amount of shooting practice you get.

A lot of successful people in a self-directed society, such as capitalistic America, are successful because they carefully map out their available time. If such planning helps to asure business success, then chances are that it will assist you in achieving your desire to become a champion shooter. That's where the Home Time Schedule Plan, shown on the opposit page, can help you. To use it effectively, you need to really understand why you are going to the trouble of even bothering to make such a plan in the first place. That's where your goal statement comes in. In June of 1978, I heard Lones Wigger, a Lieutenant Colonel in the United States Army, an Olympic shooting champion, describe a goal statement of his as he was in the process of training for the 300 meters event of the 1972 Olympics.

Worried about his shooting performance, he recounted telephoning Colonel Bill Pullum, the man responsible for developing America's world champion class shooters of the 1960's. After working through the problem together on the telephone, Colonel Pullum suggested that Wigger form a mental image of the feeling he would get when he stood on the Winner's platform, listening to the National Anthem, having won the Gold Medal. Wigger reported that he worked with that mental image all during his training, that it was with him constantly.

Wigger was participating as a panel member of the United States Women's International Rifle Organization's Schiessportschule II, an Olympic development shooting school conducted by some of America's world champion shooters, for young shooters in training. The panel was asked to define their concept of just what constituted *Mental Training*.

What Wigger had done was to identify just exactly what it was that he sought. So well was he able to do this, he told the participants, that to him that Gold Medal was already his before he stepped up to the firing line to fire his first shot in that competition. This is a very excellent example of what is meant by a goal statement. Notice that Wigger did not set the statement up as a desired wish. He set it up as being an already accomplished

© Bob Hickey

fact. This, even though the actual match was still months in the future. That is what you must do when you make up your goal statement. At the time Wigger set this goal statement, he was already a well recognized world class shooter. So his goal statement was well within his capabilities.

Your goal must be within your capabilities. On the other hand, don't sell yourself short. Your goal statement is designed to let that *Little Guy Inside* know just what you will accomplish. By using this Home Time Schedule Plan, you will be writing your goal statement twice. However, to be really effective, you should write it on a 3" x 5" note card and look at it several other times during the day. To be effective, the goal statement must be something that you are seriously wanting and that you are willing to work to achieve. As with Wigger, the goal statement kept alive his sense of hungering more after that medal than his counterparts of other nations, every bit as qualified to win that medal by dint of training and shooting experience.

So instead of becoming stale and looking at his approaching Olympic performance as just another match, with perhaps a bit more pressure than some other matches, Wigger entered it tautly balanced on the edge of his highest point of anticipation. He was "up" for the match in the very truest sense of the word. That is what *Mental Training* can do for you. It is that extra thing that the champions of the world are doing now. If you want to join their ranks and beat them, then you must master their secrets of *Mental Training*. Take a look at Figure 7–7, page 195.

> *Under*: *Daily Plan For Activity*, list the thing you will be working on, the duties you expect to do or the school subjects you'll be studying.
>
> *Under*: *Total Minutes*, record only the number of minutes you actually spend on the *Mental Training* work.
>
> *Under*: *Activity Critique*, put down what you actually did do. This will help you in your future planning.

Mental Training   Training Plans

If you notice that a particular thing keeps intruding upon your plans at a particular time, then block it in and rearrange your schedule.

Keeping track of the: *Number Of Minutes Devoted to* the various kinds of *Mental Training* will help you to plan out your future training more intelligently.

Under: *Summary Of What I Learned*, record your thoughts of the discoveries you make about yourself. Putting these discoveries down in words is a very important part of your mental training. Just as a scientist carefully records the results of his experiments, you record yours.

On the pages following this page, I have devised some training plans sheets to help you plan your training schedule.

If you will devise your own training plans, and follow them with a lot of effort, I can assure you that you will have discovered a short-cut to high level shooting performance. The best planned schedules are sometimes interrupted. The important thing is to resume following your plan as soon as possible, if a break occurs.

Mental Training   Chapter 4

AT HOME SELECTIVE AWARENESS PRACTICE TIME

DAY	HOURS TO DO TRAINING	TOTAL TIME
MONDAY:	am/pm TO am/pm	
TUESDAY:	am/pm TO am/pm	
WEDNESDAY:	am/pm TO am/pm	
THURSDAY:	am/pm TO am/pm	
FRIDAY:	am/pm TO am/pm	
SATURDAY:	am/pm TO am/pm	
SUNDAY:	am/pm TO am/pm	

At Home Selective Awareness Practice Time Total:

AT HOME GUN HOLDING PRACTICE TIME

DAY	HOURS TO DO GUN HOLDING TRAINING	TOTAL TIME
MONDAY:	am/pm TO am/pm	
TUESDAY:	am/pm TO am/pm	
WEDNESDAY:	am/pm TO am/pm	
THURSDAY:	am/pm TO am/pm	
FRIDAY:	am/pm TO am/pm	
SATURDAY:	am/pm TO am/pm	
SUNDAY:	am/pm TO am/pm	

At Home Gun Holding Practice Time Total:

Figure 4-1   Scheduling Forms.

© Bob Hickey

Mental Training   Training Plans

AT HOME MENTAL TRAINING CARDS PRACTICE

DAY	HOURS TO DO TRAINING	TOTAL TIME
MONDAY:	am/pm TO am/pm	
TUESDAY:	am/pm TO am/pm	
WEDNESDAY:	am/pm TO am/pm	
THURSDAY:	am/pm TO am/pm	
FRIDAY:	am/pm TO am/pm	
SATURDAY:	am/pm TO am/pm	
SUNDAY:	am/pm TO am/pm	

Mental Training Cards Practice Time Total:

ON THE FIRING RANGE PRACTICE TIME

DAY	HOURS TO DO RANGE FIRING TRAINING	TOTAL TIME
MONDAY:	am/pm TO am/pm	
TUESDAY:	am/pm TO am/pm	
WEDNESDAY:	am/pm TO am/pm	
THURSDAY:	am/pm TO am/pm	
FRIDAY:	am/pm TO am/pm	
SATURDAY:	am/pm TO am/pm	
SUNDAY:	am/pm TO am/pm	

On The Firing Range Practice Time Total:

Figure 4-2   More Scheduling Forms.

Mental Training   Chapter 4

TRAINING PLANS

Here is an example of a typical training plan. It is that of a high school junior. He is in his third year of shooting, and has his own rifle, jacket and glove.

TRAINING PLAN # 1

Monday:

                3:30–4:00 Home from school – do home duties
"TAST"   4:00–4:30 Thinking About Shooting Time: Review of diary. Use this time to go over the training plan for the week. Think about the next match. Set training goals.
                4:30–4:45 Set up shooting equipment for Gun Holding time.
                4:45–5:15 Gun Holding Time.
                5:30–6:00 Supper
                6:00–6:30 Do dishes.
                6:30–9:00 Homework
                9:00–9:30 Selective Awareness

Time – Total Mental Training Time: 90 minutes.

TRAINING PLAN # 2

Tuesday:

                3:00–5:30 School Rifle team practice.
                6:00–6:30 Supper
                6:30–7:00 Do dishes
                7:00–9:00 Homework
                9:00–9:30 Mental Training Cards

Total Mental Training Time: 30 minutes.

© Bob Hickey

Mental Training　　　　　　　　　　　　　　　　　　　　　　　　　Training Plans

TRAINING PLAN # 3

Wednesday:
        3:30–4:30 Home from school. Do homework.
        4:30–5:00 Gun Holding Time
        5:30–6:00 Supper
        6:00–6:30 Do dishes.
        6:30–9:30 Practice with NRA Senior Rifle Club.
Total Mental Training Time: 60 minutes.

TRAINING PLAN # 4

Thursday:
        3:30–4:30 Home from school. Do home duties.
        4:30–5:00 Homework
        5:00–5:30 Gun Holding Time
        5:30–6:15 Supper
        6:15–6:45 Do dishes.
        7:00–9:30 Practice with NRA Senior Rifle Club.
Total Mental Training Time: 30 minutes.

TRAINING PLAN # 5

Friday:
        3:30–4:30 Home from school. Mental Training Cards Session.
        4:30–5:00 Home duties.
        5:00–6:00 Supper and dishes
        6:00–7:30 Gun Holding Time
        7:30–8:00 Dry–Firing Practice
        8:00–9:30 TV watching time
Total Mental Training Time: 2 hours

CHAPTER 5

Shooter's Training Diary

When you go to a shooting match, listen to the shop talk of the world champions. You can often tell, merely by how they vocalize what happens during their act of shooting, how, in a very important way, they are truly different from the local league champion. The local league champion is often simply a "trigger puller" by comparison. A common thread running through the careers of many world champions is that, at some relatively early point in their development, they have all kept diaries or notebooks about their performance. Will a diary make you a champion? Of course it won't! What it will do is give you a focal point from which to understand what the champions are saying when you read or listen to them as you gain control over your own shooting world. You can arrange a very simple test of this assertion by obtaining some of the shooting treatises listed in the bibliography, "The Roots of Mental Training." Then read them before starting to keep your own diary. After keeping your diary and practicing this system of *Mental Training* for a period of time, a couple of months at least, go back and read again those same articles.

You will likely find that on this second reading, they have a greatly expanded meaning for you. Can you become a champion without ever bothering to keep a diary? Sure, the world is full of all kinds of possibilities! But, most of us like to hedge our bets as much as we can. Your diary is certainly an awfully good hedge.

Those who learn to record their thoughts in a diary, usually acquire the skill to analyze their shooting performances more precisely than do those who do not. By keeping a diary, you learn to penetrate to the essence of your act of shooting. Look at the power you gain over yourself by acquiring such an ability! Maybe this will not win all of your matches for you when you come up against those who merely "practice" and just "shoot," but, it will help keep you right up there.

If you should decide that the whole of this *Mental Training* program is more than you need for your desired level of competition, then do make it a point to read this chapter on how to use a diary. If you learn to use a diary properly, then you will find that you naturally have acquired a program of mental training. This chapter will show you how to establish a process of thinking which will allow you to develop your shooting skill quickly and efficiently. Remember, a habit acquired in the beginning of learning to shoot will be much more likely to be a part of your second nature as you mature in the sport of marksmanship.

If you accept and nurture your use of your diary, it will become almost a way of life. You will find you are carrying over this system of organization, trials, feedback and analysis in much of your life.

The Diary You Keep Has Several Purposes

The *Shooter's Training Diary* is your primary effort to view your shooting performance from a down—to—earth, very realistic point of view. Without it, your fantasy shows you a super—you...which works against you when you fail to measure up.

The *Shooter's Training Diary* helps you to formulate plans to improve your shooting performance, because it gives you something positive to base those plans on, instead of day dreams and wishful thinking.

The *Shooter's Training Diary* helps you to verbalize your perception of your shooting performance.

The *Shooter's Training Diary* helps you to learn to speak the truth about your shooting, because it is you that you are talking to in your diary. When you go to a shooting match, listen to the talk of the shooters and you can often tell whether they are just "trigger pullers" or if they, at some point in their shooting careers, have kept a diary. Those who have learned to record their thoughts in a

© Bob Hickey

Mental Training Chapter 5

diary, usually learn to analyze their performance as opposed to those who merely "practice" or "shoot" without giving the act of shooting any reflective thought.

THE SHOOTERS DIARY

1. GOAL STATEMENT

Each time you shoot, you should have a goal for that shooting. A goal directs your attentions to making a special effort to achieve that goal. This special effort is a uniquely mental exertion. <u>Set little goals which you can reach!</u> This will help you to learn to become goal oriented. If this happens, you will see a change in yourself. You will go from a haphazard shooter, just going down to the range to pull the trigger, to someone with a purpose. Just as nations accomplish more when they have a given purpose, so individuals accomplish much more when they have a goal in mind. If President John F. Kennedy had not established an American goal of placing a man on the Moon, "One Small Step For Man, One Giant Leap For Mankind" would probably remain yet to be taken. A goal statement will focus your effort and thus harness that of your subconscious (that *Little Guy Inside* you) toward achieving it.

The word *goal* comes from the Middle English *gol* meaning *boundary, limit*. I use it in that sense. An *Individual Shot Goal* is the limit beyond which a shot is a failure.

2. EVALUATION OF GOALS MET

A goal needs to be something that can be measured by the shooter so he can plan his future practices and train that *Little Guy Inside* to view him as a good shot.

For example, take the GOAL: "My goal is a three or better on each shot Kneeling."

A shooter knows quickly when he fires just where his hold was

© Bob Hickey

by the shot location on the target. He gets an immediate feedback when he looks through the spotting scope. The diary allows the shooter to take an objective look at his performance. The target becomes his computer read-out. The mind might become aware that a lot of shots are meeting the "three or better" goal. But the target is the official record of the position of the sights at the moment of let-off. The holes may be charted and then the proximity to the goal analyzed. as you learn to handle your own personal shooting feedback, you will find that you will probably design forms which tell only you something you want to know about your performance.

The evaluation of goals is the starting point of reality. Often we shooters experience exaggerated views of our shooting ability. Either we think of our shooting efforts as being better than they are, or we feel very inferior. In any event, both of these extremes cause a sense of bewilderment in us. We wonder, for example, why we did not do as well as we "knew" we should; or we experience a quizzical wondering at how well we did. Both of these are unsettling to us. In all of our life's endeavors, we feel more settled when we know that we have done something within our capabilities. Thus Champions go on the line in world competitions planning to shoot their average score, which they are confident they can achieve. Through hard work their average exceeds that of their competition. The evaluation of goal meeting, on a regular basis, will allow you to come to both know your present capabilities and to plan a practical program to improve those capabilities.

What do you do when you evaluate a goal? First you must look at the feedback data shown on your information gathering forms. This looking process will focus your attention on what actually happened. It will start you to thinking about your performance. No longer will you be fantasizing about your shooting effort. No more will you remember only the pinwheel bullseye or the "maggie's drawers." If you learn to use the Information Gathering Forms shown in this book, you will have an objective set of data to think about. This objective thinking is known as evaluation. With this *Mental Training* program, your thinking is done in an organized manner because the Information Gathering

Forms present you with feedback about your shooting performance. Against such raw truthful data, fantasy day-dreams are soon replaced by plans for improving performance.

3. NEW GOAL SETTING

Sometimes the goal remains constant over an extended period of time. Advance your goal only when your feedback analysis shows you that you are becoming more consistent in achieving your goal. If, for example, your goal is for a 4-ring hold in your standing position and your feedback shows you that 76% of your shots are better than the goal, then it is time to attempt a goal of a 5-ring hold.

4. POSITION DESCRIPTION

To repeatedly continue to do a thing well, most of us need to know how we do the thing, whether it be rolling a bowling ball down a wooden path or learning to knock the marble we want out of the circle. In this diary entry, our objective is to learn exactly how we shoot in each of our positions. You might think of this phase of your mental training as a getting together with "that little guy inside you." Maybe you think of him as your cheerleader or principal fault-finder. In this "getting together," you want to tell that *Little Guy Inside* just exactly what your shooting position looks like and what each part of the position feels like.

Use your diary to help you to get to know your position. By putting into words what your positions "feel" like to you, you will have made a starting point. Record the "feel" of your positions as often as you can when you start to keep a Shooting Diary. This recording of the "feel" of your position will help you to learn to "talk" to your diary.

5. EVALUATION OF PERFORMANCE

Every time you shoot, your mind analyzes how well things went. There is no way you can prevent this analysis from

Mental Training   Shooter's Training Diary

happening. So, let's get it out in the open by recording it in your diary. Even if it's nothing more than "felt good, but couldn't hit the target," get it written down. This is the way you get to know yourself. In this manner, you learn the nature of your problems. In this evaluation, when you do something satisfactorily, put it in your diary so that both you and your *Little Guy Inside* can learn to savor the sweetness of shooting victory. Remember that little achievements form the base of the pinnacle of success. For example, just a notation in your diary such as:

"5 = acceptable"

may be enough to let you know you succeeded. For you, that comment is fully comprehensible. For you to let us in on that success, we would need the following translation:

"I had a goal of a 4-ring hold. In my order of shooting my fifth bull of 5 shots met this 4-ring hold goal, since all five of the shots ended inside the four ring."

So, where *"5 = acceptable"* makes the fullest possible sense to you, say it in your diary. Remember, your diary is for you and not us. Use your words and not ours, but try to be explicit, not something like:

"Prone head position was screwing me up, shot a 93."

Later when you look this over, you need more information in order to try to correct the problem. For example, how was your head "screwing you up?" Was it too close to the sight because your sling swivel was too far out on the stock? In other words, this evaluation provides you with too little information. When making your evaluation, make note of possible influences on your shooting:

"Was very hot and I also could not steady the gun down onto the target most of the time."

© Bob Hickey

Mental Training   Chapter 5

Use your diary to record pre-match preparations and any associated physical or mental problems. For example, on the day before a match you might note something like:

> *"The whole day has been bad and I am getting a headache. I just finished a Mental Training Cards rehearsal session and could not concentrate on what I was doing."*

A pre-match notation is an important part of the information you want to acquire about yourself. By itself, one pre-match observation may not be of much help to you. But a series of such records will provide you with information about yourself, enabling you to plan ways to relieve the pre-match "headache," or if you find your match scores are very fine, you can then continue your pre-match program unchanged. Always remember, evaluation is not merely a fault-finding process. It is more important for you to record those times when you are happy with your shooting performance. For example:

> *"Overall, my shooting was fairly good."*

This does not mean you have broken the Olympic Record, but that for you at your present level of skill development, you know you've done well.

6. INDIVIDUAL SHOT GOAL

We now come to the heart of your *Mental Training Program*. Here is where you learn to program yourself for consistent performance. This is something only you can do. You may have heard your coach at one time or another say something like:

> *"Concentrate on each shot you shoot! Think only of*

Mental Training   Shooter's Training Diary

one shot at a time."

Or you may have overheard veteran rifle coaches engaged in a big of behind—the—lines range chit—chat observing:

> *"I don't believe even the best shooters we have in the country ever concentrate fully on more than 75% of their shots."*

So how do you go about improving the quantity of shots you focus your full attention on? To begin with, take notice of the thing you are attempting to do. Take a look at the target bull. Not just a glance because you have seen target bulls before, but a fully alert study. See Figure 5—1 below:

Figure 5—1

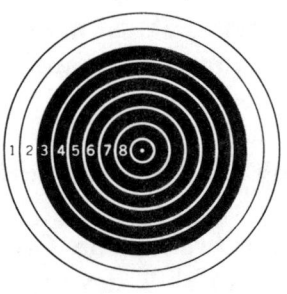

NRA International 50 foot Target Bull

Use the following method to set an initial *Individual Shot Goal*. Then, after you fire a 60—shots target as described under GOAL, conduct your target analysis to reset your *Individual Shot Goal*.

Mental Training   Chapter 5

> **Determining An Individual Shot Goal Before Firing**
>
> You need a pencil with an eraser on it. Using a razor blade, slice a thin circle off the eraser. Next, place the cut off eraser circle on the target bull. Consider now what you think you are capable of achieving on each shot. Notice that the pencil eraser makes a pretty good substitute for a .22 caliber bullet hole. Move the eraser around until you have a good idea that you can shoot one of these hits each time you fire a shot in the prone position. List that as your initial *Individual Shot Goal*. Do the same for each of your other shooting positions or or stages.

You have now set an *Individual Shot Goal*. Your shooting efforts will never be the same again. You are now different than your teammates who have not yet set up and used a *Mental Training* program. When you shoot, you now know what you are trying to achieve on each shot. This will make each shot interesting in itself for you. After you fire your first full five shots per bull practice target, then you can set your *Individual Shot Goal* from your Target Analysis Chart with the knowledge that it is a very real indication of your shooting skill level. But, in the meantime, place an "X" in the appropriate circle on your Shooter Progress Chart to keep your initial Individual Shot Goal in mind. After you do your first Target Analysis Chart, color in the proper circle with your real *Individual Shot Goal.*

The goal has to be *often attainable* to be of value to your

© Bob Hickey

progress as a good shooter. It is important for you, a new shooter, to know that goal setting for you is different than it is for an old shooter. It cannot be the "Gold at the end of the rainbow" goal. For example, saying:

"I am always trying to put my shots in the bullseye."

is not a realistic goal for you as a beginning shooter. How do you set a realistic goal?

First, you need to evaluate your present level of skill development. You have to see just where you are. In each position, you will have a different individual shot goal. You need an individual shot goal so that ;you can get an immediate feedback from each shot you shoot.

> The primary purpose of an *Individual Shot Goal* is to train your subconscious, that *Little Guy Inside*, into the firm conviction that you are a good shot who most often attains his individual goal on each shot.

How often have you heard someone say, *"Hey, I got a bull on my target!"*? If that's one bull out of ten shots, that's nine shots which were not bulls. But that guy's goal is a ten each time he shoots. If that guy is you, notice what message you are sending you subconscious. On that one shot, your subconscious, your *Little Guy Inside* felt the frustration of your failure to get a ten. What's the message that "little guy inside" gets on each failure? It is the sure knowledge that any shooter who fails to make his goal nine times out of ten is a very poor shooter. If your subconscious keeps getting the work that you can't get bullseyes, then he forms your self–image as being a "bad shot." But, doesn't everyone shoot "bad shots" in the beginning? Sure! So what's the problem? You just practice until you become better. Wrong! Wrong! Wrong!

Goal setting is easily the most misunderstood procedure in all marksmanship training. You talk to most shooters and they will tell you they are "trying to get bullseyes." Yet, that is the most frustrating thing most shooters can attempt to do. Instead, I offer a

Mental Training   Chapter 5

more practical alternative to The beginning shooter, and to the club or recreational shooter who has to report to a job each day in order to earn a living to support his family and his recreational shooting. That alternative is the "secret" of real goal setting.

> The purpose of setting a goal in shooting is to establish a consistently reachable goal so as to help your subconscious to build up the image that you are a *good shooter* who reaches his goal most of the time.

Why is it necessary that our subconscious self perceives that we are a *good shooter* who reaches his goal most of the time? Why is it necessary that our subconscious self perceive that we are good shooters when in truth, we may not be? Well, our subconscious can only perceive through what it learns from what we tell it. If we say it is cold, even though it is warm, to our subconscious self, it really is cold and it will direct the body's defenses to help protect us from the cold.

So, our subconscious perception of ourselves is very important to us. Knowing that we can change the way our subconscious views us will help us to attain better scores. This is simply because our subconscious can be trained to give us an improved view of our shooting ability. Thus, this results in our attaining a much improved self-image as far as our shooting goes.

If you believe you are a poor shooter, then you probably are a poor shooter. If, on the other hand, your subconscious knows you are a good shooter -- good insofar as you consistently achieve your own personal goals -- then you will never lose a match due to lack of confidence. And, you'll probably win more than your share of the medals.

So, how do you make the big step to "*the winner of the medals,*" if you are just getting started or have a very limited range practice schedule? Some of our best Olympic Gold medalists will give the advice of "*practice, practice, more practice and shoot every match you can enter.*" You to learn to handle the effects of competition in competition. Those same counselors will also point our that the average age of a person who wins a place on a U. S.

© Bob Hickey

Mental Training Shooter's Training Diary

Olympic Shooting Team is about 31 years. There is no substitute for range time, wisely used.

So the "secret" all we civilian coaches have been searching for is: "Five days practice, one day travel to matches, and Sunday for tournaments." Do I see a smile at this? Nevertheless, I suspect it to be truer for our fledgling Olympians than any of us lesser mortals have ever really thought. But is this the "secret"? No, but, there are many who come close to this ideal, what with shooting in a couple of leagues each week, plus a practice night and a weekend tournament. Most of us who fit into this category are known to the "inner circle" of American champions as "trigger pullers."

A "trigger puller" is a shooter who merely goes to the range for "practice" or "for a match." He does no pre-range thinking about his performance, no mental rehearsal of possible performance tactics. In short a "trigger puller" is a mental pygmy.

How do you move from "trigger puller" to become respected good shooter? You do it by adopting or devising a mental training program. This means learning to set and <u>adhere</u> to a goal you set.

The key to goal setting is knowledge of your actual performance. Often when we first start to shoot, we see only the one bullseye and not the other four shots which missed the BLACK in our 5-shot string. If not correct, this seeing only the bullseyes becomes an ingrained part of the real us, the inner self us. It is usually at least ten years from the start of our shooting training until our performance level can come close to our fantasy level of performance -- if it ever does. This mental training program is designed to correct that defect in our marksmanship training. It may still take ten years for your performance level to reach the point of all tens on a full ISU course of fire. But, in the process of reaching that level, your subconscious, by using this mental training program, will be getting positive feedback from you. You will be letting your subconscious, that "little guy inside," know that you are a good shooter who consistently reaches your individual shot goals.

Individual Shot Goals? *"Of course, I try for a ten on each shot!"* Well, if you do, and you haven't made a U.S. International Shooting Team yet, then you are one of the ones this book was written for, that is a beginning shooter. If your thinking is: "I try

© Bob Hickey

Mental Training   Chapter 5

for a ten each shot!" then that is the start of your problems in seeking a short-cut to improved performance. Even our Olympic medalists do not shoot tens all the time. "But," you say, "aren't you supposed to try for tens?" No! Emphatically, NO! For years, the NRA training filmstrip on position shooting advised "shoot within your wobble area." The problem has been how do you find out what your wobble area is? Now we have the answer, take a look at the Target Analysis Chart illustrated in this book. It is a feedback chart designed to show you graphically just what your wobble area is. With it you have a visual presentation to help you select an *Individual Shot Goal*. This will be a goal based on your actual performance level, not your bullseye fantasy.

To make this work, you need sufficient shots to establish a performance level. So, shoot at least 60 shots in a position. Here is a brief example using the Smallbore Position Course of fire. Pistol shooters do the same thing with slow fire at 50 yards or 6 ten shot rapid fire strings. I think you get the idea. Do at least 60 shots at whichever stage of fire you wish to establish an *Individual Shot Goal*. Back to the example.

1. Use the A-36 target. Why the A-36? Because with its graduated rings, it gives you a more reliable indication of your performance level.

2. Shoot 60 shots in a position.

3. Obtain a 3-ring binder for your Target Analysis Charts.

Again, why the A-36 target? It has graduated rings, from 1 to 10. This will give you a very definite and precise registration of your wobble area.

Sixty shots in a position or stage? "Can I take a break between ten shot strings?" If you get involved in this mental training program, then you are going to have to "maximize your range training time" as Lanny Bassham, one of America's Olympic Champions is fond of advising those in search of his "secrets." If you have a "walk down, hang and retrieve your targets type of range" then talk the club members into running 30 minute relays. Hang a target and shoot five shots in each bull, including your sighters on the A-36 target. The A-36 target is the National Rifle Association of America's designation for their reduction of the International Shooting Union's 50 meters target for firing at 50 feet. Surely you can stay in position for 30 minutes? If not, then you should begin training yourself to do so. You should be able to fire at least two shots each minute, if you don't dawdle over your glance through the spotting scope and learn how to unload and reload your rifle as you glance through the spotting scope.

The normal way an American views the shots he fires is tied to our present scoring system. Our system is called "inward gauging." This is because when we "plug" or "gauge" a shot, we look to see where the "plug" is in relation to the center of the bull. We "give" the highest shot value to the shooter which the edge of the plug touches on it's journey to the center of the bull. This in turn leads the shooter to a rather all or nothing attitude towards his shots. The shooter is hoping to get the shots close to the center. This tends to develop a sloppy mental attitude toward individual shot performance. This attitude is often supported by some coaches who coach by saying, *make each shot the best you can.*

This contrasts rather vividly with the British target system which requires "outward gauging." Under this system, shots touching the inside of the next outer scoring ring are scored to that *lower* value. Under this system, the shooter develops a definite mental "set" against *dropping* points in his string. This is further promoted by the way scores are presented on the match bulletin board and in the match final bulletins. The scores are reported by *dropped points.* So, in the Scottish Nationals, a shooter sees his score put up on the Bulletin Board as 5. In the American Nationals, that same score would appear on the Bulletin Board as a 395.

In essence, the *individual shot goal* is the *outward gauging* system applied to the way you think about your shooting. This should make your much more stronger, mentally, than your shooting peers who have not yet learned to think like this.

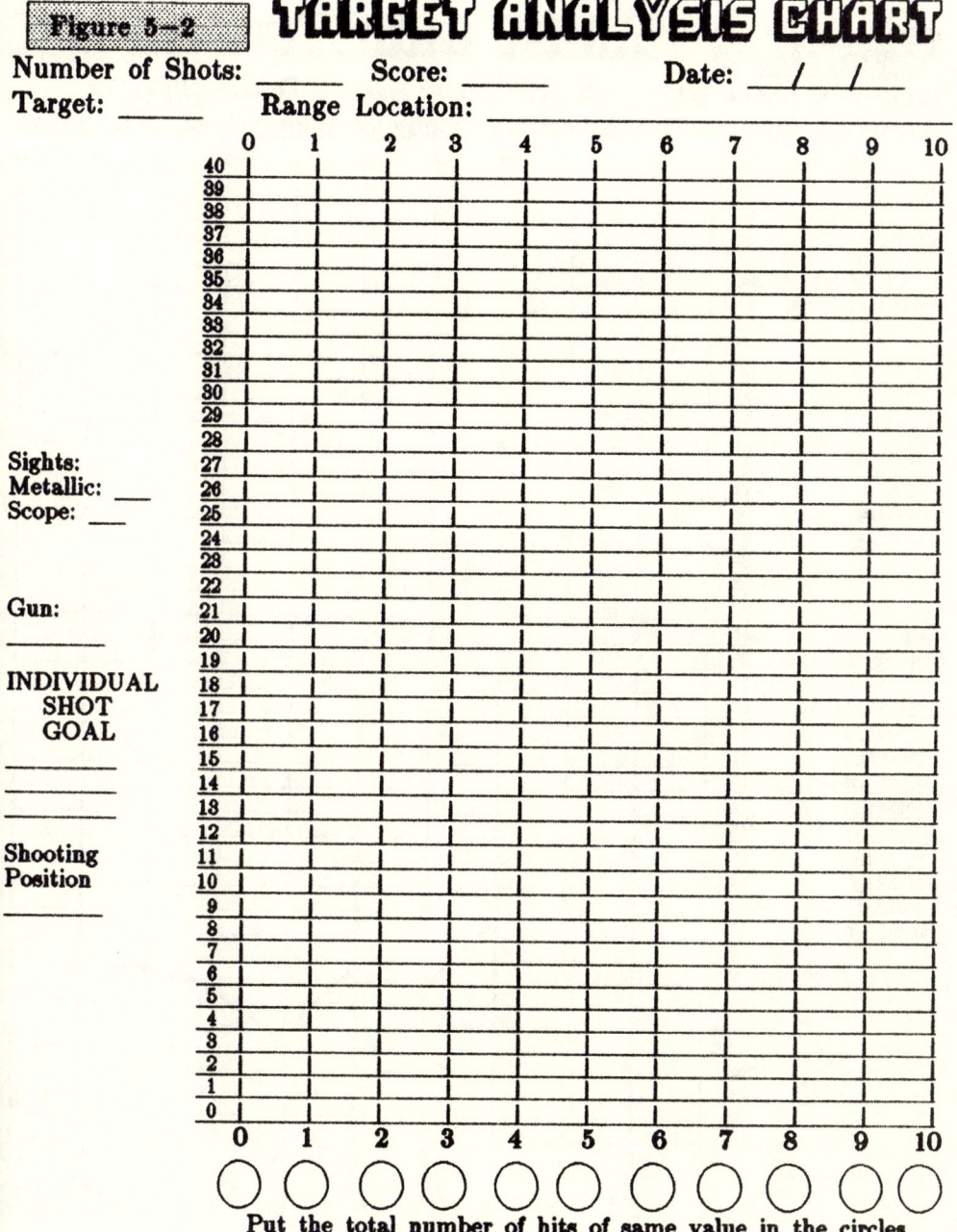

Figure 5-2

Mental Training Shooter's Training Diary

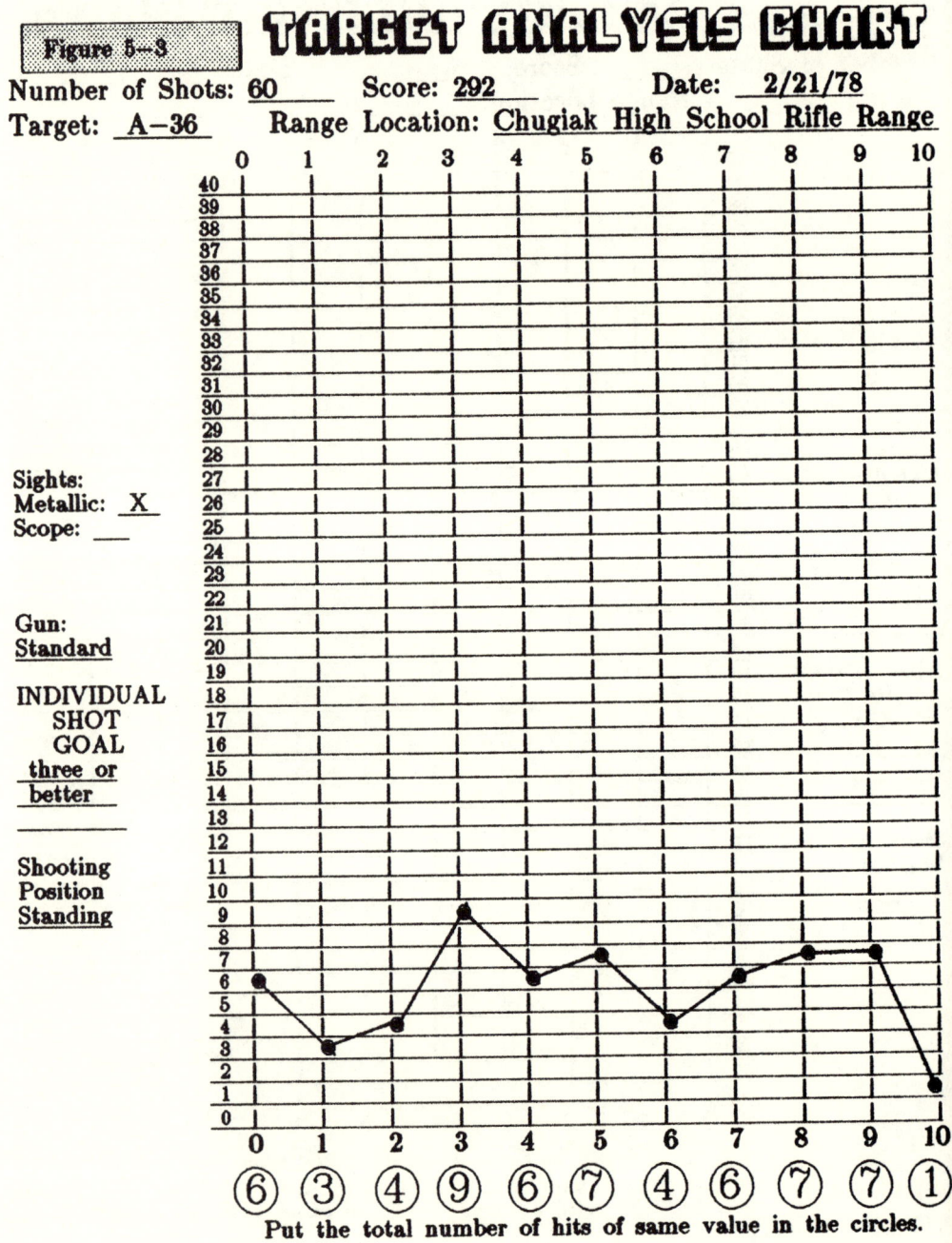

Figure 5-3 **TARGET ANALYSIS CHART**

Number of Shots: 60 Score: 292 Date: 2/21/78
Target: A-36 Range Location: Chugiak High School Rifle Range

Sights:
Metallic: X
Scope: __

Gun:
Standard

INDIVIDUAL
SHOT
GOAL
three or
better

Shooting
Position
Standing

Put the total number of hits of same value in the circles.

© Bob Hickey

Mental Training Chapter 5

Back to goal setting. After you have finished your practice, tak target home, score it and plot it out on your Target Analysis Chart. through the process together:

> 1. Record the date
> 2. Put down the total number of shots
> 3. Check off the sights used
> 4. Check the shooting position
> 5. Record the total number of hits of the same value, starting with the number of bullseyes on the right side of the chart.
> 6. Add up the numbers you placed in the boxes to be certain they correspond to the total number of shots you fired.
> 7. Then plot the hits on the graph and connect the dots.
> 8. Construct your *goal line* to determine your *Individual Shot Goal*.

Now we come to the purpose for which you plotted your shots -- goal setting. Before we begin this process, remember it is our purpose to establish a goal which will give us positive feedback most of the time, not half the time and not three quarters of the time, but *almost all the time*. Did I say *almost all the time*? Yes, I did! Well what kind of goal is that? It is the only one that will help you train your subconscious -- that *Little Guy Inside* to "know" that you are a good shot who *almost always achieves his goal.* Now if you have a low goal, keep it to yourself. No one else, except your coach, needs to know about it. Even with a low goal, a lot of your shots will be above it. They better be, otherwise you've set the wrong goal. Your shooting companions will merely see your result. Let your goal be a private matter between you and your Shooting Diary.

So how do you go about setting such a goal? Usually you want no more than about 9 to 14 shots out of the sixty which do not meet your goal. This is important:

GOAL RULE:

**Out Of Sixty Shots,
No More Than
9 To 14
Do Not Make It!**

To learn how to set this goal, take a look at the following example: First, look at the bottom part of the Target Analysis Chart as it is before you record your shot values. See Figure 5-4

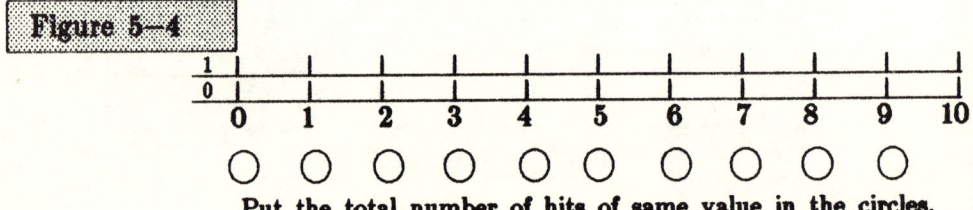

Figure 5-4

Put the total number of hits of same value in the circles.

Now look at it after it has been filled with the values of the sixty shots you fired in this, our example: See Figure 5-5

© Bob Hickey

Mental Training Chapter 5

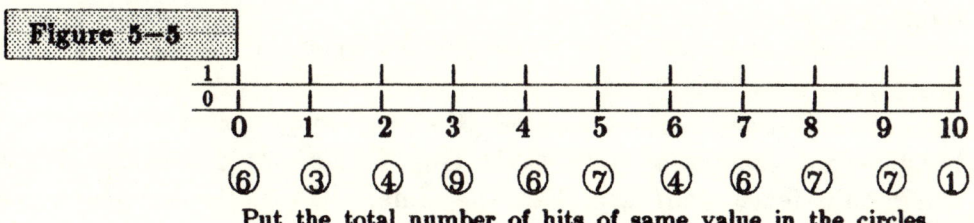

Put the total number of hits of same value in the circles.

Start by noticing the numbers in the circle at the bottom of the Target Analysis Chart. Start with the tens, then add the hits in each scoring ring, going from the inner most rings to the outer most. See Figure 5-6.

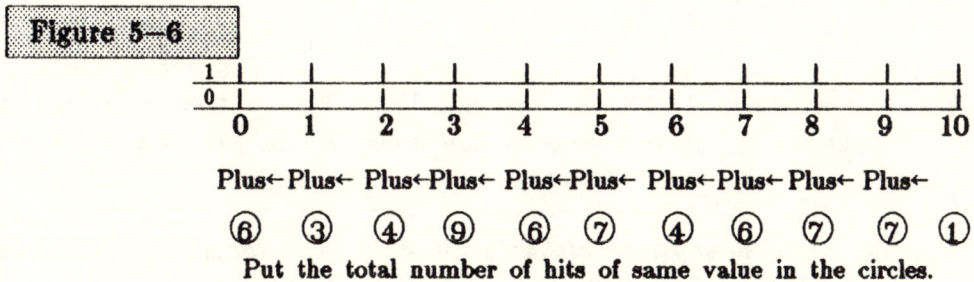

Put the total number of hits of same value in the circles.

Add the number of tens to the number of nines: See Figure 5-6.

The sum of the nines and tens is eight. So, your goal cannot be a nine or better because, if it were, you would have ONLY eight positive feedbacks to your subconscious when you glance through your spotting scope., More importantly, you would have 52 *negative* feedbacks. So you must proceed to the next shot ring in setting your shot goal.

Add the sum of the nines and tens to the number of eights: See Figure 5-6. No goal in sight yet. Fifteen positive feelings for the *Little Guy Inside* and 45 bad feelings for him. Not good at all for that *positive* self-image we are creating.

So add that sum to the number of sevens: See Figure 5-6.

Twenty-one out of sixty shots is still only one-third positive feedback. Not nearly good enough. Go on and this sum to the number of sixes: See Figure 5—6.

Twenty—five, no good! Getting the idea? Go on to the fives: See Figure 5—6.

Thirty—two, you've passed the half—way point. Can you imagine how confused your *Little Guy Inside* would become if you could only reach your goal half the time? Go on to the fours: See Figure 5—6.

Thirty—eight! That means twenty—two negative feelings of not achieving a goal of a four. Too many! Go on to the threes: See Figure 5—6.

A—ha! We found our goal. It's a "three or better." Look at this! We have 47 *positive* feelings for that *Little Guy Inside* to savor! That means, that out of sixty shots, he gets a negative feedback only 13 times. See Figure 5—6.

A caution, do not set a goal merely "intellectually" and then proceed to feel a disappointment when you do not get a bullseye. The Target Analysis Chart does not lie. It is a true reflection of your performance as recorded by the holes in that ultimate feedback chart of each shooter, his target!

Another point to remember, when you set a *goal* in this manner, *Blind yourself to higher goals until your target analysis chart shows you that your performance level has advanced.*

7. TARGET FEEDBACK ANALYSIS

This again is something you do at home. It is part of the time you schedule and devote to your shooting training outside actual range practice.

Use range time for firing shots at targets. Consider each hole your bullet puts in the target paper as your own feedback of your shooting performance. In other words, the hole in the paper helps to confirm the sense impressions your mind related to you about the shot as it was fired. A glance through your spotting scope and the position of the bullet hole acts as a very positive feedback, confirming those at—the—moment—of—firing sense impressions.

Consider this: The hole in the target is a fact! Its nearness to the exact center of the bull can be precisely measured. In the beginning of your awareness of what your mind tells you about the shot before you glance through the spotting scope, you may notice some contradictions. Don't worry about them at the beginning! The position of the shot hole is not a lie! But neither may your mind-sensations be a lie either.

As you become more experienced, you will become more aware that man has not yet been able to invent the perfect lot of ammunition, Eley Ten-X not withstanding.

Even the best ammunition, produced under the most stringent manufacturing care in the world, will not group consistently, shot upon shot in an indoor 100 yards shooting tunnel. I observed this upon a visit to the Imperial Metals Industries, the factory which produces the Eley brand .22 caliber ammunition in Birmingham, England. At the Eley plant, I watched as shots were fired into test groups and was even permitted to fire some shots in the group myself. I watched as the tester cut off a slice of the nose of the bullets and then fired it into the group. He then showed me how a nick in the base of the a bullet would throw it outside to the group. But, even in these very controlled conditions, in which the bullet was fired from a rifle locked in a vise, at a blank sheet of paper on a roll, at the end of a windless tunnel, the shots did not impact one on top of the other. The shots made holes near each other, forming a "group."

For is an example of what a group of five fired outdoors, looks like: See Figure 5-7. This group was fired at fifty yards in the prone position. Now remember, a normal course of fire, in prone events, consists of 40 shots. That breaks down into eight of the kinds of groups depicted in Figure 5-7. That's right, in every class of competition, many big tournaments are won with perfect scores of 400 out of 400 possible points.

© Bob Hickey

Figure 5-7

If the ammunition is not capable of achieving the consistency of putting one bullet on top of the previous bullet when fired in these optimum conditions, then try to understand that your mind may not be lying to you just because the shot hole may not be where your mind senses it went. However, do not blame the ammunition for each such misjudgment. Most commercially available .22 caliber target ammunition will be quite reliable for

Mental Training   Chapter 5

indoor gallery shooting at 50 feet. I suggest that you place complete reliance on your ammunition as you begin to analyze your individual shot performance. So, let's regard the shot hole as a reliable feedback factor. Consider that the hole would not be where it is if the sights had not been located where the hole ended up. Regard each shot hole as the feedback of your shooting effort. You will find that you will have two different types of Target Feedback Analysis:

1. *Immediate Analysis*: On the firing line, you will find that your mind will automatically provide you with an on–the–spot analysis by your own *Little Guy Inside*:

> "*Dummy! Don't 'cha know better than to jerk the trigger?*"
>   OR
> "*Boy! That's it! Now you're grooving them! Keep it up!*"

Go with this *Immediate Analysis*, but try to allow your *Little Guy Inside* a chance to work for you. Rehearse your *Individual Shot Goal* all–the–way for that *Little Guy Inside*. Do not dwell on the bad performances, *think only of your good shooting efforts*.

2. *After Shooting Analysis*: So much for your instant shot analysis. That's what you do at the range, during individual practice session. Now the rest of your target analysis is to be done at home or during an "off" relay. If you practice with a club and you have a coach or club leader who scores the targets for you, you're lucky. It frees your time so that you can put your attention to more shooting or studying the results of your performance. But try to cultivate the habit of using this free time for extended practice or analysis of your shooting efforts. Try to avoid non–shooting related gossip sessions or horse–play. Range time is too valuable to waste. To hold out in your mind the idea that such non–shooting activities help relax you from the grind of competition, is to beg the question. They also get your adrenaline pumping. This means you must exert a much greater effort to calm your body after such activities, before you return to the firing line for your next competitive event.

Now, in your home, find a place where you can work without interference. For you, such a spot might be in your own room. Next, take your target and:
1. Count the number of hits of each value, such as the number of tens, nines, eights, sevens, sixes, etc.
2. Write the total number of hits of same value in the boxes at the bottom of your Target Analysis Chart. 3. Next chart a graph of your hits.
   a. Go to the line of the hit value until you intersect the number of hits of that value.
   b. Make a large dot at that intersection.
   c. Draw a line connecting your dots.
4. Now compute your *Individual Shot Goal*. Your *Individual Shot Goal* is the scoring ring which has 76% of your shot hits in that ring and higher. Out of 60 shots, that would be 46 hits or better.

The object of this procedure is to draw your attention to the results of your shooting performance and to let your *Little Guy Inside* know what you expect. This gives you a much more reliable indication of your skill development than achieving an NRA Indoor 50 foot Rifle Qualification medal or even winning a local match. Strive to develop your skill to such a degree that all of your shots form one dot, at the top, of the right hand side of your graph. In other words, when all of your shots are tens, you have a "perfect" graph. The "taking—a—look at" which you do after you've drawn your graph is your target feedback analysis. The Target Analysis Chart will allow you to monitor your shooting performance. Consistently maintained, your Target Analysis Charts will graphically show you your progress and help you to make intelligent decisions on the amount of practice you should devote to each shooting position. Remember, you want to move the dots on your chart from the left side of the graph to the right side of it. If you are fortunate enough to belong to a club with a concerned coach, share this phase of your shooting analysis with him. He may be able to help you to schedule and monitor your range practice time to better effect. Remember, each time you practice, fire enough shots to

Mental Training Chapter 5

make use of the Target Analysis Chart worthwhile. Fire at least five shots at each bull, so that you shoot sixty shots in a position on the NRA's A-36 indoor International 50-foot target, each time you practice.

8. NUMBER OF SHOTS MEETING SHOT GOAL

This is actually a part of your target feedback analysis. Here you take a look to see how many of your shots actually met your *Individual Shot Goal.* Just make a note of it:

"47 shots 3-ring or better."

9. PURPOSE OF SHOOTING

It is important for you to know why you are shooting. For example, your purpose for shooting is:

"Qualification for Friday's match."

You now know you have a different situation than if you merely wanted to practice your kneeling or standing position. If you have to qualify for your position on the team, that's much like having a mini-match. It is your chance to see how you perform under a pressure condition. It is a valuable self-indexing tool. Savor it and use it to record the difference between the way your shooting positions feel in practice as compared to how they feel in a pressure situation.

Perhaps your *purpose of shooting* might be:

"To practice Mental Shot Rehearsal before firing each shot."

OR

"To practice an aggressive attitude toward my trigger let-off."

In any case, verbalize it by writing it down in your diary.

© Bob Hickey

Mental Training

10. ORDER OF SHOOTING

This part of your diary is a memory saver. Here you number the order in which you fire your shots. In matches, on the indoor NRA International A–36 50–foot target, remember, start with your top sighting bull, then move down to your bottom sighter. But, in the beginning of your shooting, you may wonder:

"How many shots at the sighter?"

Try at least six at the top sighter and then confirm the fact that you are sighted in by firing two more at the bottom sighter.

So far, so good! Now comes your major decision of the match! We're assuming that you would like in on one of the secrets of how to shoot your target bulls in a manner that will maybe save you a point in a tight prone match.

Do You Fire The Target Bulls
in The Order In Which They Are Numbered?

See Figure 5–8.

Figure 5–8 Target Numbering System

1 2 3
4 SS 5
6 SS 7
8 9 10

No! Absolutely not!

Those bulls are numbered so that ties can be broken in a uniform way each time. That is the only use for the printed numbers. So for you, as the shooter, just ignore the numbers.

Consider this! You very carefully took time to check and

adjust your rifle's "natural point of aim" at your initial sighting bull before you fired any sighters. You were mindful not to allow your left elbow to move once you had arranged your natural point of aim at your sighting bull, nor to permit your left elbow to move once you started firing your sighters. Look at how many times you must shift your point of aim if you shoot the bulls in the order they are numbered: See Figure 5-9.

Figure 5-9   Points of Aim shifts

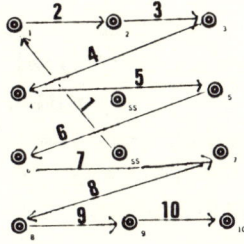

Ten natural points of aim shifts! You can certainly do it. Lots of beginning shooters do. Is there a better way? Yes! Doesn't it make more sense to keep the natural point of aim you already established for the sighters and merely adjust your breathing process to shoot at the two record bulls above and beneath your sighters for the first two On Record shots? This is within your primary natural point of aim. After shooting these bulls then adjust your natural point of aim to the left side string of bulls. Shoot them! Go now to the right side string of bulls. Adjust your natural point of aim for this side. Shoot them! Result: *Two* natural points—of—aim shifts as opposed to *ten* the old way! See Figure 5-10.

Figure 5-10   New Points of Aim Shifts

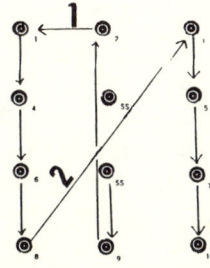

In using this order of shooting, go ahead and fire at the bottom middle bull first, since you just finished your sighting shots

Mental Training — Shooter's Training Diary

in the sighter bull above it. Then go on to the top middle bull. Then proceed shooting down through the left side of the target and then the right side bulls.

Use this in practice so it becomes a habit that you need not think about in a match. Consider this your usual order of shooting. In practice, since you are not shooting for score, or group, but are shooting for your individual shot goals, fire five shots at each of the bulls on your target all from only one position. Your spotting scope will give you immediate feedback as to whether or not you achieved your *Individual Shot Goal* on each shot you fired. You need to get used to staying in position for extended times and firing many shots in one shooting position. The reason you need to do this is so you can train the pathways to your mind to perform skillfully enough to pump shot after shot into the center of the aiming mark.

11. DATE

Day Of Week	Month	Day	Year

Here's a simple entry. Just put down the information in the blanks. Simple though it be, do it each and every time. It will help you keep an accurate record of your progress.

12. TIME

Time: __:__ a.m./p.m.

Easy! Just put down the time you start to shoot. Important from the standpoint of how well you perform at different times of the day. Significant only after you have a lot of recorded practice sessions and matches to compare.

13. LOCATION

Mental Training   Chapter 5

Tell where you are shooting. Just enough to keep the range identified in your mind as the years sweep past you. You may also want to record special characteristics of ranges, other than your home range, in order to review conditions just before you fire another match there.

14. AMMUNITION

Brand:

15. LOT NUMBER

Lot Number:

Keep a record of your ammunition so that you can keep track of the brands and ammunition lots you have success with. Ammunition is identified by manufacturer by numbers, called lot numbers. Often these lot numbers will identify the year of manufacture.

It is also good to record the number of shots fired, so that you will have reasonably accurate count of how many rounds have gone through your barrel.

16. EQUIPMENT PROBLEM

Make a note here about anything regarding your equipment. Malfunctions should be noted because they certainly do affect your performance. List equipment you lack, either because you forgot it or there is not enough range or club equipment for you to use. For example:

"No spotting scope; I can't see what I am shooting."

OR

"The bolt keeps sticking about every other time. I have to

© Bob Hickey

force it down."

17. EQUIPMENT MODIFICATION

Use this part of your diary to keep a record of any changes you make to your shooting equipment. For example:

> *"Changed front sight: From: 2.7*
> *for prone position   To: 3.0"*

Comment on whether you feel this change affects your shooting performance:

> *"On second target, I put a piece of heavy cardboard on my stock. It seemed to help; head felt more comfortable."*

18. PERFORMANCE PROBLEM

Identify problems you have with your shooting positions. If you observe something happening, jot it down. That's what your diary is for:

> *"I cannot steady the gun. It keeps bouncing and swinging around. I seem to be tensing my right shoulder muscle."*

OR

> *"I think my head position is screwing me up because it is tipping slightly to the right. Tomorrow I will try canting the rifle into my face."*

By listing these problems, you can then attack them because you have written them down. If you cannot think of a solution to try immediately, put it in the back of your mind. Think about it every so often, then leave it alone. You may be surprised to find that later, when you read this problem again, a solution may just "pop into your head." This is your creative subconscious at work.

19. PROBLEM ANALYSIS

When you notice a problem, try to figure out the cause. For example, if you find you are noticing the heat more than your relay mates, you might speculate:

"I had on an extra T-shirt and this may have caused the heat."

This trying-to-figure-out-the-cause is known as "problem analysis." Remember, you do not have to be right each time in your attempt to isolate the cause of your problem. But...write your selected "cause" in your diary. Future such observations, when the same problem occurs, will tell you whether this "cause" was more probable than your new "cause", if it is not the same. And it is entirely possible that both "causes" are correct problem causers at the time the problem occurs.

20. SOLUTION TO TRY

After identifying your problem, your primary effort will be to try various things which will eliminate the problem or come to grips with it so it does not hinder your shooting performance. For example, if you have a problem with your head position in the prone position, you might suggest to yourself in your diary entry:

"Try to increase angle between arm and gun."

Make a little drawing to illustrate what you are thinking of trying. It is your diary, so try to draw these things out. Your work is not going to be put on display in an art gallery. Drawing it out will help both you and your *Little Guy Inside* to see just

Mental Training Shooter's Training Diary

exactly what you are thinking of trying. See Figure 5-11.

 Make Pictures To Help You In Your Diary

Try to increase angle between Arm & Gun.

21. DISTRACTIONS NOTICED

Jot down notes about those things at the range which distract you. This will help you to learn how to cope with unexpected problems which come up. You must learn to accept the unexpected and not permit it to interfere with your match performance. In order to do this, you must become flexible in your approach to your shooting. You cannot always control the conditions under which you will fire all of your matches. Accept the problems which crop up in practice and deal with them as your own personal learning situations. For example, you might sometime experience a problem such as:

> "Rita took my target on standing and got me mad. I lost 12 points on my first 3 shots."

OR

> "The NRA Referee was smoking in a chair right behind my firing point, and I didn't want to make him mad by getting out of position to tell him it was bothering me."

If you do not come up with a satisfactory way of dealing with the problem at the time, use your diary as a monday-morning-quarterback to help you to decide how you should

Mental Training — Chapter 5

have dealt with the distraction. For example, you might have told Rita that you do not like to have people messing around with your targets on the range. If that doesn't work, you might just ask her out for a date. Then, with respect to the smoking problem, you might have gone to the Range Officer and told him you were having problems with the smoke on the firing line. Or you might ask your coach to handle this one. See how MONDAY–MORNING–QUARTERBACKING works? Should it occur in another match, you now have some pre–thought out alternatives.

22. MISCELLANEOUS OBSERVATIONS

This is the place to record those things about your shooting or things connected to your shooting, which do not fall under any of the other categories of your diary. For example:

> *"Head cleared up at about 8:45 p.m. and I got caught up on Selective Awareness Training goals."*

As part of your preparation for each tournament, set goals for your matches. When you do, always make an after–match evaluation list comparison. This will help you to see whether you are viewing your skill level realistically.

23. FUTURE PRACTICE PLAN

Try to use this to help you and that *Little Guy Inside* keep ahead of your practice requirements. For example:

> *"I need to go over my standing position soon and see if I am doing anything wrong."*

But this is a negative thought. A better use of this area of your diary is to use it for entries such as:

> *"I need to go over my standing position and record it*

© Bob Hickey

Mental Training   Shooter's Training Diary

in detail in my diary, since I've been performing very well in it recently."

Always go for the positive. In other words —— *Accentuate The Positive!*

HOW TO USE THE RECOIL CHART

PURPOSES:

1. To teach the shooter to follow through by directing his attention to observation of his rifle's recoil.
2. To stimulate the shooter into making the "scientific method" a part of his shooting training.
3. To allow the shooter to see that even when his attention is on something other than the Act of Shooting, his shots will be fired.

METHOD: For coaches, when working with groups.

1. Have the shooters divide into pairs.
2. The shooter is to record the number of the shot in the segmented area, indicating the direction of the recoil.
3. The shooter is then to record the area of the shot hole by putting the number of the shot in the proper segmented area and drawing a small circle around the hit number.
4. Under comments, have the shooter observe the relationship between recoil and shot hits.
5. Have each shooter's buddy do the same thing for his shooter.
6. Upon finishing, the shooter and his observer buddy compare notes and observations.

© Bob Hickey

Mental Training   Chapter 5

RECOIL CHART FORM

Figure 5–12

DATE: ___/___/___   Name:

Coach's Observations:

DIRECTIONS: PLACE THE NUMBER OF THE SHOT IN THE DIRECTION OF THE RECOIL.

COMMENTS:

© Bob Hickey   139

Mental Training   **Shooter's Training Diary**

DIARY FORM

Figure 5-13

DATE: __/__/__   Name:

Coach's Observations:

1. Goal Statement:
4. Position Description:
6. Individual Shot Goal:
9. Purpose Of Shooting:
10. Order Of Shooting:
12. Time: 13. Location:
14. Ammunition: 15. Lot Number:
16. Equipment Problem:
17. Equipment Modification:
18. Performance Problem:
19. Problem Analysis:
20. Solution To Try:
21. Distractions Noticed:
22. Miscellaneous Observations:
2. Evaluation Of Goals Met:
3. New Goal Setting:
5. Evaluation Of Performance:
7. Target Feedback Analysis:
8. Number Of Shots Meeting Shot Goal:
23. Future Practice Plan:

© Bob Hickey

Mental Training Chapter 5

Figure 5-14 — MATCH SCHEDULE FORM
RECREATIONAL SHOOTING FORMULA
From where will the money come, to where will it go?

	Monthly Income	Match Name	Fee	Match Expenses				Total Expenses
				Gas	Food	Motel	Ammo	
Jan								
Feb								
Mar								
Apr								
May								
Jun								
Jul								
Aug								
Sep								
Oct								
Nov								
Dec								

© Bob Hickey

Mental Training   Shooter's Training Diary

DUEL MATCH CONTRACT

DIRECTIONS:

1. Select a person close to your ability level and offer a challenge for a mtach at the next or a future practice session.
2. If the *duel* is between shooters of different skill levels, adjustment points will have to be mutually agreed to when the match is set up.
3. Be certain the prize is something of significance. In an actual match, the prize might be a bronze medal of small economic value. The point lies in the significance of the prize to the participants. it is a *real* prize if there is an *inner humiliation* at having failed to win it. So too, the *duel* match prize should give you an *inner sense of responsibility* as you attempt to win it. This *inner sense of responsibility* must be able to generate a determination to *not lose* because of a strong feeling of the value of the prize. A *coke* match just fails to meet this *sense of responsibility*.
4. What kind of prize generates this absolutely necessary *sense of responsibility*? It will vary with each pair of shooters. As an example, two juniors attending different high schools practice evenings with the same **NRA Senior Rifle Club**. Their prize consists of the loser having to wear the winner's high school booster sweatshirt to classes and school sporting events until the next *duel* match. On the adult level, a shotgunner wins his first belt buckle at a regional tournament. At home with his club, he offers the belt buckle as his end of the prize of a *duel* match. If he loses, he gives up the belt buckle to the winner of the *duel* match. If he wins, he collects what the other shooter put up. The other shooter would have put up something he would not want to lose either. Remember, if you put up something you know in your mind that you can afford to lose, then the match will be of marginal value to your training. This is true, even if in the mind of the other shooter, what you put up is something he really wants.

Mental Training   Chapter 5

Duel Match Contract

Figure 5-15

Date: __ __/__ __/__ __

Date of Match:

Course of Fire:

Duelist #1 Prize Offered:

Duelist #1 Signature:

Duelist #2 Prize Offered:

Duelist #2 Signature:

- -

Thing to work on in match:

After match comment:

© Bob Hickey

CHAPTER 6

Alpha State Training

Alpha state is a state of mind where you remove all distractions from your awareness and allow your reflexive impulses to be your performance. Remember, all of your shooting training is designed for the reflexive reaction of your trigger finger to the perceived perception of what your eye sees with respect to the position of the sights on the target. Therefore, you must work to achieve the kind of state of mind which will permit that reflexive reaction to occur without a block. This is Alpha State.

How does this book help you to achieve this condition of Alpha State? It does so by giving you the following programs, each carefully designed to train your mind and your attitude toward your shooting, so that you will end up in that special pre-shot attitude called: Alpha State. These programs and the way they fit into the overall *Mental Training* program are:

1. *Mental Training Cards*

    A program to develop an interest in how each shot feels. This is a program designed to help you train your mental recall of good shots. It is a background helpful to the mental shot rehearsal program you will work on later in the *Mental Training* Program.

2. *Gun Holding Practice Program*

    A program designed to help you to become objective about your effort to reduce the movement of the sight pattern. This program, by channeling your attention to your sight pattern, is designed to promote your interest in each individual shot. By doing this, it will decrease the number of shots upon which you do not concentrate fully during the course of a match or practice.

Mental Training Chapter 6

3. *Selective Awareness Training*

A program designed to help you to "internalize" your approach to your shooting. This next step in the "turning inward" of your approach to shooting is a very important step in your training to achieve Alpha State when you are on the firing line. This program will focus your attention on the muscles of the act of shooting. That is, you will look at the muscles involved in achieving the tension necessary to get the maximum performance out of your shooting effort. This will help that *Little Guy Inside* you to get "inside" those muscles and really "feel" the tension of shooting and the tension of the muscles *at rest* and under induced INTENSE tension. Often the tenseness of the muscles in a match will differ from those same muscles in practice training. This may be especially noticeable at the beginning of your shooting career. This Selective Awareness Training program is designed to give you a formal way of recognizing any change in the tension of the muscles of shooting. It will give you an invaluable practice at "looking inward."

4. *Training Plans Program*

What is this? Training Plans Program? A part of Alpha State Training? Yes! And double yes! This mental training program is a training program designed so each of its parts dovetails and complements each of the others. The Training Plans Program is designed to help you to learn to "turn inward." When you sit down and make a plan under this program, it lets both you and your *Little Guy Inside* know where you are going and how you plan to get there. It also gives that *Little Guy Inside* a clue as to how much you are willing to "put out" to achieve your ambition. The Home Time Schedule Plan is also specifically designed to help you acquire the "inward looking" ability to aid you when you take up Alpha Training. Learn to follow it and it will lead into the habit of vocalizing what you discover about yourself and your shooting so that your *Little Guy Inside* knows full well what you want him to know. This is another way of saying that you will learn to interpret what is going on inside you. By doing this vocalization, you will be bringing it to the attention of your external sensors. It is then reintroduced to your brain so that your subconscious can help you

© Bob Hickey

Mental Training Alpha State Training

perform in the way you want to in your shooting.

5. *Your Shooting Diary*

I think you know now that most definitely your Shooting Diary is an integral part of this program to prepare you to get the most out of your Alpha State Training. For most of you, your diary will be the first halting steps you take to coming to friendly grips with your own *Little Guy Inside*.

Two good examples of diary entries were provided by Marie Alkire, Executive Director of the United States Women's International Rifle Organization and are reproduced below. The first is a diary entry for a practice shooting session. The second is for a tournament.

FICTICIOUS DIARY ENTRY FOR PRACTICE SESSION

Date: December 6, 1977   Wednesday
Place: Kansas State University
Time: 7:30 pm
Weather: Gallery.
Goal for Day: Improve standing and kneeling hold by experimentation. Practice 30 shots in each position.
Mental Condition: Excellent spirits.
Physical Condition: Very tired.
Comments: Experiment. Move left hand from under champber to under scope block forward about 1 1/2 inches. This seems to give me better control over the rifle and helps dampen out little involuntary jerks. Score improved greatly as shooting progressed, primarily, I think as I got used to the new arm angle. Two observations: the left elbow belongs centered on the tip of the hipbone, and make sure to move the left leg also to align column. Moving the right leg alone throws off the position and muscle tension.

Kneeling: Another experiment: I've had a feeling of the rifle floating randomly around. I tried tightening the sling, which seemed to drastically worsen the problem. So I tried lengthening the sling. This produced a feeling of looseness which was very unsettling. Tentative solution: leave sling length alone and move hand stop/sling swivel in (to rear) from 4 to 4 1/2 inches. This helped to decouple

© Bob Hickey

the rifle from my pulse while maintaining tightness and control and a compfortably high position. Check the weight distribution on the left knee. Make sure it is over the knee. Also, the body weight should be shifted forward somewhat off the ankle and onto the right calf. This helps stabilize the position. Slumping shoulders down seems to help also.

Tomorrow: Shoot some from prone and then continue to test kneeling change. Practice all three positions.

FICTICIOUS DIARY ENTRY FOR TOURNAMENT

Date: December 9, 1977
Place: Tabor Head, Marion, Maryland
Time: 8:00 am
Weather: Gallery. Tabor's range and lighting are okay. Very dark at line, with indirect, yellow, fairly good overhead target lights.
Goal for Day: Shoot in 560's.
Mental condition: In good spirits, enjoyed the match.
Physical Condition: Tired from trip.
Match: Indoor 3 position 1/2 course.
Equipment Note: If not rested, open front aperture. Rear: 1.3 mm.
Prone: Started rough — a little hesitant with overhold. In an attempt to combat this, I rushed a shot and then found the midpoint good, fairly quick cadence. Thereafter, very strong. Good attention to point-of-aim, semi-sub-conscious trigger control, good follow through. Score: 195.
Stand: I was intentionally very aggressive, very positive, trying to correct for and learn from yesterday. It worked! My conscious was occupied with shooting quickly and aggressively, which forced trigger control to sub-conscious. One thing to watch for is snap shooting. Make sure sight picture is good. Additionallly, follow thru, shoot and follow-thru, concentrating thereon. Score: 179.
Kneel: I relaxed well — perhaps too well. Point-of-aim a bit low. Took 10 minutes settling down and sighting. Realized the rifle was too low, so raised buttplate slightly. Re-sighted, and had 4 1/2 minutes for 6 shots. The cause, I think, was change in target height at this range. I rushed two shots, one so badly, I jumped on it. I then settled and slowed down and shot well, with a good hold and

good trigger control. Score: 188.

A potential experiment: The raised buttplate (about 3 mm) helps naturalize and stablize the hold.

See what Marie's fictionalized diary entries do? They focus the mind's attention on specific details. Each experiment is recorded. The thoughts surrounding the experiments are noted. These diary entries can be very valuable for future reviewing. Couple these diary entries and other entries like them with a computer database and you can see that this can be of considerable benefit to a shooter. With the cross indexing available on the personal computers today, diary solutions can be instantly displayed on the computer terminal screen so future shooting problems can be checked against past problems and their solutions or experiments for solving them. These diary entries are really good examples of a person doing all of the right things with his, or in this case, I suspect, her, diary. These are the types of diary entries I think you should emulate.

If you are ever fortunate enough to have an opportunity to read through a world champion's diary you might wonder, how could I ever think like that? The multiplicity of detail would more than likely overwhelm you. Of course, there has to be a place you begin, and I think the examples of Marie Alkire's fictionalized diary are good examples to follow in starting out with your own diary. So, take heart and get started.

Now, to the subject of this chapter, Alpha State Training. Basically, it's thought of as a way to relieve anxiety. Now, you know how much we shooters need to relieve anxiety! Every match we go to takes its toll through pre—match, and actual—match "jitters." Alpha State Training is advocated by many as the way to achieve this desired relaxation from such anxiety.

The word, *relax*, is one of the most over—worked and perhaps most universally understood words in our vocabulary. There is probably not a coach in the country who has not advised his team members to "relax" at some point in his coaching. The shooter then "tries hard" to relax. He "tries hard" for two reasons:

1. *The coach says to relax.* 2. *The shooter knows it is in his/her best interest to relax and thus avoid the*

over control that an extraordinary amount of tension brings.

But, "lo and behold," even with these best of reasons and the avowed intention and the determination to relax, he is as tense or more tense than before. Why? How do you solve this problem? You know the meaning of relax, you want to relax, so what is the problem? There is a dilemma your subconscious is faced with here. That *Little Guy Inside* knows that you are shooting and that you need to "do well." But, you are anxious, which means you do not feel confident that you are going to do well. This creates a bit of stress. This naturally causes the small muscles around your blood vessels to tense under the stress. When this occurs, blood pressure goes up. So, learning a technique to relax is a very real tool the shooter needs to have available to use in matches which mean a lot to him.

For example, you are a beginning shooter. Your coach is watching and you are on the firing line in a match. Suddenly, you are aware of things -- the lighting is different, the shooting mat is too thick, your left elbow is sinking into the mat, this throws your sling out of whack, your eye is suddenly too close to the rear sight, the shooter next to you is looking at you and she's a pretty little blond, or if you are a girl, the shooter next to you is really sharp and he's just noticed you with a grin, and oh, they must have the heat up to 100 degrees. Is that cigarette smoke? Notice, the stream—of—consciousness just will not stop. This is what some people call *rumination.* The available scientific research seems to indicate that alpha training will inhibit this type of mental activity during the period the person places himself in Alpha State. This is important to you as a competitive shooter.

This book is for the beginning shooter. Alpha Training can begin when you first start your marksmanship training. It is not necessary for you to shoot a score of 250 out of 300 or any other such magical number.

But, you might like to know something about that thing called *alpha* before your allow yourself to get involved with it. First, just briefly, you need to think a bit about your brain. Your brain is a source of electricity. There are machines which can identify various kinds of electrical patterns, or waves, given off by the brain. Scientists have given some of these waves names:

THETA WAVES

ALPHA WAVES

BETA WAVES

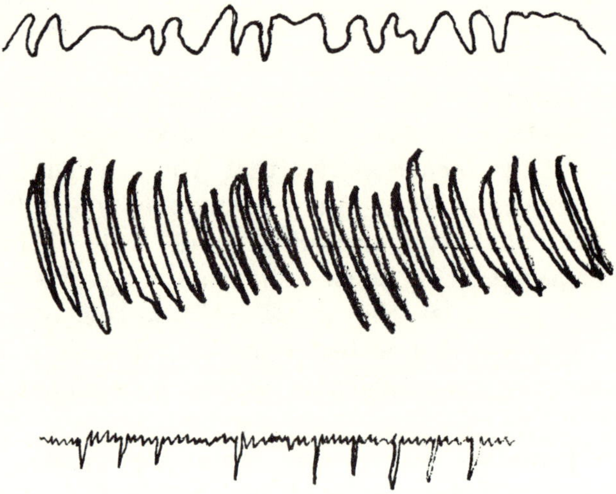

Figure 6—1   Brain waves illustrated.

Alpha waves are very common throughout the brain. Research has discovered that it is possible for a person to train himself to modify the output of these waves by giving his brain various instructions. For example, by visualizing a horrible, frightening and very sudden automobile accident, the brain will send a message to various muscles causing them to tense.

The tenseness causes a stimulation of muscle cells that the muscle tension itself produced. This appears to bombard the mind with messages which distract the attention of the mind from other activities. For shooters, the implication of this is enormous. In other words, when your rumination causes a muscle tensing thought, your subconscious is distracted from its work of getting you a good shot in a match. This distracting rumination need not be of the shocking variety to actually cause emotion generated energy.

Now, not all of this rumination is detrimental to the

Mental Training   Chapter 6

achievement of our shooting goals. In fact, now that we know about the effects of rumination, we can make it work for us instead of being controlled by it's created distractions.

Rumination Control Training

1. MENTAL TRAINING CARDS

Practice with these will give you a chance to rehearse the possible thoughts you will have as you shoot over your course of fire in your mind. It will give you a chance to learn to direct your rumination under relaxed conditions. You will also be able to identify those ruminations, stream-of-conscious thoughts, which are unwanted. You will be able to devise strategies for dealing with those intruding, unwanted thoughts.

2. GUN HOLDING PRACTICE

In the Gun Holding Practice program, you hold the gun in your shooting position. While holding the gun, you must direct your whole attention to reducing the size of the sight picture. Your efforts in this practice are to VOID your mind of rumination which has nothing to do with your practice effort. However, you will more than likely find that it will take very much practice to redirect that stream-of-conscious which flows unbidden through the attention you try to focus on the task at hand. So, this again is a very good way to practice rumination control training. This will allow you to be in better control of your destiny during the firing of your practice and match scores.

3. DRY-FIRING PRACTICE

The objective of your dry-firing practice is to learn to split your attention between making your sight pattern as small as you can, and learning to allow your *Little Guy Inside* to let the trigger release when ALL IS RIGHT. You should closely observe the nature of the rumination during this process. Then develop a strategy to

© Bob Hickey

use whenever that unwanted rumination is observed.

Strategy For Dealing With Unwanted Rumination

1. Stop the Act of Shooting sequence. You may stop it by either: leaving the gun in position and re-establish the SET of your mind before starting the Act of Shooting sequence over again; or by breaking your position and taking a brief breather before going on.

| THEN |

2. Begin the Act of Shooting again.

The Act Of Shooting Is:

⋆A.
    Assume your position, and bring the gun up to firing position

⋆B.
    Look to your sight pattern

⋆C.
    Align your position as necessary. Sometimes it means hunching your body around so everything "*feels*" right

⋆D.
    Initiate your target shooting breath control technique

⋆E.
    Void your mind of all rumination except for a vague attention to your *Individual Shot Goal*

Mental Training   Chapter 6

★F.
    Give your *Little Guy Inside* the remembrance of the technique and then the feeling that you felt when you achieved your best recalled *Individual Shot Goal*

★G.
    Allow the shot to be fired as you give your attention to your sight pattern.

OR

3. Conduct a Selective Awareness muscle tension inventory.

THEN

4. Initiate a muscle relaxant effort to eliminate or reduce the improper or unwanted tension. You see, without having practiced your Selective Awareness Exercises, the muscle relaxant effort would be unfamiliar, thus taking a greater effort to effect this relaxation. The reason you initiate a Selective Awareness muscle tension inventory upon noticing a bit of unwanted rumination during practice or a match is that sometimes the rumination causes an excitation of the brain. This may inhibit messages of the increased tension in the muscles being relayed to those areas of the brain which would otherwise let you consciously appreciate or become aware of that increase in muscle tension.

    So, as shooters, we want to develop Alpha State. This is that state of mind where rumination or stream–of–consciousness is brought to a halt or inhibited. This is the condition you want to develop when you are shooting. It is a condition where that *Little Guy Inside* is allowed to shoot the shot for you by a reflexive reaction. When you assume control, you break that Alpha State and cause a partial blocking of that reflexive pathway you have developed between your brain, which controls the reaction of your trigger finger and your eye.

    In considering Alpha State Training as an aid to improving your marksmanship skill level, focus on why you do this. The mind is a wonderful part of the human system. Out of our total body weight, this less than three pounds portion of us is the most important part. Without out brain, we cease to think and be aware. But, important as the brain is to us, it is utterly dependent upon the messages it receives from the exterior sensors. For example, your eyes report visual sightings for your brain. Your nose warns of offensive or new odors. Your mouth also acts as a sensing machine for your brain. The skin is a massive system supplying many sense sensations to the brain. The essence of the brain is that part of it identified in psychology as the subconscious. I like to think of it as my *Little Guy Inside*. After receiving the messages from these sensors, and the transmitters in the muscles, of their condition, that *Little Guy Inside* issues his instructions. That *Little Guy Inside* only knows those thing his internal sensors tell him. But, conversely, we cannot see into our bodies, without specially constructed machines to observe what is happening there. We cannot even look at our own face without a mirror. And, even the mirror distorts what we observe. In the looking-glass, we see ourselves reversed. The purpose of Selective Awareness Training is to reveal the inner workings of our body to us. With this information, our *Little Guy Inside* can get a grasp of exactly what we want our muscles to do. But, before our *Little Guy Inside* can help us, we must bring the inner workings of our bodies out into the open, where our mind's sensors can grasp the information as feedback by those specially designed sensors.

We must be careful about the nature of the training program we adopt for our purposes. You, as a shooter, "want to do it like the champion." What you must remember, is that not all of the champions have been consciously aware of being in Alpha State during their shooting. Not all have set up a program to consciously place themselves in this condition during their shooting. Not all have set up a program to consciously place themselves in this condition during their matches. This Alpha State is a label applied by observers to the apparent condition which various of our rifle champions seem to place themselves in during their shooting. When in this state or condition, the shooter is marked by the following

Mental Training Chapter 6

characteristics:

> 1. Intense concentration on the attempt to place his shots in the ten ring or his *Individual Shot Goal.*
> 2. Blocking out of non-essential external stimuli.
> 3. Control of internal rumination.

I recall a conversation with Jack Writer regarding the training method he used to practice control of his rumination during matches. He didn't use the word "rumination." He called his method, "thought control." Writer described "shooting the course of fire" over in his mind many times before the day of the match came around.

For example, he described going over and considering a number of different thoughts which might go through his mind during the shooting of a match. In the 1968 Olympics in Mexico City, Writer said that of all of the thoughts he had considered, there was one he had not. He had considered many possibilities regarding his point totals and his ranking in relation to the rest of the field of competition, during each of the shots of his shooting strings. Now, that is a total of 120 shots Writer had to break down and consider in his mental efforts on thought control. That is a lot of hours of thought training. If this is the first you have heard of such training, remember, the champion works hard to be and stay a champion. Do the work, do not short cut yourself.

Back to Writer. One thing he had not considered, was the possibility that he might be out in front by a considerable margin, after his standing position. This brought thoughts to his mind he had not considered and this bothered him. You see, he had developed a training technique of considering his potential thoughts in advance of his matches. This gave him a very definite advantage over his fellow competitors. He was able to recognize the activation of his rumination process and thus he could stop and "get his mind back in order."

This training method is borne out by research in alpha training, as a valid method for control or rumination. The importance of being able to control your mental process is perhaps underscored best in the words of Jack Writer in June of 1976, speaking at *Schiessportschule I*, sponsored by the United States International Women's Rifle Organization at Phoenix, Arizona, and published in their *Schiessportschule Dialogues I*.

> *Bob, I've never told you this before, but I was up in Alaska a few years ago giving clinics to Bob Hickey's group and they had an award presentation which would include me shooting a ten shot air rifle match with one of the juniors up there. I had more pressure on me in that little ten shot match than I had in the Olympics or any world championship I have ever shot. I had a day or two to think about shooting the match. I'd never done anything like this before. I could sit down and think, "Now, I'm one hell of a better shooter than this kid is," but it didn't help. I still had the pressure. I thought, "What if he beats me!" This is a good example of not having anticipated the situation. Physically, I knew how to go out, hold up the rifle and shoot the match like any air rifle match, but mentally I couldn't anticipate how my thoughts would be running when I actually went up there to shoot. I wasn't able to get my mind straight on it. If I could do this every day for a week or two, it would be no sweat, because each time, I'd learn a little bit more about myself and how I'd react in that situation and pretty soon, I'd have it all squared away upstairs and I'd beat the kid real good. I knew how I was going to react in Munich. I didn't know how I would react in Alaska. I was nervous in Alaska and I wasn't in Munich. I prepared myself for one a lot better than I did for the other.*
>
> *Let me tell you, I spent a lot of time thinking about what I did wrong shooting that little ten shot air rifle match. I tried to pin down what specifically, not just generally, but what specifically*

Mental Training Chapter 6

caused me to have pressure. It was a good experience for me in progressing in shooting.

Jack Writer won this TV match, 92 to 87. I call it a TV match, because we had cameras on the targets and monitors in the auditorium for the spectators to observe. His opponent for the evening was David Ash, who later went on to coach championship teams in the collegiate arena. So, my point is, it is still possible for a World Champion to win even when faced with the unanticipated. However, the Champion gives himself as much of an edge as possible in each match. Incidentally, David Ash, the junior with whom Writer competed in this TV match was an Alaskan juniors, who on our club's trip to England in 1970, had won the Junior Air Rifle Championship of the National Small–Bore Rifle Championships of Great Britain, held at Bisley, England. Ash later became coach of one of America's eminent university rifle teams, Tennessee Tech University. As coach, his team won the United States Collegiate National Rifle Championships in 1977. In addition, an individual on his team, Rod FitzRandolph, won National Collegiate and Junior titles that year. Not a bad job of coaching for the man, who as a junior, was the unwitting cause for a greater amount of pressure on an Olympic gold medalist than the Olympics itself.

So, knowledge of what to expect and planning to meet what you know about, are unique elements of your mind working. And, the mind at work, is like a perpetual motion machine of continually charged electricity. But, like the battery of a car whose alternator is shot, there comes a time when things grind to a halt and the charge is no longer available to start the engine. If the *body is the engine and the mind is the electrical charge to cause the movement*, then it is important to avoid overloading the brain with work when it is all involved with coping with the pressure of a match and trying to get us a good score. We can relieve some of the brain's overload by working out ways to keep our rumination to the object at hand, namely restricting our stream–of–consciousness thoughts in things such as:

"Let the hold tighten up onto the bull"..."Hold up at

© Bob Hickey

Mental Training Alpha State Training

Alpha waves have been known to the world since their identification by German scientist **Hans Berger in 1928.** Since that time, much research indicated that, with training, man was able to control the production of these waves. This was alleged to be beneficial to man because an increase in Alpha would show a corresponding decrease in anxiety. There was evidence that the production of Alpha was closely related to a state of relaxation.

The usual manner of training a person to control his Alpha waves is to seat him in a room in a comfortable chair. Often the room is darkened. He then would be attached to a biofeedback machine, which would report back to him the condition of his Alpha waves. Now, it is important for you to know that you do not need to be hooked up to a biofeedback machine in order to learn how to control your Alpha waves. The purpose of the machine is to give you a visual or audible indication of your success in controlling Alpha. The biofeedback machines we use in our rifle club are small hand held devices. We obtained them from Thought Technology, of Canada, for $29.95 several years ago. (*Coaches working with junior clubs may read aloud the following verbatim during club training sessions.*)

ALPHA STATE RELAXATION TECHNIQUE

1. Put your shooting mat on the floor, lay yourself on it, on your back, and put your kneeling roll under your neck.

2. Loosen any tight clothing, belt, shirt collar button, etc.

3. Put your hands, palms down, on the mat next to your body.

4. Breathe only through your nose. Keep your mouth closed during the training session.

5. Look up towards your forehead and keep looking upwards as

Mental Training Chapter 6

you allow your eyelids to shut. Continue to look upwards as you go through this session.

6.

Focus on the most peaceful and quiet place you can recall or imagine.

7.

Hold your peaceful place, in your mind. Examine it carefully as you continue.

8.

Now you must begin to systematically relax the muscles of your body. Hang on to the idea of peace and relaxation you have imagined in your mind as you proceed through the relaxation of the parts of your body.

TOES

Get inside your toes, feel them move. Now transfer that feeling of peace and relaxation to those toes. Let them wallow in a sea of peace and tranquility.

FEET

Let your mind explore the muscles on the bottom of your feet, get "inside" your feet. See what they feel like. Then bring your feeling of peace to them. Notice how soft they now feel.

LEGS

Think of your calves as being genuine friends, as keeping your peaceful image, you bring the inner muscles of your legs under the serene caress of your mind. Now, allow the harmonious calmness of your peaceful image to help relax those muscles, and give the same peaceful sensation you have from the image you are holding in your mind.

THIGHS

Now, pass through the softened muscles of the legs and get into the muscles of the thighs. Feel yourself letting loose of

© Bob Hickey

the stringiness of the muscles. Permit the quietness and calmness of your peaceful mind image, to enter and remain.

BUTTOCKS
Move into the muscles of your buttock area, permit a loosening of the tension as you slip into these muscles. Feel the tension flowing outward from the insides of these muscles.

ABDOMEN
Move now to the interior of the muscles of the abdomen. Just sort of allow a slumping down of the muscles, just as if you are expelling a deep breath. Let your breathing become deeper and more regular as you notice a softening of these muscles.

CHEST
Take a little deeper breath and exhale slowly, and a little deeper breath and exhale slowly. Continue to breathe like this as you now feel into these muscles.

LOWER BACK
Now study the tension of the muscles of the lower back. Feel them? Now, reduce the tightness of the muscles of the lower back. Allow the muscles to sort of slump down onto the mat.

UPPER BACK
Examine now, the muscles of the upper back. Continue breathing deeply and regularly. Let your peaceful and tranquil mind image flow into these muscles as you continue to breathe deeply and regularly.

HANDS AND FINGERS
Move into the muscles of your hands and now your fingers. Let go of these muscles and feel them soften and loosen.

LOWER ARMS
Allow a feeling of calmness to pass through the muscles of the lower arm. Move inside the muscles as you start the calmness to start passing through to the inner part of the

muscle. Spread the feeling of calmness throughout the muscle.

UPPER ARMS

Bring that feeling of calmness to the muscles of the upper arms. Slip inside the muscle to smooth the calmness over the inner parts of the muscle. Observe the whole muscle relax. Continue breathing deeply and regularly.

SHOULDERS

Probe the muscles of the shoulders. Have the consciousness of being on the interior of the muscles of the shoulders. Let the gentle calmness flow outward from the center of the shoulders through the muscles. Continue to breathe deeply through the muscles. Continue to breathe deeply and regularly. Become familiar with the diminishing tension as you bring a feeling of peace and smoothness to the muscles of the shoulders.

NECK

Now relax the muscles of the neck. Move inside the muscles at the front of the neck and...now the back of the neck. Spread a feeling of peace as you slip inside these muscles.

HEAD

Now is the time to relax the muscles of the head. Now the cheek muscles. Now relax the muscles at the top of the head. Continue to breathe deeper and more regularly as a feeling deep and wonderful peace and soothing comfort enter all parts of your head.

9.

Your mind is now filling all parts of your body with calmness and peace. You are now feeling very comfortable and relaxed and very safe in the feeling that is is so good for you and you like it very much.

10.

If you find any part of your body which is tense, go to that part of your body, and still breathing very, very deeply, allow the calmness of your mental image to bathe it in softness and relaxation.

11. You will notice now a sense of pleasant warmth spreading all through the relaxation area of your body.

12. It is warm and pleasant, you are now dipping into that warmness and soothing comfort. Your are feeling the warmth spreading about your body and it is a good, relaxing feeling and you want more of it. You enjoy being able to block out everything but what you want. It is a warm and pleasant feeling.

13. Now is the time to come up out of the warmth, but very slowly. You are still breathing very deeply and regularly. Your are out now and your breathing is becoming more normal. You are feeling very relaxed and you have had a wonderful experience. You want to do more of these training sessions and it will be easier each time you do them. You feel very good about getting inside each of your muscles. You are feeling more in control of your muscles now. Your head is straightening and you are now opening up your mind to a feeling of fresh vigor and attention. Open your eyes now and notice the feeling of being refreshed.

That is the technique. It has been in use for many years. There are many similar and related relaxant techniques. Any of this kind of technique will be valuable for learning to relax enough so that your brain will produce Alpha waves and let you experience the feeling to that you can recognize your own state of relaxation.

This method was adapted to reinforce the techniques of *Mental Training*.

Mental Training   Chapter 6

Alpha waves are in plentiful supply during the time you are passive, or not concentrating. But, the moment you begin to concentrate on something, your brain gives off what might be thought of as bursts of sustained static, called Beta waves. The Beta waves are crowded together above fourteen cycles per second. These Beta brain waves continue while you are doing work requiring concentration:

    scoring a target, filling out a tournament registration card, talking to someone, eating a candy bar, etc.

This also tells us that when we go onto the firing line to shoot, that Alpha is going to be suppressed because of the nature of the task we have set ourselves. Recognizing this, *Mental Training* sets up a program to train you to look inward and to avoid "concentration" on your task. Concentration means to direct one's mental powers or efforts to a problem. It implies that the goal of the concentration is sort of static. For example, when the coach tells us to "concentrate on trigger control," we direct our entire mental awareness to "making" the trigger finger work "right." This overrides our attempt at achieving Alpha State because this "concentration" act produces so much Beta. It has the effect of blocking or inhibiting the reflexive pathways for the act of shooting.

But, if we avoid "concentration," what is left? **Attention** is the key. Attention creates interest in the task. Concentration brings all of the mind's effort to bear in focusing on a task. This creates a "blocking" of the subconscious as the conscious self takes charge of getting the thing done properly and thus blocks out the subconscious so that it cannot foul things up. Notice yourself the difference in doing two similar tasks:

1. When you are concentrating HARD on the task.
2. When you are interested in the task, but not really bearing down and **concentrating** on it.

This was borne home to me when I "reupholstered" my five-fingered shooting glove. I do not ordinarily sew or work in leather. I became "interested" in figuring what I needed for the job. I also was very interested in laying out the glove as a pattern for my replacement covering of neoprene rubber. My attention remained very high as I bang my stitching. I took my time, and days ate into days. Then I noticed the calendar and a match I planned to compete in was close upon me. I decided I would like to finish the glove and use it in that match. I immediately began **concentrating** and trying to speed up my needle pushing. disaster followed, with a needle and then it's mate breaking in my extra effort. I seemed to tire more quickly than before. So too, with your shooting! The extra effort of **concentrating** adds an additional burden to the mind. It is even suspected of setting up a blockage of some of the pathways by which your subconscious expects to "really" assist you in your efforts to get shots in your *Individual Shot Goal.* Perhaps there is a modicum of truth to the saying: "*Man is his own worst enemy.*"

Mental Training is not a "quickie" cure for "wild and crazy" shooting performance. It is a program you must "get into" and then stay with until you have achieved your dreams. For example, Selective Awareness Training needs to be done several times a week. This gets your attention focused inside those muscles. Notice it is not a "concentrating" on those muscles. It is an attention to them with a view of recording actual observations. Attention is a "wondering at" what is happening, not as with concentration, an effort to "make it happen."

In summary then, Alpha State is that condition of the brain where the electrical impulses which create the brain waves known as Alpha waves, occurs in a shooter on the firing line. A young novice shooter, once described a feeling he experienced as:

> "*It was sort of like a blanket has descended over the range area. The background noise and everything seemed to retreat into the background and the shot seemed to fire itself.*"

© Bob Hickey

Mental Training Chapter 7

CHAPTER 7

Coach's Corner

Added to the book at the suggestion of:
 Marie Alkire, Executive Director of the United States Women's International Rifle Organization and Dr. William Cole, EDGE Institute, Inc.

This chapter involved an extensive amount of research, as can be borne out by a glance at the sources cited in "The Roots of Mental Training," at the end of this book. The more research I did, the more I found that the old-tried-and-true techniques used by American coaches over the years did not allow maximum use of *Mental Training*'s new programs. I, therefore, had to develop an entirely new set of coaching techniques and methods.

These techniques, when used with this program, will actually save the coach some time. It will also cut down on the amount of paperwork the coach has to do. There will be an increase in the quantity of paperwork done by a shooter who is in an old, traditional junior shooting club.

The coach who switches to using this program with his team will find that he will have to allocate his time on the range differently than is the case now. For example, most time on the rifle range is new spent in firing rounds down range. Your attitude is probably that range time should be used for shooting. That's the attitude of most Americans. I want to change that attitude. I think I have a program which will help you to become a "super coach." A Class "C" coach is a person who never discovers the secrets you are reading about. This program will allow you to become a Class "AAA" coach over night. But it is your decision. You owe it to your shooters to make the change. I will show you how to make this changeover with the least amount of effort. All

Mental Training   Coach's Corner

I'm going to do is to re-channel the direction of your coaching and the amount of time you spend doing various things on the range. As you know, the coach of a Junior Shooting Club is a very busy person. In fact, he is often kept so busy doing a thousand and one different things, he finds he has little time for coaching. He is a:

1. Record keeper
2. Arranger of matches
3. Scheduler of building use
4. Collector of money for: dues, ammo, awards, matches
5. Assembler of rifle equipment for junior use
6. Disassembler of rifle equipment after use
7. Custodian of the range
8. Aribiter of squabbles
9. Interpreter of rules
10. Fixer of broken equipment
11. Morale builder-upper
12. Chauffeur

    My experience comes from 30 years coaching junior rifle clubs. So, coaches, I know you will still have to do all the things listed above regardless of what coaching method you use. This book comes from the trenches of volunteer coaching done in junior rifle clubs. It comes from my search for a "better way." It also comes from my frustration of not being able to find a better way to offer my kids the help they needed. This book is not designed for the World Champions, they have their way. This book is designed for the volunteer worker in the junior clubs of our country. It is designed to help coaches prepare their shooters to acquire the mental attitude necessary for them to become consistent achievers of their personal goals.

    For example, look at Figure 7-0. Help your shooters gain a realistic awareness of their skill level in each of the shooting positions, or stages. Set up a day each month when the shooter fires for his shot group record. If the shooter is training for smallbore rifle competition, have him shoot 60 shots, 5 shots at a bull, and then put his best and his worst bulls in his diary as shown in Figure 7-0.

Mental Training   Chapter 7

NEW COACHING PROGRAM OUTLINE:

1. New shooter observation of shooting demonstration
2. New shooter discussion of observation
3. Firing practice
4. Position inventory of new shooter's position
5. Shooter's recording of coach's position
6. Gun holding practice
7. Dry firing practice
8. One-Shot matches
9. Mental training cards practice
10. Selective awareness training
11. Alpha state training
12. Shooter maintains shooting diary

Figure 7-0   **AMMO GROUP RECORD**

DATE:
POSITION:

DIRECTIONS:

1. Fire 5 shots per bull.
2. Cut out and paste the bulls below:

```
   Use this form to
 maintain a record of the
grouping quality of your
rifle.  Do this at least once
a year; more often if you feel
the rifle barrel is "going
out."  DO THIS IN THE PRONE
POSITION.
```

```
      This form can also
   be used to graphically
    illustrate your progress-
ing skill levels in each of
the shooting positions of
PRONE, STANDING and KNEELING.
This way, as you progress,
your LITTLE GUY INSIDE knows
exactly what your grouping
   looks like.
```

© Bob Hickey

Mental Training Coach's Corner

INITIAL OBSERVATION SESSION

You have a new group of youngsters who most probably do not know very much of what target shooting is all about. As with all basic training courses, the first step in this new marksmanship training program is to show them. But this time, your "showing" will have a different purpose than merely demonstrating what range target shooting is. It is your purpose to involve these "potential" new shooters in the process of mental training right from the first moment of their participation in your marksmanship training program. This is what the Initial Observation Form is designed to help you do. If you are an already established junior rifle club, then you have the raw material necessary to put on a New Shooter / Old Shooter firing demonstration. The old shooter should be one of your shooters who can demonstrate all three or four positions, probably with at least a year of your club shooting training. For my new shooter, I usually use an eighth grader, one who is thirteen years of age. For my old shooter, I use a high school junior, a boy or girl of 16 years of age. If you do not have OLD SHOOTERS in your club, then I feel certain that a coach of a nearby town with such youngsters, could help you out.

© Bob Hickey

Mental Training Chapter 7

INITIAL OBSERVATION FORM

NEW SHOOTER **OLD SHOOTER**

1. Tell how each shooter gets ready to shoot. Does each seem to know where his/her shooting things are? Does either do a lot of joking or fooling around? Do they seem serious or are they happy-go-lucky?

2. Tell, in detail, exactly how to load the gun, based on how you see each of the shooters doing his/her loading.

3. Tell, very exactly, what the trigger finger of each shooter does as he/she gets read to fire, and then fires the shot.

© Bob Hickey

Mental Training   Coach's Corner

SECOND PAGE INITIAL OBSERVATION FORM

NEW SHOOTER   **OLD SHOOTER**

(4)   In position rifle shooting, number the order in which the shooters fire at their record bulls (the ones around the edge of the paper.) Look through the spotting scope to observe this. Put the order number in the circles.

(5)   Tell what the shooter's aiming eye does just before the shot fires, and just after it fires.

(6)   Watch 3 shots and mark the direction of muzzle jump. Put an arrow in the circle to show the direction of the recoil.

© Bob Hickey

Mental Training Chapter 7

THIRD PAGE INITIAL OBSERVATION FORM

NEW SHOOTER | **OLD SHOOTER**

⑦ Tell what the fingers of the trigger hand are doing just before the shot fires and just afterwards. Do the fingers seem tight or loose?

⑧ Describe the shooter's breathing process.

⑨ Describe the relationship of the spotting scope to the position of the shooter. Tell how far away his non-aiming eye is from the scope's eyepiece, 5 inches, 6 inches, etc.

⑩ Describe what the trunk and hip of the shooter do in the position.

© Bob Hickey

Mental Training   Coach's Corner

FOURTH PAGE INITIAL OBSERVATION FORM

NEW SHOOTER		OLD SHOOTER
(11)	Describe what right leg is doing in shooting position.	
(12)	Describe what left leg is doing in shooting position.	
(13)	Describe what the right ankle and foot are doing in the shooting position.	
(14)	Describe what the left ankle and foot are doing in the shooting position.	
(15)	Describe what the shooter is wearing and any help you think he/she gets from it.	

© Bob Hickey

Mental Training Chapter 7

Procedure:

Position the shooter—demonstrators three firing lanes apart on the firing line.

Carefully point out that the firing line is considered the SAFETY LINE, and that no one is ever allowed in front of it while the range is active.

The next part of the procedure differs from most current American junior shooting club practice, thus a big explanation. Most American marksmanship demonstration sessions for new beginning shooters are marked by the demonstrators showing what the positions look like. They usually never fire any shots in that position, certainly no shots in the standing position. And should they fire any shots, the viewing students are continually being admonished to stay well back and not go near the shooters while they fire. That's the current practice. Now take a look at this new procedure:

The students are advised that they are to approach as close to the shooter as they can. "Put your nose right up next to the shooter's trigger guard, so you can see what his finger does as he fires the shot."

The concept here is "movement" from new shooter to old shooter and back again. As instructor, position yourself so that you can control access to the shooters and maintain vigilance to ensure that no one moves in front of *The Safety Line*. Try to have an assistant to the outside of each shooter to control this situation.

Before moving to the next shooter, the student should have written down an observation, following the outline of the Initial Observation Form. From 9 and 10 year olds, expect only a couple to three words. I learned this when I ran a Cub Scout pack through the program. Twelve and 13 year olds can usually manage an incomplete sentence, while high school youngsters will write more complete thoughts. Beginning adult shooters will fill the spaces provided and need to finish on the back of the form. I noticed this in the college courses I taught for the University of Alaska, Anchorage. Try to avoid being overly helpful in pointing out what to look for.

Allow time for a discussion of the students' observations after the demonstration of the three or four positions is completed. During the process of preparing to shoot, the following points should be highlighted in the discussions. Both shooters keep rifle on shooting mat as they place sling on arm. This can be highlighted as a safety precaution. By laying down first, and getting the sling on the arm and then the rifle, the rifle is not being waved dangerously in directions other than down range.

Often the *old shooter* will have his loading block loaded, his body positioned with respect to his spotting scope, and will have checked his position and sights more economically than the new shooter.

The shooter keeps the rifle on the shoulder and pushes the cartridge all the way into the chamber. The bolt is then closed in the following manner. The shooter locks the bolt handle down by placing the thumb of the hand under the trigger guard. The palm of the hand faces forward. Using the thumb as leverage, the trigger finger and the next two fingers, placed on top of the bolt handle, depress the bolt handle and complete the locking of it into position. This technique is especially useful in teaching the habit of safe loading to new shooters and making it an ingrained part of their loading procedure. Many youngsters experience some difficulty in closing the bolt handle. This technique overcomes that difficulty. It also helps to prevent accidental discharges of rifles when bolts are slammed home and locked in the same motion. It should be explained to the new shooter that this is a sensible safety precaution. Many indoor gallery ranges may have exposed steel girders in the ceiling, such as our range does. Other ranges may be located in the basements of multi—use buildings. (I remember as a junior I fired in the basement of our

Mental Training Chapter 7

local YMCA and dances were occasionally held on the floor above. The floor was unarmored and could easily have been penetrated by .22 bullets.)

(3) Break the trigger finger into the parts in front of the knuckle and the parts in back of the knuckle. Further break it down into the underneath part of the finger and the top part of the finger. The describe what each part is doing.

(4) Here look for efficiency of firing technique. Do you fire the target bulls in the order in which they are numbered? No! Those bulls are numbered so that ties can be broken in a uniform way each time. That is the use for the printed numbers.

You very must carefully take time to check and adjust your rifle's "natural point of aim" at your initial sighting bull before you fire any sighters. Be mindful not to allow your left elbow to move once you arrange your natural point of aim at your sighting bull. Be careful not to permit your left elbow to move once you start firing your sighters. Look at how many times you must shift your point of aim if you shoot the bulls in the order they are numbered: See Fig. 6-8.

You would have ten natural points of aim shifts! You could do it. Sure, lots of beginning shooters do. Is there a better way? Yes! What you do is to keep the natural point of aim you already established for the sighters and merely adjust your breathing process to shoot at the two record bulls above and beneath your sighters for your first two record shots. This keeps your sights within your primary natural point of aim. After shooting these first two record shots, then adjust your natural point of aim to the left side string of targets. Shoot down through them! Then go now to the right side string of the target. Adjust your natural point of aim for this side. You have the choice of starting to shoot

© Bob Hickey

Mental Training   Coach's Corner

from the bottom of the right side or the top. I usually choose to begin from the top, but this is merely personal preference. Notice, with this technique, you have two points of aim change, as opposed to ten the old way. See Fig. 6-10.

(5) Here look to see what the aiming eye does during the Act of Shooting. Does it blink? What happens after the shot is fired? Does it close reflexively?

(6) At this point, you should carefully observe the firing of three shots. Focus on the muzzle of the gun. What direction does it jump upon being fired? There are three circles provided on the form. Draw an arrow in the circle pointing to the direction the muzzle jumped. As you observe the firing of the shots, try to be alert for the ways the shooter attempts to control muzzle jump. Attempt to determine the degree of muscle tension which is devoted to trying to control muzzle jump. See if muzzle jump is consistent from shot to shot.

(7) Here, the shooter is directed to look at the fingers of the trigger hand. As a coach, you can direct the attention the knuckles. In your, after shooting, discussion, try to bring out observations of apparent finger grip tightness. And, at this point in the discussion, have the shooters respond and comment on the degree of tension they exert through the fingers of the trigger hand.

(8) In this observation, the shooter needs to learn to describe the breathing process used by the shooting during the firing of the shot. In the discussion, after the student has read aloud his/her discription of the breathing process, have the student perform the breathing process. Then ask the shooter whose breathing process the student described and then imitated, critique it.

⑨

In the discussion about this point, the focus should be on whether the eye of the shooter is *close* or *far* from the eyepiece of the spotting scope. Ask the shooter demonstrator to comment on why the eye is placed where it is.

⑩

The effort here is to help the student to identify how his/her trunk and hip are to look when in the shooting position. After reading aloud the description of this observation, have the student assume the shooting position, without the gun. Have the shooter demonstrator critique the position.

The effort here is to help the student to identify how his/her right leg is to look when it is in the shooting position. After reading aloud the description of this observation, have the student assume the shooting position, without the gun. Have the shooter demonstrator critique the position.

⑫

The effort here is to help the student to identify how his/her left leg is to look when it is in the shooting position. After reading aloud the description of this observation, have the student assume the shooting position, without the gun. Have the shooter demonstrator critique the position.

The effort here is to help the student to

identify how his/her right ankle and foot are to look when in the shooting position. After reading aloud the description of this observation, have the student assume the shooting position, without the gun. Have the shooter demonstrator critique the position.

The effort here is to help the student to identify how his/her left ankle and foot are to look when in the shooting position. After reading aloud the description of this observation, have the student assume the shooting position, without the gun. Have the shooter demonstrator critique the position.

Here, the students should note hats which keep the sun from the eyes of the shooter and earmuffs which keep out the noice of the shot firing and the conversation of people behind the firing line. For rifle shooters, the students should note shooting jackets and shooting pants and speculate on in what way they are helpful to the shooter. The shooter demonstrator should then be allowed to demonstate the way in which the articles help in the production of good and consistent scores.

Mental Training Chapter 7

SHOOTER OBSERVATION FORM

Coaches, both you and your young charges need to have a formal way of recording your observations of good master shooters. Use the Shooter Observation Form to formalize your observations.

Many beginning shooters want only to "shoot." It is your task as a coach to change this attitude. When the shooter is in the process of working on his Act of Shooting, his attention is necessarily restricted to the internalization of his own point of focus. To expand his awareness and develop a skill level beyond his own horizons, your shooter has to see how the master shooter handles tactical situations. He has to "get inside" the master shooter and get the feel of his mind.

The shooter and the coach can learn to do this by shooting the match with the master shooter. Take the Shooter Observation Form to the match with you. Then situate yourself behind the master shooter you have chosen to observe. Get a good spotting scope and stay with your master shooter throughout the entire match. Jot down questions as they occur to you. Then after the match or the relay, discuss the questions and the tactics used in the match situation. Most master shooters will respond in a positive manner to such inquiries. However, should you encounter a "bad egg," excuse yourself and continue your observations. The shooter cannot hide from such observations. The holes in his target and his psychological reactions, if you observe him closely, cannot be hidden from you. Plan on selecting some special tournaments for observation of master shooters.

This is a part of the championship attitude. If you are always competing, then you are not availing yourself of that very essential ingredient of a master coach or shooter: that of developing and extending your faculty of observation.

© Bob Hickey

Mental Training Coach's Corner

> Figure 7–1

SHOOTER OBSERVATION FORM

Name Of Shooter:
Name Of Range:

DATE

Shot #	Shot Value	Sun	Wind	Mirage	Comment
1.					
2.					
3.					
4.					
5.					
6.					
7.					
8.					
9.					
10.					

QUESTIONS

© Bob Hickey

Mental Training   Chapter 7

HOW TO BE A BETTER COACH

As a coach, you have several options open to you. First, you can rely on your experience as a shooter, to coach others. Experience is a good, sometimes harsh teacher. There is a problem in relying on only the experience you have as a shooter. Often, that experience is one dimensional. Another option is to study how to be a good rifle coach. Fortunately, the National Rifle Association has developed a series of coaching schools for you to attend. You can start at the NRA's Class C coaching level and advance progressively in the NRA coaching system as your skills increase. Having attended the NRA Class C school, you can take the advice of the instructors and continue to study after completion of the course, or you can rest on your laurels and strut around with your Class C hat on your head. If the hat rests upon pride, rather than humility, then you are not living up to your promise as a coach.

So, how do you live up to your promise as a coach? Attending an NRA coaching school will give you an excellent basic foundation. But, if you do not intelligently build upon that foundation, then it will become moldy and decay. If you attended the Class C coaching school for the prestige you think it will give you amongst the members of your club, be careful you do not become the butt of unkind jokes behind your back.

The most important thing you need to do, whether you have graduated from one of the NRA coaching schools, or have been drafted by your club to serve as coach of the club's junior division, is to get organized. You must organize to become a good coach. You need to develop more experience than merely depending upon your own personal shooting background. How do you get this experience? You get it by devoting many weekends to studying shooting and how shooters shoot.

You will often see the better shooting coaches peering through spotting scopes at rifle matches. Have you ever thought about what they are doing? They are not merely following their favorite friend. What the better coach is doing is observing how the master shooters on the line are handling the range conditions. As a coach, there is little you can do to help a shooter once the command *Commence Firing* is sounded. However, what you can do is to observe how that shooter handles windage and mirage problems which come up during the course of the match. But, also pick a master shooter and observe how he handles the same range problem.

© Bob Hickey

Mental Training   Coach's Corner

That is one of the things you can do as a coach. Expanding your knowledge of shooting in this manner is a natural and easy thing to do. If your shooters are entered in the match, it is even easier. In any case, you should make an effort to attend shooting matches where you can accomplish such studies. Organization. Yes, the best coaches organize for victory. Coaches, your organization is the key to your shooters victories. With the proper organization, you can help insure your team members successes. The type of organization I am referring to consists of several things.

First, naturally, there is the range time to be organized for the best utilization of that time on the range. Here is where you would organize your practice schedule around 60 shot strings instead of 10.

Secondly, you need to help your shooters to integrate mental training into a system of at–home–practice.

Thirdly, you need to arrange things so that you can better prepare your shooters for their up–coming tournaments. Once you have seen to their shooting and mental preparation, you need to generate feelings of self confidence in your team members. You can do this by starting to maintain a photographic file of the ranges you shoot regular matches on. By sharing these photos with your new shooters, you can help overcome some of the pre–match jitters. You should do this at all levels of coaching. For example, in preparing for our first club shooting trip to England in 1970, I asked for an exchange of pictures of the shooters firing the match. This was to give our young shooters a chance to study conditions they would find when we fired against the British juniors on their home turf in England. Now, of course our photo file is available for any future trips our club takes. Everywhere the coach goes, so should go his camera.

Now, in an age of expanding high technology, the video camera is a tool which can be used to record *live* range files. And, with the availability of affordable computers, you can even maintain your coaching files on a personal computer. I use a Kaypro 10 for my coaching files.

Another type of file, you as a coach need is a range plan file. For this purpose, use the *Rifle Range Observation Form*, Figure 7–2. When using this form, draw in the principal features of the range. Obviously, you need to locate the direction of the sun with reference to the firing line. Then you need to draw in any natural obstructions of the wind patterns on the range. In other words, is there a bank of trees along one side of the range? Is there a stream crossing in front of the target line which can be a source of mirage?

© Bob Hickey

Mental Training Chapter 7

By going over these with your shooters prior to the day of the tournament, and stressing the possible problems which might be encountered on that range, you help guide their self mental preparation. A coach stressing this type of training will find his shooters approaching the tournament with a better idea of just how they are going to be able to achieve their goals for the tournament. This type of preparation is especially valuable if you made your range drawing during a day a tournament was being fired on the range. If you have made use of the *Shooter Observation Form*, figure 7-1, then you can share with your shooters examples of how some master shooters dealt with problems they encountered in that day's shoot.

You need to develop some type of system to help jog your memory of such events. You do not need to use my forms, develop your own. Make them meaningful for you to share with your shooters. If you start to think and to coach like this, then you will share in the raising of the esteem in which shooting coaches are held in this sport. You will be doing your part in raising shooting coaching to the status coaching is held almost universally in other sports.

Another file you need to establish for yourself is a *reading file*. This is the file you keep of marksmanship and coaching articles you come across in your reading. One way to expand your reading of such articles is to subscribe to magazines and newsletters which publish articles about marksmanship and coaching. Some of the better ones are listed at the back of this book on page 252 under *Sources of Works Cited*.

Mental Training   Coach's Corner

Figure 7-2

RIFLE RANGE OBSERVATION FORM

Contact Person: Phone: DATE

Name Of Range:

N ↑

Draw the features of the range on this Plot

1) Firing Line Direction of
2) Wind
3) Sun
4) Humidity
5) Wind Obstructions
6) Target Lines
7) Climate during the shooting month
8) Range Surroundings
9) Monthly Rainfall Humidity

Shooting Range Plot

WIND   **SUN**

Comments

© Bob Hickey

Mental Training   Chapter 7

POSITION INVENTORY

PROBLEM:
        Frequently people new to shooting do not always seem to grasp what the coach tells them about their shooting the first time he says it. Many times the coach will observe the shooter making a similar error time after time.
        Often he is not a stubborn person who isn't listening to the coach. The coach's message has just not gotten through to him. So, what we must look at is the method to give the shooter the assistance he needs to make the corrections needed for his positions, in order to become a better shooter.

SOLUTION:
        Here is a way of helping both the coach and his shooters to achieve the goal of helping the shooter better his or her performance. Conduct an inventory of your shooter's positions. Do this each shooting session at which you would normally expect to be offering coaching advice to your shooters. Use the form titled: *Position Inventory*, Figure 7-3.

This form will help you to do several things:

    1) This is an excellent device for really allowing you to work with either one shooter or a dozen shooters and offer meaningful assistance.
    2) It prepares the shooter for maintaining a shooting diary.
    3) It helps the shooter to learn to use his self-talk, or his subconscious, as a *little guy inside* to guide his self-improvement.
    4) It frees the shooter to do the best job of shooting he can without worrying that his coach will be coming up making suggestions to him, or having to shift his position every so often.

        Take the plunge, start using the coaching forms shown in this

© Bob Hickey

Mental Training   Coach's Corner

book. Notice that you as a coach do not have to learn anything really different. For those of you who do not feel comfortable with writing or filling out these forms, I suggest that you plan to schedule one of your shooters to act as the coach's *recorder*, one night a week. Provide the *recorder* with a clipboard, a supply of Position Inventory Forms and a pencil. Then proceed with the following method:

PROCEDURE:

    1) Stand back from the firing line so that you do not distract the shooters as you talk to your *recorder*.

    2) Tell the *recorder* the suggestions or criticisms you have for each shooter. Don't "think" for the shooter by telling him exactly what he is doing right or wrong, but bring him to this by suggesting the problem may be such and such and ask him to think about it, thus developing the habit of individual problem–solving that is critical to successful performance of an individual sport.

    3) Have the *recorder* write them down. You have to be prepared to speak slower than normal and to repeat some things three or four times. But, I believe you will find the rewards are worth it.

    4) After practice, gather your shooters around a table and distribute the position inventories. Have the shooters copy the suggestions and criticisms onto a copy of the Coach's Observation Form to keep in their notebooks.

    5) The shooters are to record their reactions or responses to these suggestions in their diaries.

    6) More important, for the criticisms, the shooters must plan solutions or write out justifications for how and why they are shooting in the shooting position they have adopted.

Mental Training Chapter 7

Figure 7–3

POSITION INVENTORY

Shooter: Phone:

Name Of Range:

Shooting Position:

DATE

Label the position of the shooter on this form with comments:
1) Gun Cant
2) Head
3) Trunk
4) Shoulders
5) Hands
6) Arms
7) Hips
8) Legs
9) Feet
10) Eye blink
11) Follow through
12) Trigger squeeze
13) Loading technique
14) Shooting gear

GOAL PLANNING SUGGESTIONS:

© Bob Hickey

187

Mental Training   Coach's Corner

ONE SHOT MATCHES

Here is a method which will help you to teach your shooters to internalize their individual shot awareness. It will stimulate competitive feelings and at the same time equalize the differences between skill levels. Quite a claim! Let's take a look at just what is a *One-Shot Match*.

First, have your shooters assume a shooting position on the firing line. I suggest the Prone position until you feel they are ready to proceed into the other positions. If pistol shooting, then use the slow fire phase. In this match, the shooters are timed for one minute, with all the proper firing line commands. During this one minute, the shooter must fire his shot, write down his *call* and *estimated shot value* and also write *a complete sentence showing his thought at the moment before trigger let-off*. Shooters are not allowed to use spotting scopes for this exercise. When the minute has ended, the coach proceeds to call out to the shooters just what their shots' values and locations are.

"POINT ONE: 8 at 6 o'clock."
"POINT TWO: 10 at 2 o'clock."
"POINT THREE: 10 at 4 o'clock."
"POINT FOUR: 8 at 5 o'clock."
"POINT FIVE: 7 at 12 o'clock."

After he has done this, the coach calls out the match rankings of the shooters. If there are any ties, the coach calls them out as tied. Have the shooters record their match placement on their *One-Shot Matches* form. Give the results of the match above as follows:

"POINT ONE: Second Place."
"POINT TWO: First Place."
"POINT THREE: First Place."
"POINT FOUR: Second Place."
"POINT FIVE: Third Place."

The coach does all of his evaluating through a spotting scope. So, do not try to break ties. Also, I believe you will find it advisable not to permit the shooters to either plug or challenge shots

Mental Training   Chapter 7

after the target is returned to the coach after the ten *one-shot matches* have been completed. You see, the purpose of the *one-shot matches* is to instill in your shooters a *sense of responsibility* for each shot they fire. If you allow them to think that it is possible to change results later, then you effectively eliminate their feeling of a *sense of responsibility* for each shot.

One of the results of this technique, is that your shooters will begin to conceptualize the shot call and location. They are allowed to change their sights at will. But since they do not have a spotting scope, their visualization of their shots is a completely mental one.

After completion of the ten *one-shot matches*, discuss with each shooter the thoughts he had just at the moment of let-off. You may also have a group session for this.

PURPOSES:

    1. To help the shooter learn to give his attention to one shot at a time.
    2. To sharpen the shooter's mental competitive edge.
    3. To help the shooter learn to mentally prepare to fire his first shot close to the Range Officer's Command, *Commence Firing!*
    4. To give each shooter some positive feedback, since under this method, he will have a good chance to *beat* some *good shooters* during these *one-shot matches*.
    5. To help the shooter to visualize the shot in his mind, by having the shot value and location of the hit, called out by the coach, the shooter not having a spotting scope.

METHOD:

    1. Have each shooter hang one target.
    2. Each shooter is allowed 10 shells, both pistol and rifle are to single load.
    3. No Sighters
    4. All shooters fire from the same position. In rifle training, all might fire in the PRONE position. In pistol training, all might fire with the center fire pistol.
    5. The firing line commands are given for each shot.

© Bob Hickey

Plus the additional command is given of *Pencils Down!"* after *Cease Firing!*

6. Time Limit: *one minute*, <u>strictly timed</u>, no more, no less. In this one minute the shooter must:

   a) Fire the shot.
   b) Write a sentence stating his thought just prior to firing the shot.
   c) Record his estimates of the shot value, and location, on the top left side of the diagonal lines provided on the form.

7. Coach calls *Cease Firing!* after one minute. Then calls out the value and location of each shooter's shot.
8. The shooter writes out the value of the shot and its location, as called to him by the coach, onto the bottom right half of the diagonal line.
9. The shooter makes any sight adjustments necessary.
10. The coach then calls out the *Match Winner*, and any ties with the score of the match winner, are also treated as being in *First Place*.
11. All other shooters and their placement in the match are also called out.
12. The shooters copy their match placement down on the *One-Shot Match Form*.
13. The remaining *One-Shot Matches* are conducted as above until all ten shots have been fired.

Mental Training   Chapter 7

Figure 7-4

ONE SHOT MATCHES

Shot #	Value Called	O'clock Called	Actual Value	Actual O'clock	Write Your Thought At The Moment Before Trigger Let-Off
1.					
2.					
3.					
4.					
5.					
6.					
7.					
8.					
9.					
10.					

Match Results And Tactical Planning Practice

#	Place	Feeling About Result	Plan & Prep For Next Shot
1.			
2.			
3.			
4.			
5.			
6.			
7.			
8.			
9.			
10.			

© Bob Hickey

Mental Training   Coach's Corner

AGGRESSIVE TRIGGER RELEASE CHART

DIRECTIONS:

1. Here, coaches, we want to overcome trigger–release hesitation. This often comes from too deep thinking about an apparent or real trigger problem. We get to thinking that the trigger is irregular in weight of let–off. At other times, the trigger seems to go off too quickly. When your shooters recognize that they are actively thinking about the *trigger problem*, first of all, check it out with a trigger pull weight. Then, if it checks out properly, have the shooter do about eighty aggressive trigger–release let–offs, using the following directions.

    2. As you look through your sights, decide to fire as soon as possible, after settling into position on your sight pattern.
    3. Think *quick and smooth* as you swing into your sight pattern.
    4. For each shot you fire, which is preceded by an *aggressive trigger–release* attitude, draw a line through the appropriate box in your string on the chart.

5. As an alternative, record the value of the hit in the box of an *aggressive release* shot. Record the value to see if this aggressive trigger release training is a help or hindrance to you. By keeping track of this in your files or in your computer database, you can determine the effectiveness of this training for your shooting.

Mental Training Chapter 7

Figure 7-5 Aggressive Trigger Release Chart

DATE: __ __/__ __/__ __

Shot #	STRING #1	#2	#3	#4	Comment
1.					
2.					
3.					
4.					
5.					
6.					
7.					
8.					
9.					
10.					

Shot #	STRING #5	#6	#7	#8	Comment
1.					
2.					
3.					
4.					
5.					
6.					
7.					
8.					
9.					
10.					

© Bob Hickey

Mental Training   Coach's Corner

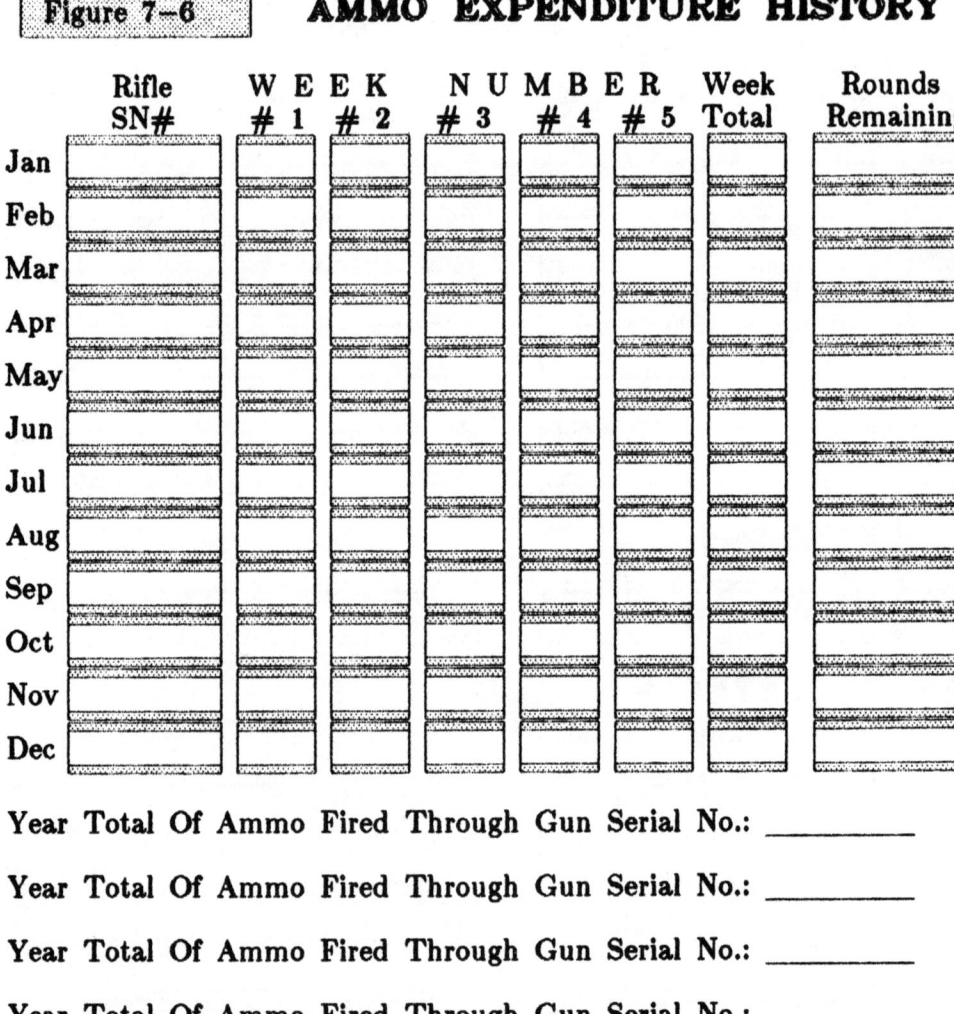

Figure 7-6   **AMMO EXPENDITURE HISTORY**

Year Total Of Ammo Fired Through Gun Serial No.: _____

Year Total Of Ammo Fired Through Gun Serial No.: _____

Year Total Of Ammo Fired Through Gun Serial No.: _____

Year Total Of Ammo Fired Through Gun Serial No.: _____

© Bob Hickey

Mental Training Chapter 7

Figure 7-7 — HOME TIME SCHEDULE PLAN

GOAL STATEMENT:

Time Block	Daily Plan For Activity	Total Minutes	Activity Critique
2 – 3:30			

Number of Minutes Devoted To:

M T Cards	
Gun Holding	
Dry Firing	
S A T	
Future Training	

Total Time Devoted To Home Training:	

Summary Of What I Learned:

Mental Training Cards:

Gun Holding:

Dry Firing:

Selective Awareness Training:

Future Training:

© Bob Hickey

CHAPTER 8

Computerize Your Shooting Data Records

With computers becoming more and more cost effective to own, shooters should seriously consider purchasing one. Using a computer is an easy and quite natural thing for shooters. It need not be frightening. I naturally assume two things. First, your shooting equipment receives priority in the allocation of your financial resources. Secondly, you want to receive the best value when spending your money on non-shooting accessories. For the value, I like the computers produced by Kaypro Corporation of Solana Beach, California. I like their reliability and portability. Make no mistake, the computer is a valuable accessory for the modern shooter.

But, what kind of computer is best for shooters? You see much about *IBM compatibility* if you read computer magazines. Of course you must expect to pay extra for this compatibility. Unless you know that you personally need *IBM compatibility*, don't bother! Most CP/M computers are less expensive and what is more, in some cases, they run faster. What does operating a computer consist of and what can you do with one to help you with your shooting?

SHOOTER'S DATABASE LOG PROGRAM

The purpose of the Shooter's Database Program is to provide a computerized *shooter's database* to track shooting performance, based upon the scores entered into the random records provided by the program. Use it to do your record keeping for you. If you have tried to keep track of records of your shooting performance for any length of time, you know the problems associated with information tracking in all the notebooks you somehow acquire as you chart your progress, let alone trying to find anything you once put it down in any notebook. Comes the computer to the rescue. The computer is the shooter's helper. But, a computer is good only as long as it will do your bidding. For example, the computer you get

Mental Training   Chapter 8

to keep track of your shooting records should be a serious computer. By serious, I mean it should be capable of operating in more than a games format. Some of you may want it for compatibility with a computer in your workplace. For some of you, IBM compatibility may be a must. If you need IBM compatibility, then buy a computer which is IBM or one which will give you the compatibility you need.

I have developed a database computer log program for keeping track of shooting records. I wrote the program in 8080 assembly language. This database log program will fit on most of the new lap size computers, *providing they use the CP/M operating system*, and do a good job for you. For those who have a computer, or who acquire one, this shooter's database program is designed to allow you to keep track of your shots for each shooting session. What it does is to provide you with a means of storing information you log into the program. It stores this information on a disk and then redisplays it on your computer screen whenever you wish. It is available for $39.95, plus $4.00 for shipping and handling. You must specify the name of the disk format you wish. Disks shipped to addresses in countries other than the U.S.A., please add $10.00 (U.S. currency or International Postal Money Order) for shipping and handling.

However, I cannot provide an operating system for any disk. I have agreed to make the program available on disk for a period ending June 1, 1986. If you want one after that date, please contact me and I will see if I can help you. *The program is provided in source code format.* The source code takes up 48.875K of space on the disk. In some cases, I will provide a .COM program also. The .COM file takes up 3.625K of space. This means you will not have to compile it. However, due to a lack of standardization in computer terminal handling characteristics, I cannot provide a .COM file for all of the formats listed. Order the program from the address below:

ASCII
P.O. Box 770222
Eagle River, AK 99577-0222

Mental Training Computer Use In Shooting

The *Shooter's Database Log Program* is available on a disk containing the program in the following 5 1/4" inch disk formats:

TABLE OF DISK FORMATS AVAILABLE

---------- Single sided formats ----------

Fmt	Description	Fmt	Description
A1	Kaypro	L1	Heath w/Magnolia (DD)
B1	Osborne 1 (SD)	M1	Superbrain (JR)
C1	Osborne 1 (DD)	N1	Superbrain (40 trk SS)
D1	Xerox 820 (SD)	O1	Cromemco CDOS (SSSD)
E1	Xerox 820-II (DD)	P1	Cromemco CDOS (SSDD)
F1	TRS-80 I (Omikron CP/M)	Q1	Cromemco w/Intl Term CPM
G1	TRS-80 Mod III (MM CP/M)	R1	DEC VT180 (DD)
H1	IBM PC (CP/M-86 SSDD)	S1	ACCESS (SSDD)
I1	Morrow MD2	T1	LOBO MAX-80 (DD)
J1	NEC PC-8001A	U1	TI Professional (DD)
K1	Zenith Z-90 (48 tpi DD)		

---------- Double sided formats ----------

Fmt	Description	Fmt	Description
A2	Kaypro	J2	NEC PC-8801A
B2	TeleVideo TS-802	K2	Zenith Z-100 (DD)
C2	Hewlett Packard HP-125	L2	Datavue
D2	Otrona Attache	M2	Superbrain (QD)
E2	IMS 5000	N2	MAGIC Computer
F2	EPSON QX-10	O2	Cromemco CDOS (DSSD)
G2	Sanyo	P2	Cromemco CDOS (DSDD)
H2	IBM PC (CP/M-86 DSDD)	Q2	Cromemco w/Intl Term CPM
I2	Morrow MD3		

TO USE THIS PROGRAM

Upon getting the disk, as with any computer program, you make a copy of the master disk. Make the copy on a disk which has been formatted with your operating system. The program is not copy protected. Put the copied disk into drive A of your computer.

Type: MT SHOTS↵

(↵ is the symbol I use here to indicate that you tap the key labeled

© Bob Hickey

Mental Training Chapter 8

Return on the computer keyboard.)

SHOTS can be any legal file name of your choice. It is the file which will hold your data. You can name as many different files as the disk will hold. You can put up to 65535 records in a single file. For filenames, you might name a file PRONE, or TIMED, or even 300YDS, just keep it 8 letters or less.

The program is designed as a log to record, store and provide for retrieval, the scores you enter. Should you want to use it as a part of a team training program for a number of team members, it is designed to be just as suitable as it is for an individual recording scores for personal use.

In using this with team members, a good strategy for a coach to use is to set the computer up on the range or in a target scoring area. Then have the shooters record their scores into the database as described below. The coach can then review the shooter's progress either with the shooter at the end of the practice session or, by himself, at home. Much of the introspective review the shooter learns to do when reviewing his scores is learned when there is the guidance of a coach. When the coach is available to aid the shooter in his interpretation of the shooting progress, there are many shortcuts which can be achieved. Having another human being focus on your shooting progress can have many beneficial effects on the development of your progress awareness.

One double density disk should serve 50 team members for quite a few practice sessions. When shooters drop off the team for one reason or another, it is easy to archieve their file onto another disk and erase their file on the active disk. Should they again become active, the coach can then move their old file from the inactive disk to the active one. The process of having each member of a team use this program is similar to the way it is used by an individual for his own use. For use with several members of a team, have each of them bring up the database with their last name (limited to no more than 8 characters), plus the month. For example:

MT SMITH.FEB⏎

If you have quite a few shooters on your team, you may wish to

© Bob Hickey

Mental Training   **Computer Use In Shooting**

have them enter their last name and the year of competition. For example: MT SMITH.86↵

Terminal Coding is for the Kaypro Computers. However, the code for other terminals can be easily substituted.

A typical database log display is shown in Figure 8-1.

Figure 8-1   Shooter's Database Log Screen Read-Out

```
     123456789112345678921234567893123456789412345678951234567896123456789712345678
 1   ┌──────────────────────────────────────────────────────────────────────────┐
 2   │ ---------- TARGET ANALYSIS RECORD ----------                             │
 3   │                                                                          │
 4   │ Date: 3/8/85                    Name of Range: Home                      │
 5   │ Type Of Gun: Air                Shooting Distance: 10 meters             │
 6   │ Sights: Iron                    Wind Direction: n/a                      │
 7   │                                 Lighting: ok                             │
 8   │ - SCORE RECORD -                Temperature: 76                          │
 9   │ Number of Zeros        : 0                                               │
10   │ Number of Ones         : 0      ----- FOOD/DRINK -----                   │
11   │ Number of Twos         : 0      Time Since Drink: 2 hrs                  │
12   │ Number of Threes       : 0      Time Since Food: 1 hr                    │
13   │ Number of Fours        : 0                                               │
14   │ Number of Fives        : 1                                               │
15   │ Number of Sixes        : 0      Other Observations: Follow through.      │
16   │ Number of Sevens       : 11                                              │
17   │ Number of Eights       : 16                                              │
18   │ Number of Nines        : 10                                              │
19   │ Number of Tens         : 12                                              │
20   │                                                                          │
21   │                                                                          │
22   │                                                                          │
23   │                                                                          │
24   │ Hit Any Key To Continue:                                                 │
     └──────────────────────────────────────────────────────────────────────────┘
     123456789112345678921234567893123456789412345678951234567896123456789712345678
```

The numbers around the edge of the screen of the computer terminal illustrated above show a requirement for the use of this program. The terminal must be able to display 24 lines and 80 columns of text.

CHAPTER 9
THE ROOTS OF MENTAL TRAINING

The world of shooting needs to acknowledge the roots of Mental Training. Here, I have extracted the pertinent thoughts of the marksmen of the world, who have advanced the level of performance of our sport, by sharing their knowledge with all of us. For copies of the original articles, contact the publishers of the articles or books. I believe it to be instructive to show where ideas originate. From my research, and from the sources cited in *Roots Of Mental Training*, I think it is clear that no nation has a monopoly on shooting knowledge.

This chapter is a tribute to those shooters, coaches, trainers and sports medicine researchers who have shared their knowledge with us. I have quoted extensively from those articles not likely to be readily available in local library retrieval systems in order to accurately illustrate the thoughts of the authors of the articles. On the other hand, for those books and articles readily available in the commercial marketplace, or likely to be available in local libraries, I have merely cited the book or article.

I have annotated the works cited, when I could identify their influence on my thoughts and ideas. These are compilations of notes taken from my coaching notebooks. When coaching, whenever I read an article which stimulates my thinking, I have a habit of jotting the reference down in a notebook. Such a notebook is a valuable working tool for any coach. I find myself referring often to these notes when designing a program for teaching a particular point or when designing a chart to teach the point. I hope these annotations will help others see where I started in this book.

© Bob Hickey

WHAT IS MENTAL TRAINING

Anderson, Gary L., "The Anatomy Of Firing A Shot – Part I," *Precision Shooting*, Jan. 1970, Page 6+
A technical discussion of the factors which make up the process of firing a shot. Coaches and trainers will also find much to interest them in this article. Club shooters just starting to take a technical interest in their shooting should read this, put it aside and return to it again after three months. I find something new in it each time I reread it. Discussed in the article are aiming, breathing, muscle control and trigger control.

Anderson, Gary L., "I Attempt To Run 1 To 2 Miles Daily," *Precision Shooting*, June 1963, Page 63+.
This is about much more than merely "running one or two miles a day. The principle thread running through this article is that the shooter needs a purposeful system of preparation.

Anderson, Gary L., "Klingner's Fleeing East Germany Results In Gold Medals For West," *Gun Week*, Sept. 1969, Page 7.
This article stimulated the development of several ideas in the coaching of my junior and collegiate rifle teams and ultimately for incorporation in this book, *Mental Training*.
When I was seeking a program to substitute for the NRA Basic Junior Shooting Course, I remembered Klingner's. I wanted a program which could be designed to accept a methodology containing 80% to 90% mental training. The NRA Training Course offered, at that time, only about 5% mental training.

Anderson, Gary L., "Mental Training Most Important Element In Making Good Shooter," *Gun Week*, Nov. 21, 1969, Page 1+
Anderson identified four elements which shooting training must include:
1. Physical training
2. home training or dry firing and air gun shooting
3. range training or actual shooting
4. mental training

He discusses "disciplining of the thought processes," "method of analysis","scientific method","shooting diary", the most important aspect of "thought training", how a "good trainer" interacts with his shooters, "development of concentration", and "fixing of mental standards." The aim of mental training must be, according to Anderson, that "the shooter must train himself to stop his hold and begin a new hold whenever extraneous thoughts enter his mind. This includes thoughts of physical pain. The shooter should also train himself so that wind changes will break his concentration."

© Bob Hickey

Backes, Clarus J., "Science of Athletics's," *TWA Ambassador*, Jan. 1978, Page 37+.
>Report of the University of Denver's Department of Physical Education's Human Performance Laboratory's methods of testing and training athletes for top performance. Backes discusses 1) The Athletic Motivational Inventory, "designed to measure those personality traits found most often in successful athletes, such as drive, emotional control, mental toughness and determination." 2) In addition, he includes comments about the use of the Cattell Personality Factor 16 Test: "designed to measure introversion, extroversion, intelligence, submission and self-control."
>What is the champion's personality? Dr. Marvin Clein, Chairman of the university's Department of Physical Education answers, "Those engaged in team sports tend to be extroverts, while those engaged in individual sports, such as race-car driving and tennis, are usually introverts. It's a matter of concentration: introverts tend to shut off outside stimuli, so they don't perform as effectively where teamwork is a factor. But they have a greater ability to focus their energies on a single, personalized objective, so in individual competitions they do well." This idea of introverts being able "to shut off outside stimuli," if true, is of crucial importance to persons responsible for directing shooting research in their clubs or associations. The production of Alpha waves seems to also depend to a good extent upon the ability to shut off outside stimuli. Coaches need to determine if their shooters are shutting off their awareness of such factors as wind and lighting factors during their shooting.

Barlow, J.A. (Brigadier), *The Elements of Rifle Shooting*, Gale & Polden, Ltd., Aldershot, Hampshire, Great Britain, 1932.
>Barlow, back in 1932, observed, "it is within the capability of almost anyone to become a really good rifle shot, provided only that he is mentally and physically fit. Notice that the word "mentally" is put first. This is because shooting, like all other games worth playing, is very largely a matter of mental control when once the rudiments have been acquired."

Eccles, John C., "Physiology of Imagination," *Altered States Of Awareness*, Sept. 1958, Page 31+.
>For coaches who want the theoretical background for why mental rehearsal is a valid part of the sportsman's "bag-of-tricks." Detailed, and complex, but clear.

Fitz-Randolph, Kurt, 1978 World Championships Report, *The International Shooter*, Vol. I., No. 3, Dec. 1978, Page 12.
>The youngest shooter on the U.S. World Championship Smallbore Rifle Team (18 years of age at the time), reported on

his preparations for and, his shooting performance in, the 1978 World Shooting Championships. Important for youthful insight into such high level competition. "The kneeling stage is where I had the most problems. My heart raced, I failed to perform, got caught on the wind, and shot horrible. What I'm trying to say is prepare yourself mentally before you start shooting."

Freeman, P.C.(Dr.), "Mental Training — Another View," *The Rifleman*, Spring 1974, Vol. LXXXI, No. 491, Page 28.

Good Questionaire for introducing the elements of mental training to new shooters or coaches. Mrs. Freeman's article seems to be an extrapolation of Hart's "Brain—Compatible Teaching" theory. It is not, because, of course, Hart's article was published in the Nov/Dec 1978 issue of *Today's Education*.

In her questionnaire, Mrs. Freeman utilizes "Perceptual Games" designed to "sharpen your visual discrimination and speed up the visual sequencing skills needed to take you from the incorrect to the correct sight picture." She points out "We have words to describe all this so we can reinforce these patterns by talking ourselves through shooting routines, aloud or in inner language."

I find a key thought regarding *Mental Training*'s Selective Awareness Training program in Mrs. Freeman's comment, "Where a skill is being learned involving sensory information from various sources and in sequence each part is learned separately and then put together." The idea behind the *Individual Shot Goal*, I see in Mrs. Freeman's assertion, "Confidence is not something we can demand of ourselves, it grows in us as a result of being aware of our strengths and our weaknesses and creating the right conditions for success, not just in shooting, but in our lives generally. Just as experiencing failure leads us to be anxious in case we fail again, so also being successful increases our confidence. Success is more obvious if only we measure it in small steps —— in other words don't aim for the high score, aim for one less 8, one less 9 as a success progression, keeping records so that you have visible proof of growing success."

Guerin, Tom, "Prone vs. Position —— Tempest in a Teapot," *Precision Shooting*, Jan. 1972, Vol. 16, No. 9, Page 15.

Guerin pointed out "The man is a computerized servo system with all of the sensors and decision making processes to determine the exact instant when the shot should be fired." Further, "The placement of the fired shot on the target is the final stimulus to the man's decision process. If the shot goes astray, an error message is entered into the computer, and the criteria for firing the next shot is altered." Guerin's thought provided the stimulus for much of item number 5 in the section of this book on how to use a diary.

Hart, Leslie A., "Brain—Compatible Teaching," *Today's Education*, Nov/Dec 1978, Page 42+

In this article, Hart asserts, "The brain controls all emotion and all goal—seeking behavior." He further points out, "The brain is a pattern—detecting apparatus." Importantly to shooters, Hart notes, "Stimulus—response psychology gave us the impression that the brain is passive and that what is taught will be what is learned.

But now there is wide agreement that the brain is intensely aggressive." Situationally, he establishes himself and his theory, "The new brain—based theory of human learning I have put forward defines the process of learning as the extraction of meaningful patterns from confusion. What we call "insight," seemingly very mysterious, appears to be simply the recognition of the key patterns that apply to a situation or problem." He goes right to the heart of a mental training program,

> *A second major concept gives us a definition of learning that is of immediate use to replace the old, fatuous "change of behavior" versions. Many brain researchers agree that the brain operates by programs, or goal—oriented sequences.*

It is hard to ignore his point "...It is easy to see infants building such programs. Using a spoon is hard at first, but gradually it becomes automatic." This is of importance to *Mental Training*'s Alpha State Training program. It is, in fact, the theory on which *Mental Training* is based. "We can," Hart says, "define learning, then as the acquisition of useful programs. We can see, too, that children can only use programs they have already built and stored in their brains. Ordering, scolding, punishing, giving a low mark——none of these will enable them to use programs they don't possess." That is why this *Mental Training* program changes the amount of shooting done in practice sessions. It is why home programs of mental rehearsal are so necessary. It is as Hart points out,

> *Nor do students acquire programs by being told or talked at, or by explanations, recitation, or taking tests...Learning (apart from briefly remembered "right answers") appears to be achieved only by the learner's own efforts, especially through repeatedly performing programs correctly. This suggests strongly that teacher should use methods that prevent the learner from "doing it wrong," and should avoid useless chiding or correcting after the fact.*

Mental Training follows Hart's suggestions by "Providing high input and letting the student extract patterns, combined with building programs by correct performance, may well lead to enormously better learning outcomes."

Here is how *Mental Training* meets this theory proposed by Hart:

HART'S THEORY	*Mental Training* Program
1. "The brain has a huge neo-cortex...but, it "shuts down" under pressure or threat everything but the barest rote learning is inhibited.	1. The goal of *Mental Training's* program: make the shooter feel at ease and secure in his shooting skill by the nature of the *Mental Training* program.
2. "Learners...need to manipulate materials in their own way and at their own pace."	2. *Training Plans* help you to organize shooting training within the time frame you have available. *Mental Training Cards* provide you with training materials which are easily accessible during otherwise wasted time segments.
3. "Learning proceeds more rapidly and surely when the student deals with real objects, real problems, real situations as opposed to contrived problems. In part, this is because dealing reality is complex and requires ex-	3. Notice that in *Mental Training*, the shooter researches into his own shooting problems. That is why the Duel Matches Program is so important a part of the beginner's training. To be a real match situation, the shooter has to know in his own mind that the loss of the prize which,

© Bob Hickey

acting patterns."	he will give up, has enough meaning for him so that he has an enhanced sense of responsibility for each shot he fires.
4. Children "must verbalize what they are doing.	4. The Shooter's Diary is the method used to show the shooter how to verbalize what he is discovering about his shooting.
5. "Learners should be encouraged to use their brains in intuitive creative, and pattern-detecting ways."	5. Again the Diary is designed to encourage this using of the brains to assist them in developing their potential in line with their goals.

Dahl, Winston A. (LTC, Infantry, Commanding), *International Running Target Guide*, United States Army Marksmanship Unit, Ft. Benning, Georgia, 25 Jan 74, 70 pages.
    Has some discussion of "mental discipline." Has some good points in the section titled, "Why Can't You Be A Winner?" In earlier editions of *Mental Training*, I warned readers against this section. I have reconsidered that warning. I believe its guidance on how to handle typical situations of frustration is very valuable to the shooter wishing to learn how to manage his own frustrations. For those interested in getting involved in the international running target game, this is a good book to get your hands on. For example, there is a well written discussion of reticle choice in one of the chapters, along with illustrations.

Parmentier, Stanley J. (Colonel, Infantry, Commanding), *International Running Target Guide*, United States Army Marksmanship Unit, Ft. Benning, Georgia, 1979, 100 pages.

Essentially the same book as the 1974 edition cited above. The interesting thing is, in the five years since the '74 edition was published, the U.S. Army decided that no significant progress had been made in mental training for it's international running target shooters. The information on mental training was reprinted verbatim from the '74 edition for this edition published in 1979. So, if you can get your hands on the earlier edition, rest assured that you will have the most up–to–date information.

Hinds, Sidney R., Jr. (Colonel, Infantry, Commanding), *Pistol Marksmanship Guide*, United States Army Marksmanship Unit, Ft. Benning, Georgia, 1978, 146 pages

This manual is an outstanding piece of work, of even higher quality than the U.S. Army's usual standards in the marksmanship guides it has produced over the years. For example, Annex III of this manual has an excellent discussion of the "Processes of the Human Nervous System Relevant to Equilibrium, Trigger Control and Hearing." Really an excellent piece. The section on mental discipline is the same as that published in the International Running Target Guides cited above. So, there is nothing new there, but Annex II is great. It goes into enlightening detail about the "Optical Properties of the Human Eye Relevant to Sight Alignment." This manual, in Annex I, "Characteristics of the Human Body Relevant to Stance, Position and Grip," does a good job in explaining the necessity for shooters to develop means of relaxation during shooting practice and competitions. For example, consider the following excerpt from page 110:

> *b. During the period when the muscle is at work, a decomposition of certain substances which are part of the muscular fibers occurs in the muscle and lactic acid is formed. During the intervals between individual contractions, the muscle momentarily rests. This relaxation contributes to the restoration of the state which has existed prior to the contraction, and the muscle proves to be completely capable of operating again. However, if any muscle is in the contracted state continuously, fatigue develops rapidly; protracted contraction of a muscle can soon reduce it ot the state of complete debility. c. When assuming the firing stance, at which time the shooter must achieve the greatest immobility of his body, the muscles perform static work. That is that work which is least favorable from the point of view of muscles fatigue. Taking this into consideration, the shooter must, especially when shooting for long periods of time, devote a great deal of attention to devising a system that allows alternating breaks between periods of assuming the firing position. This will make it possible for the muscles to regain their working ability to the greatest possible extent.*

Mental Training Chapter 9

Parmentier, Stanley J. (Colonel, Infantry, Commanding), *International Rifle Marksmanship Guide*, United States Army Marksmanship Unit, Ft. Benning, Georgia, 1980, 149 pages.

    More pages than the Pistol Guide you say? Sure, but 72 of the pages are devoted to "The United States In World Competition." For you marksmanship historians, this is a gold mine. But, of course, it does only leave 77 pages of test on rifle marksmanship. These 77 text pages are very well written. In addition, the manual contains photographs of many American Olympic and World Champions shown with their rifles in the their shooting positions. This is a valuable addition to any library.

Dahl, Winston A. (LTC, Infantry, Commanding), *International Skeet & Trap Guide*, United States Army Marksmanship Unit, Ft. Benning, Georgia, 10 Dec 73, 53 pages.

    If you are thinking of taking up skeet or trap shooting, this is a manual you should obtain as soon as possible, at least from a mental training point of view. This manual contains some information on mental training which has been omitted from similar sections of the more recent rifle and pistol guides. For example, the following, from page 10, is one of the things omitted:

> *All emotions are nervous processes arising in the cortex and subcortex of the brain. When you are experiencing nervousness, changes take place as a result of the imbalance of the exciting and depressing processes in the nervous system. One factor becomes dominant in the various parts of the brain. If the exciting processes are dominant, agitation in one's movements is observed. You may walk about nervously before your squad is called, unable to find relaxation. Sometimes the reverse is true, the depressing nervous processes are dominant. This results in low spirits, indifference, sluggishness, and sleepiness. This condition is known as "pre-tournament apathy." When agitation is the result of the disruption of the nervous processes in the subcortex sections of the brain, certain changes take place in body activity. The cardio-vascular system undergoes change. The pulse is faster and may at times reach 120 beats per minute. The breathing is fast and shallow. you become hot and perspire. Nervousness is reflected in the tone of your muscles and in the erratic manner in which you move parts of your body. This aggravates the situation still further because you become aware that you have lost the steadiness of the hold. The coordination is upset. This make s itself felt in the form of indecisiveness. A feeling of concern arises for the value of the score. Under such a condition you may deliver a shot without assurance and precision.*

© Bob Hickey

Peot, Joseph J. (Colonel, SigC, Commanding), *Rifle Instructors And Coaches Guide*, United States Army Marksmanship Unit, Ft. Benning, Georgia, 17 Jun 65, 113 pages.
>This is the most readable guide the U.S. Army has yet produced which I have reviewed. It is still the standard by which I judge the new manuals which come out of Fort Benning. It has the benefit of being an original. The guides produced since them have become clones of one another. This guide is still comprehensive and should be obtained by anyone just starting or thinking of getting into the highpower rifle game. It is a guide which is directed toward those individuals and coaches interested in the American National High Power Rifle Matches. It has a good section on the Infantry Trophy Shooting.

Jaramillo, Jesus M., (Columbia), "Perfect Shooting," *International Shooting Sport*, June 1974, Page 16.
>Jaramillo advises "it is necessary to practice intensively over long periods, so that the brain gradually learns what is a perfect shot." Further, he points out, "The ability to exercise this degree of mental control is something which the majority of shooters never attain...Why is that? The reason could lie in a lack of proper autogenic training, or perhaps in the lack of the urge to win, or some other personal factor which not everybody possesses, but which could be taught to every shooter."

Key, Wilson Bryan, *Media Sexploitation*, The New American Library, Inc., 1976.
>The chapter titled, "The Commercial Appropriation of the Unconscious," is good background preparation for understanding the essence of mental training.

BASIC MENTAL TRAINING

Anderson, Gary L., "Some Notes On Instructing New Shooters," *Precision Shooting*, Jan. 1972, Vol. 16, No. 9, Page 12+.
>According to Anderson, "The first experience in a new position is most effective when it comes from a dry holding exercise. The student should be asked to aim at a target and hold the rifle as still as possible. This is designed to teach him right from the start that concentration on his hold or wobble is the most important part of getting a good shot...The next experience should be dry firing to give the shooter the feel of firing a shot in the position and also to teach him what an important home training exercise dry firing or dry holding can be...The dry fire exercises before live firing begins in any position should be used to teach the shooter the wobble area concept. This technique teaches him to squeeze the trigger during reasonable holds rather than to press the

trigger when the sight picture is perfect." Then Anderson points out, "Perhaps the most important motivational factor for new shooters is to get them into competition as soon as possible, but always with shooters of their own skill and experience level...The sooner a shooter can get a taste of the excitement and fellowship of competition, the more likely he is to become a real target shooter."

Anderson, Gary L., "Tactics in Shooting," *International Shooting Sport*, Sep. 1977, Page 6+.

Anderson was the first to point out that "Shooting tactics are those things which a shooter does to take advantage of or minimize the negative effects of the variable in shooting." He identified three broad categories of shooting variables with which a shooter has to deal in making his tactical decisions:
1. shooter performance. Such things as hold, trigger timing, nervousness and fatigue are never constant, and as they change the shooter must adapt his techniques to match these changes.
2. weather
3. those things every shooter hopes won't happen: slow or irregular target service, harassment by match officials, "the small minority of match officials who think they're not doing their jobs unless they let the shooters know they are around."

Anderson also gives examples of different types of tactics to use for various problems which come up during the course of firing match. For example, "In more important matches, I normally decided to open up my shot acceptance standard so that I just tried to fire nines in the first two or three shots standing. Once I go settled into the record shot routine, I could change back to trying for good nines or tens. The reason for being satisfied with nines in the first few shots was to avoid shooting any bad shots while I was still unsettled."

Anderson, Gary L., "Shooting in the Wind," *Precision Shooting*, Mar. 1972, Vol. 16, No. 11, Page 14+.

Here Anderson delves into the tactics of shooting--equipment considerations as well as methos to use in matches and practice. For example, "The way the muscles are used to hold the rifle must also be changed." Good discussion of ways muscle tension is used in the standing position. "The shooter has to know by experience just how good he can shoot with the hold he has...Knowing what standard of acceptance he should set is one on the important things he can learn by practicing in the wind."

© Bob Hickey

Anderson, Gary L., "Sport Shooting Psychology," *Precision Shooting*, Mar. 1974, Vol. 18, No. 11, (Reprinted from Sept. 1970 P.S.).

Anderson attributes to Bill Pullum, the claim "that as much as 90 percent of a world record shooting performance is mental and not physical." He lists five basic mental factors needed for a shooting sports champion:

1. **Motivation.**
2. **The disciplining of the thought processes.**
   Olympic gold medalist Bernd Klingner says a good athlete has his ability in his body and a champion has his ability in his head.

3. **Concentration Sequence.**
   We know that it is best to have as little to concentrate on as possible--that is, as much of the shooting process should be relegated to the sub-conscious levels of awareness as can be done. Through the conditioning and learning processes that take place during training may formerly conscious shooting actions are slowly relegated to the sub- or semi-conscious level.

4. **Mental Standards of the Competitor.**
   The task of a shooter is to establish rigid mental standards that are high enough to win. A shooter will never consistently fire a score that he has not already established as an attainable mental standard...What the body does is determined by what the mind says it can or should do...What the mind does not think, the body cannot do! This is the key to the 1180's and 1190's that will be the rifle scores of the future.

5. **Control of Pressure.**
   Many good shooting techniques are developed to produce good practice results when the muscles are calm and the pulse slow. Nervousness brings very definite physiological changes to the body such as a faster pulse and more active muscles. The best techniques are adapted for these and not practice conditions...One of the most effective ways to combat pressure is through mental preparation...Discus thrower Al Oerter and I discovered that we both use the same technique to do this. We both prepare for a competition by mentally rehearsing every conceivable circumstance we could face in the competition. Makhmoud Umarov (USSR Olympic Silver medalis and world champion in pistol shooting) said, "Before the

shooter can defeat his opponent, he should have conquered him in his imagination." If the match has been thoroughly rehearsed in the shooter's mind, then he will be so much better prepared to deal with unexpected circumstances that always seem to shake most competitors.

Anderson, Gary L., "The Training Effect," *Precision Shooting*, Feb. 1972, Vol. 16, No. 10, Page 15+.

The "training effects" are the "changes which marksmanship training...produces in the physiological and psychological responses of the shooter's body." Anderson lists several "training effect indicators for beginning shooters:

1. **Hold quality**
   a beginner's training should strive to steadily improve his ability to hold the rifle still
2. **Hold control**
   the important question here is how well the shooter is able to keep his basic wobble area centered on the bull
3. **Trigger control**
   means first of all the elimination of trigger mistakes, like jerking, through training and increased mental discipline

Anderson wants us to know that, "It also means the development of a sense of subconscious timing that allows the trigger to be released in coordination with his hold control." According to Anderson, the beginning shooter should also strive for "position consistency."

Coaches will be interested in reading this article for the description of the "Advanced Shooter Training Effects," so they will have a better idea of what constitutes an "advanced shooter."

Anderson, Gary L., "Trigger Control," *Precision Shooting*, Dec. 1969, Page 8+.

Anderson provides us with a good discussion of the continuous squeeze, time release and interrupted squeeze trigger methods, with charts and diagrams. He says, in this article, that "Primary concentration is focused on the hold for most of the time the shooter is attempting to fire a shot. The direct relationship between the intensity of this mental control over the hold and the quality of the hold when the trigger is released cannot be overemphasezed."

AUER, Victor, "In Defense of a Sport," *Precision Shooting*, Nov. 1971,

Vol. 16, No. 7, Page 12+.
"Dry firing," Auer tells us, "indoors is an important part of the position shooter's training where he can practice breathing, pulse and muscular control...The shooting sports operate in reverse from every other Olympic sport. All track, gymnastic and swimming events require the sudden or prolonged excitation of voluntary and primary muscle, while the good shooter must learn to relax and isolate these muscles so that he can concentrate on learning to control his involuntary reflexes and responses...as the beginning shooter gradually develops his skills he learns: to control his breathing, to actually will his pulse to slow down as he squeezes the trigger, and even to exercise control over his nervous system...Ideally, the aspiring position shooter practices holding exercises every day or night."

Auer, Victor, "The 1972 Olympics in Munich: A Critique," *Competitive Marksman*, Nov/Dec 1974, issue 1-3, Page 9.
Well worth reading for the insight into an Olympic Shooting Competition, problems and suggestions.

Carson, Gavin, "Russian Success Formula Made Easy?", *The Rifleman*, Winter 1975, Vol. LXXXII, No. 498, Page 36+ (From the *South African Marksman*, October 1975).
This article reports on a lecture given to the Australian team during the "recent" World Championships in Switzerland, by two Russian shooting coaches, Max Polikanian and Vladimir Haidurov. They "stated that by far the most important thing for a shooter to do, be he novice or expert is to dry fire. They said that in order to become really proficient, a shooter must have stability (mental and physical), trigger control, concentration and "use of sight"--and all of these can only be learned by continuous dry firing...Most shooters lack the self-discipline necessary to do the amount of serious practice necessary, which is why so very few become great...The two men said that their most difficult task was to teach a top shooter to work, and this again was done with dry firing. Dry firing teaches doggedness, purposefulness and perfects technique."

Davis, Roy Eugene, *Secrets Of Inner Power*, Frederick Fell, Inc., New York, 1964.
For a flavor of this book, look at some chapter headings:
Entering the Creative Silence
Converting Ideas Into Realities
The Art of Releasing Tension
Awakened Imagination

Fifth European Air Weapons Championships -- Eight Gold For U.S.S.R -- but no new Records, *The Rifleman*, Spring 1975, Vol. LXXXII, No.

495, Page 10+.
> A very fine profile of an international championship tournament.

Gonzalez, Jose, (Mexico), "Dry-firing As the Foundation of the Training," *International Shooting Sport*.
> For beginning shooters and recreational shooters, Gonzalez makes a telling point, "I do believe that training is compatible with other activities, such as work and studies." He goes on to say, "All shooters who really want to improve their scores should take the time to practice dry firing at least one hour every day, and they will find it very helpful to fit this particular exercise into their daily routine...It is recommended to make note of each dry-shot, as in that way the shooter will attach greater importance to his practice. It is not easy to make this estimation, but you will gradually learn how to do it."

Gonzalez, Jose, (Mexico), "The Olympic Shooter and His State of Mind," *International Shooting Sport*, April 1969, Page 32+.
> "In all sports," Gonzalez tells us, "the physical activity, mainly carried out by the muscles, is guided by the activity of the brain, in other words one's mental state determines the correct execution of any piece of work...Acquisition and refinement of a technique is the work of the brain, so is the application of the certain method during the physical work which eventually becomes a mechanical procedure...The presence of shooters of other nationalities, members of the Jury, leading personalities, and strange people in general are some of the factors that influence the shooter before each international championship. The fact that the whole environment is new to him, can rightly be said to have a great influence on his frame of mind, as such unusual circumstances indicate the importance of the competitions and make the shooter excited."

Kern, Steven R., "Bill Rigby, Biography & Interview," *Competitive Marksman*, July/Aug 1974, issue 1-1, Page 9.
> This article provides some good insight into training techniques. "For a major match, Rigby practices holding exercises for one month and tries to get in some extra range time...He does a lot of dry-firing and holding exercises using a scope sight; like trying to hold the 1/2-inch dot on a 20X scope in the ten ring for several seconds."

Parish, David, "Rifle Captain's Report," (41st World Shooting Championships), *The Rifleman*, Winter 1974, Vol. LXXXI, No. 494, Page 12+.
> An international match from a team captain's perspective. A reading of this report will help prepare you for off-range problems as well as during-the-shoot problems.

Rotaru, Nicolae, (Rumania), "Some Aspects of the Shooter's Tactical and Psychological Preparation," *International Shooting Sport*, June 1970, Page 59+.

Rotaru informs us that "the placing of the shooter in several difficult situations during his training, is an absolute necessity in order to train him to solve the "tactical matters" which occur during competitions." He continues, "This important side of the training (has been) proven very often, to be not only necessary, but also essential, both to competitive shooters, but also to the beginner." *Mental Training* provides this type of training by encouraging duel matches between teammates. "Coke" matches are a good prelude to duel matches, but they are only to be considered in that light.

Shooting for a Coke is usually too insignificant a prize to be taken very seriously by the shooters. Then too, a Coke match is usually a spur-of-the-moment type of match, whereas a duel match is should be the result of a pre-agreement between two shooters as to match conditions and the prize. The shooters need to be aware of it and to think about it for at least several days prior to the duel match. In a Coke match, there is often little or no enhanced sense of responsibility present during the firing of the match.

During the shooter's training preparation, Rotaru says, "Among the main tactical aspects, to which we have to pay special attention are: developement of tactical thinking; the carrying out of the main trainings and of the test events in the same competition conditions or in more difficult conditions." He lists eight other aspectrs, but these two help form the program of *Mental Training*.

Additionally, Rotaru advises, "Before the competition, the shooter will have a look in his training notebook, in order to see whether he has omitted anything...The success in a contest depends greatly on the thinking manner of the shooter, on how to concentrate his attention to fight against distrust in his own forces, on patience and perseverence...The psychological preparation plays an important part in the athlete's training." You can see that his list of the things a shooter needs to pay special attention to reads like a primer of mental development. Notice some other items on his list:

1. **development of the tactical thinking**
   (analysis of the actions and of the results) during the firing
2. **exigency in observing the training program**
3. **training of the willing qualities**
   in order to overcome the typical difficulties
4. **development of attention**
5. **development of ability for a better self-control**

6. formation of the capacity to overcome emotions
7. development of the self—critical spirit
8. formation of the analysis capacity and independent evaluation of the situations
9. Formations of the responsibility sense against the results obtained in competitions

"The purpose of this preparation," according to Rotaru, "is to eliminate the distrust in (one's) own possibilities, decreasing the nervous tension which is dominating the shooters during the event." He points out the role the coach "has to play in order to know the shooter's temperament and how he (will) act in all circumstances." Rotaru further advises, regarding the relationship of a shooter to his coach that, "between them should exist a spiritual relation." In other words, without affection going both ways between a shooter and his coach, the shooter will always remain a shooter without a coach. If this is the case, then the shooter is very much in need of *Mental Training* to help him develop his own shooting advancement program.

SHOOTER'S TRAINING DIARY

Anderson, Gary L., "Anatomy of Firing a Shot — Part II," *Precision Shooting*, Feb. 1970, Page 5+.
> Here, Anderson discusses the sources of information and how they fit into the process fo firing a shot. "Once the ready position is prepared and the hold is started, the shooter must still wait four or five seconds for some muscles, which were actively moving during the position preparation, to reduce their activity and for others to gain full control over the hold...Continued concentration on hold control should be broken by the report which can be heard only after the bullet has left the barrel...There is no need for an exaggerated follow—through."

Anderson, Gary L., "New Developments In The Standing Position," *Precision Shooting*, Aug. 1970, Page 9+.
> Anderson has a good review of the early 1960's standing position development. Good discussion of the rationale behind the muscular tension you must maintain in the muscles used while in the standing position. "I always kept the muscles in my legs quite tense. The importance of using the leg and feet muscles to stablize the hold helped us realize that it was really the function of the legs to hold the position still and to correct for hold deviation. It is the legs that do the work in standing; the function of the upper body is to form a unit which does not cause any extra movements for which the legs must do the correcting.

Bruce, Bob, "Dropping Points——or some of the ways by which those 9's and 8's appear", *The Rifleman*, Winter 1977, Vol. LXXXIII, No. 503, Page 18+.

    This is an article which will appeal mostly to the creative coach, who is seeking help in training his team in outdoor shooting. Bruce has several excellent visual aids described in this article. I have a bit of a problem with Bruce's "controls." Two he says are mental and two physical. As he listed and then explained them, I came to the conclusion that all four are "mental controls." For example, "The second is a physical control——control of the ability to relax the muscular system, especially for the four or five seconds before the shot is fired so that the "system" hangs on aim. In order to find out how much was involved in establishing complete relaxation, I asked a medical friend if he could tell me just how many "muscle systems" the human frame has——from the waist up. Here are the figures he gave me: In each finger and thumb, 240; arm, 76; neck, 22; shoulders, 32; jaw and face, 40; chest, 32; abdomen, 16; and back, upper and lower, 200; for a total of 658...The fourth is the physical control used in outdoor shooting. It is a monitoring of the conditions at the firing point and down the range——a subconscious which picks up the signs and makes signals so that the shooter takes note and action."

    Regardless of the case made for these being "physical" examples, I have adopted them as a part of my *ulMental Training*ul program. Bruce's second "control" fits very nicely into the *ulSelective Awareness Training*ul program in *Mental Training*. The "fourth control" is what I see being attained by shooters who have reached the point in their training to place themselves in **Alpha State** during their shooting, thus a uniquely mental state.

Calderaro, Giuseppe, Dr. (Italy), "A Psychotechnical Portrait of the Sport Shooter," *International Shooting Sport*, April 1972, Page 22+.

    Dr. Calderaro reports on the results of psychotechnical examinations, which have been made from 1961 to the date of this article, with approximately 200 top class shooters at the Medical Sports Institute in Rome. Useful in setting up a mental training program.

Csaba, Dr. & Dofa, Jozsef, Dr., "Mental Training——an important aspect," *International Shooting Sport*, Aug. 1975, Page 21+.

    Drs. Csaba and Dofa discuss the "Videomotor Phenomenon," which their research projects established "proved that, during the mental projection of a movement, there was a detectable increase in the electrical charging of the muscles...It became apparent during these experiments that variations in temperature also affect muscular tension."

    Mental training is important because "it is the visual situations which are most easily mentally recalled, involving the remembering of various practical experiences such as the fore—sight centered on the target...Later, the memories which come to the fore are more likely to be of the actual feel of the movement (kinetics). It is when this stage has been reached that mental training begins to have effect...After four to six weeks, the sportsman is able to envisage more and more individual aspects, and after continuous practice is able to mentally sense almost every muscular tension throughout his body...Naturally, mental training relies on actual physical practice and will not work without effective training."

Emptaz, Gilbert (France), "Rifle Shooters Training," *International Shooting Sport*, June 1975, Page 18

Emptaz observes, "Training does not mean the expenditure of a lot of ammunition, or improving one's score every time one shoots. Training means that every factor involved in shooting must be observed, analyzed, and the finding evaluated. These relative factors are of an (a) **tactical**, (b) *technical*, (c) *psychological*, and (d) *physical* nature." Emptaz lists recommendations for tactics, technical preparations, psychological preparations and physical training. Here are some examples from his lists:

1. **Analyze and recognize the effects of various influences in order to control them**
2. **Practice "dry firing"**
3. **Implement and analyze your training plan**
4. **Be frank and honest with other shooters, but most of all with yourself**
5. **Relative muscle groups must be studied and developed**
6. **Nerve stimulants, such as nicotine (which results in poor resistance to fatigue), alcohol (which raises the heart and breathing rate), coffee, etc, have a detrimental effect upon a shooter**
7. **Shooters will achieve the steadiest possible stance when they completely relax the chest and arm muscles**

Emptaz points out in no uncertain terms, "Psychological training plays an extremely important role in the achievement of high scores." With respect to relaxation, he identifies two methods, "There are two methods of relaxation, the Jacobson Method and the Schultz Method. With the Jacobson Method, relaxation is achieved by first tensing and then relaxing the various limb and muscle groupings...The Schultz Method achieves relaxation by a mental process called introversion. The shooter thinks about relaxation and then allows the appropriate limb or muscle to relax. Using this method, he can should be able to get the best out of every limb and muscle."

Farris, Edmond J., *Art Student's Anatomy*, Dover Publications, Inc. 1935.

Fixx, James F., *The Complete Book Of Running*, Random House, New
    York, 1977.
>Not much here for shooter, but "Appendix B — The Physiology of Running, " is an unexpected find when the book is done. Good background for coaches.

Garcia, Jose Gonzalez, (Mexico), "The Physical Aspects of Shooting with
    the Small—bore Rifle," *International Shooting Sport*, Feb. 1971, Page 17+.
>"The function of the muscles," according to Garcia, "is the trickiest, as they must have a certain tension in order to keep the rifle steady without producing fatigue or cramp. The tension of the muscles must be maintained in a manner which refines and supports the position...There is nothing worse for a shooter than to eat too much or to drink alcohol, coffee or tea before a match, as the organism will then have to carry out a piece of work that accelerates the blood circulation and makes the heart beat fast. The consequence is palpitation and a faster pulse, not to mention a whole series of other digestion processes which result in bad scores."

Mathe, Jean, Dr., (Translated by: David Macrae) *Leonardo DaVinci,*
    Anatomical Drawings, Miller Graphics Distributor, Printer: Industria Grafica Se Tuset, Barcelona, Spain.

Loesel, Heinz, Dr. (Germany), "Medications — No Help In Improving
    Performances," *International Shooting Sport*, April 1977, Page 35+.
>Dr. Loesel states unequivocally, "None of these "performance improvers," depressants or tranquilizers, is of any use to the target shooter. **They disrupt the stimulatory signals transmitted from the sensory organs to the central nervous system,** *thereby slowing down the inter—relationship process,* **which causes incorrect positioning of the body.** These medications also lead to malfunctioning of the balance and visual organs, the accomodative and adaptive faculties being especially vulnerable, and to problems with the auto—sensory faculties...**Alcohol is counter productive to the achievement of high scores because "stimulative substances," by causing the secretion of catecholamine, generally raise the blood pressure, leading to an increase in the heart and pulse rate, thereby affecting the dilation and movements of the pupils.** They also encourage feelings of fear and anxiety and lead to an increase in tonus activity in both the passive and active states...All of the pharmaceutical substances used for doping purposes, achieve their objectives only by blocking the body's defense mechanism, or by mobilizing reserves of capacity which are intended for use only in extreme emergencies and are

therefore sub—conscious protective reactions. They are to be avoided for these reasons and also because the resulting dependence upon these drugs is a danger to the athlete's health...*According to present sports psychological knowledge, a shooter will be able to attain lasting success only when he is able to reach the optimum state of readiness for a competition by learning to achieve tranquillity or to activate the mental and bodily processes through intensive psycho—regulatory training.* Nor may he neglect a thorough mental training to extend to his sensory faculties."

Meik, Mirosvikov, (U.S.S.R.), "The Acclimatization of a Shooter to a Competitive Atmosphere," *International Shooting Sport*, April 1972, Page 19+.

Meik suggests the creation of match tensions during practice, "Although various attempts have been made to reproduce match pressure artificially, one must acknowledge that participation in competitions produces the best psychological training...The psychological training must be carried out in a precise and systematic manner. The pressures and more importantly, the tensions, during training must be great enough to achieve the desired effect." It is precisely for this reason that duel matches need to be arranged prior to the day of the match. In the prize arranging, the shooter must, in his own mind, feel that he is going to experience some loss of face if he loses. In this way, the tensions felt during *Mental Training*'s duel match will be those felt in match competition and the shooter will be able to devise techniques for shooting under match tensions. Meik points out, "To achieve a rapid and satisfactory acclimatization to stress, the following characteristical qualities are decisive:

1. **a low excitability**
2. **a well controlled aggressiveness**
3. **a high intelligence quotient**"

Montes, Jose Ignacio Valesco, Dr, (Spain), "Psychological Preparation of the Shooter," *International Shooting Sport*, Sept. 1975, Page 18+.

Dr. Montes discusses nervousness, "Emotional Tension," its symptoms and methods of combating its effects. He identified and listed the following symptoms:

1. **Tachycardia** — increase in pulse rate.
2. **Hypertension** — increase in arterial pressure.
3. **Tachypnoea** — increase in the rate of breathing.
4. **Digestive Spasms** — felt by the shooter in the form. of stomach ache, intestinal spasms or a loosening of the bowels. An attack of diarrhoea may even develop which disappears after the competition. The cause is excessive intestinal activity, as op—

posed to to an infection.
5. **Polyuria** — frequent passing of urine.
6. **Perspiration** — is one of the manifestations most noticed by the shooter and the one which most disturbs him. The perspiration itself is usually cold and thick, as well as abundant and is mostly located under the armpits, upon the forehead and on the hand. As perspiration on the hands can interfere with one's grip of the weapon, the use of Magnesium Carbonate, which interrupts the production of perspiration for a period, has been found beneficial.
7. **Vasoconstriction** — produces a cold sensation primarily in the extremities.
8. **Muscular Trembles** — due to emotional tension, there is a noticeable increase in involuntary muscular activity which stiffens the shooter and causes a state of trembling which can be slight in the upper part of the body, but stronger in the lower regions leading to motions, which shooters call "shaking" or "trembling".
9. **Lack of Coordination** — Involuntary movements may occur and there may be muscular "tics"
10. **Mydriasis** — produces a marked enlargement of the pupil of the eye. By interfering with the natural ability of the eye to adjust to variable light conditions, it has serious effects upon aiming.
11. **Loss of Attention** — because of all the problems we have mentioned, the shooter becomes worried and distressed, so that his attention is directed towards everything except shooting properly.
12. **Loss of Concentration** — emotional tension breaks the capacity to concentrate and the shooter notices that when he is shooting, his thoughts are dwelling on matters which have nothing whatsoever to do with his present circumstances.
13. **Tachpsychiae** — is the increase in the speed of thought processes, in which things are seen, etc. Everything happening around the shooter appears to accelerate.

"...If Emotional Tension is normal," Dr. Montes, continues, "as we have already stated, it is therefore impossible to suppress it. The only alternative left to us, is to accept and accustom ourselves to it, so that it becomes just as familiar as one's shooting glasses or trigger. By doing this we will have taken the first step towards shooting well."

It follows, then, from Dr. Montes' observations, that some of one's training should be devoted to scheduled inter–squad, or inter–club, duels with meaningful rewards to the winner and non-desired consequences to the loser. In this program of <u>duel</u> <u>matches</u>, if the prize if of little value or the loss of little concern, the duel is of small worth in the shooter's training.

Mutke, Peter H.E., *Selective Awareness*, **Celestial Arts, Millbrae, California, 1976.**

Rigby, William R.(Bill), "**The Realities of Shooting Standing,**" *Precision Shooting*, Sept. 1972, Vol. 17, No. 5.
  Rigby discusses the elements which contribute to shooting 10's in the standing position. He points out, "Above the diaphragm the body and rifle become a unit; this "body-rifle" is controlled by muscles in the stomach, legs, back, and buttocks. The shooter must acquire a sense of awareness about his body which tells him when he is in the correct position and the right degree of muscle tension is applied to the different areas." Rigby's concept of timing as "the decision making of shooting," is at variance with the theory of <u>Alpha</u> <u>State</u> <u>Training</u> in this book, *Mental Training*. Rigby contends "Emotional enthusiasm is as important to timing as it is to hold. A high pitch of enthusiasm results in more efficient observation, more exact decision, and must faster execution." This is diametrically opposed to what I have advocated in *Mental Training*. Where Rigby's theory advocates an active involvement of the conscious, *Mental Training*'s advise to allow <u>the</u> <u>little</u> <u>guy</u> <u>inside</u> to fire the shot. Where Rigby advises that you cultivate a high degree of enthusiasm in approaching each shot, *Mental Training* suggests the cultivation of a spirit approaching boredom in order to allow your subconscious to take over for you in the firing of the shot. Take a look at both theories. Try them. See which works for you.
  Rigby helped clarify my thinking about the purpose of my <u>Gun</u> <u>Holding</u> <u>Program</u>, "A useful variation of dry firing is holding exercises with a scope sighted rifle without manipulating the trigger. The objective is to attain skill in using the muscles to hold the point of aim in a certain minimum area...One of the critical factors of hold is the muscle tension applied to the different areas of the body. This should be one of the first areas a shooter investigates after he learns a good position." Rigby also gave me the idea for aggressive trigger release training. "The steps of decision and execution can be improved by adopting a more aggressive attitude toward firing the shot."

Stevens, John O., *Awareness: Exploring, Experimenting And Experiencing*, am Books, Inc., 1971.

Weinstein, Lew, (U.S.S.R.), "Holding, Aiming, Firing," *International Shooting Sport*, Oct. 1963, Page 138 (Methodical Training with the "Free Pistol").

© Bob Hickey

Weinstein points out, "Each muscle consists of a great number of muscle fibers. The most important property of these muscle fibers is their ability to contract. This activity is controlled by impulses sent out by the central nerve system...functional relations between the work—to—be—done and the state of tension of the muscles are established in the cerebral cortex as resultant from the training."

Gray, Henry, *Anatomy, Descriptive And Surgical*, Bounty Books, New York, 1977

TRAINING PLANS

ALKIRE, Marie
   I am grateful to Marie Alkire, Executive Director of of the United States Women's International Rifle Organization, for sharing her work on training plans with me.

Anderson, Gary L., "The Training Plan," *International Shooting Sport*,
   Aug. 1971, Page 15+.
       This is a very fine discussion of training plans. Anderson goes into detail about yearly through weekly plans. He also has a chart graphing out a yearly training plan. But, he says, "In the end, every training plan is individual, but it must be governed by a firmly fixed goal and an intelligently planned concept of how to reach that goal. this is the only purpose of the training plan."

SELECTIVE AWARENESS TRAINING

Anderson, Gary L., "The Dynamics of Score Improvement," *Precision Shooting*, Aug. 1972, Vol. 17, No. 4, Page 14+.
       With respect to the source of score improvement, Anderson says, "The basic and ideal movement of shooting scores is in a pattern of gradual improvement. Gradual improvement is a good indication that the training program is regular and well—planned." He points out, "A graphic picture of a shooter's scores will show his rate of improvement which in turn also tells a lot about the intensity of his training program." An integral part of any training

program, according to Anderson is the acquisition of a good basic shooting position. He says, "A shooter who has adopted an inherenently poor position will never be able to perform any better than the maximum capability of that position." More importantly, he notes, "consistency depends on learning how to think and react to the problems and mistakes that are encountered in the course of a match."

Anderson, Gary L., "The End of the Season...or the Beginning?," *Precision Shooting*, Oct. 1972, Vol. 17, No. 6, Page 18+.
    In this article, Anderson looks at the value and nature of planning. "Whenever a position is changed, many parts of the body have to learn new habits...If he does this, his body and mind will have enough time between then and the most important matches in the summer to really learn the new habits and actions involved in the change." The diary "will also show him what things should be emphasized during his fall training." Anderson also looked at goal setting, "Too many shooters just keep on letting the months and years catch up with them without ever setting any firm goals. They apparently do not realize the beneficial effect of having an attainable goal or set of goals...Whatever a shooter's goals are, they do give him something concrete to attain, compared to the vague idea of just continuing to shoot in hopes of getting a good score."

Anderson, Gary L., "Jerking Trigger Most Dramatic Error For Competitive Rifle Shooter," *Gun Week*, Feb. 12, 1971, Page 10.
    Anderson isolates the basic cause of a "jerk," "It becomes a jerk...when he fails to isolate the muscles in his trigger finger and other muscles that should be holding the rifle still get into the act too." I find **the individual shot goal** concept, which I developed in this book, in Anderson's statement, "The new shooter who still has trouble keeping all his shots in the black is only inviting a jerk if he tries to shoot tens. He should be concentrating on keeping his shots inside the black instead of in the ten ring...Controlling the jerk is basically an effort of the will, of the shooter's mind. If the shooter can develop the mental discipline needed to accept his wobble area and not try for perfect shots."

Anderson, Gary L., "Shooting Records Systems," *Precision Shooting*, May 1972, Vol. 17, No. 1, Page 17+.
    This is an analysis of the types of records used in providing the shooter with a framework for reflective thinking about shooting. Anderson discusses:
        The Shooter's Notebook
        The Scorebook
        The Shooter's Diary
        Shooting Calendar

© Bob Hickey

Anderson, George B. and Pamela J. Johnson, *Physical Fitness Digest*, DBI Books, Inc., Northfield, Illinois, 1979.
    If you include physical fitness activity in your training plan, I suggest you get this book. Discusses your body type and even shows you how to evaluate your physical fitness through a step test, a flexibility test, a muscular strength test and a muscular endurance test. If you feel you need to develop your strength, this book shows you how with isometrics, calisthenics, weight training and with machines and gadgets.

Bassham, Lanny R., "The World Class Shooter," *Competitive Marksman*, Nov/Dec 1974, Issue 1—3, Page 3.
    Bassham asks, "How does one become "one of the best in the world in shooting?" He then shows us the dedication and training those who achieve this distinction, have to adhere to.

Buys, Donna, "A New Way To Make Pain Disappear," *Family Weekly*, Oct 1, 1978, Page 13.
    Ms. Buys discusses "guided imagery" as a means of getting in touch with the 90 percent of our brains--some call it the unconscious--that most of us do not use.

Cordell, Franklin D., and Gale R. Giebler, *Psychological War On Fat*, Argus Communications, Niles, Illinois, 1977.
    Goal setting very helpful.

Gallwey, W. Timothy, *Inner Tennis, Playing The Game*, Random House, New York, 1976.
    Much of this is applicable to marksmanship training.

Gatty, Ronald, Ph.D., *The Body Clock Diet Book*, Simon and Schuster, New York, 1978.
    This book is an expansion of a government research project the author was involved with concerning the relationship between eating your heavy meal early or late. The research definitely indicated that those eating their heavy meal early consistently lost weight.

Koestenbaum, Peter, *Managing Anxiety*, Prentice—Hall, Inc., Englewood Cliffs, New Jersey, 1974.
    There is much to learn from this book. For example, on page 93, "What, specifically, is journal—writing? It is the ability to **become** the writing." That is the essence of the Shooting Diary as seen in *Mental Training*.

Mischel, Walter, "How Children Postpone Pleasure," *Human Nature*, Vol. 1, No. 12, Page 51.

Good basic background showing how people learn to abstract symbolic skills..."As a result of follow—up experiments, we have been able to specify just what kind of thoughts about a goal or reward help children to delay gratification or make the wait difficult...As their symbolic capacities mature, children become able to focus on the abstract qualities of an incentive, rather than on its exciting or arousing qualities. This new ability allows them to pursue goals without constantly feeling frustrated because they are still out of reach."

Prokop, Dave, (Editor), *The Dart Book*, World Publications, 1978
Put Chapter 7, "Mastering the Mental Aspects" by John Reichwein on your should—read—list. He talks about **positive intention** as being superior to **positive thinking**.

ALPHA STATE TRAINING

"Alpha Rhythms: Back to Baselines," *Science News*, Vol. 109, No. 10, Mar. 6, 1976, Page 148.
This is a report on the results of research reviewed in a paper presented at a meeting of the American Association for the Advancement of Science, by Martin T. Orne and Stuart K. Wilson, dealing "specifically with attempts to teach people to control alpha waves through biofeedback." Their work has relevance for target shooters "If the feedback light itself was inhibiting alpha, then what appeared to be learning to control brain waves may have been nothing more than learning not to attend to the visual stimulus that was blocking alpha production." Their results supported their hypothesis, "that apparent augmentation of alpha density occurred only when it had previously been depressed and seemed to involve the individual's gradually learning to ignore the stimulus that had been responsible for alpha suppression in the first place." A shooter, observed having done this might be thought to be in "alpha state."

"Alpha Wavesand Anxiety: No Link?," *Science News*, Vol. 106, No. 19, Nov. 9, 1974, Page 294.
Describes research by Martin T. Orne and David A. Paskewitz of the Institute of the Pennsylvania Hospital and the University of Pennsylvania, to test the theory that since alpha waves "accompany anxiety, then increasing alpha waves via

feedback efforts should reduce anxiety...Our most striking observation," Orne told SCIENCE NEWS, "is that contrary to previous research, alpha density is not linked with arousal of anxiety...that alpha and anxiety are not concurrent phenomena."

BLAIR, Wes, "Psychology of the Match Competitor," *The American Rifleman*, Mar. 1969, Page 30+.

Extrapolates from a study he made "of gold medal match winners in the smallbore, pistol and highpower categories and found that success hinged on 3 factors...Each winner had gone through a rigorous training schedule...each had developed the ability to focus intense concentration on each shot...each possessed a fierce determination to excel and win." Advocates using practice sessions "to improve your position, timing, technique, and winning attitude. if you don't have a coach, get one." Notice his explanation of the method used to learn how to concentrate, "The basic techniques of concentration are few. First clear your mind of all extraneous thoughts; make it a complete and total blank. Next, focus all your attention on the target subject. With practice, competing thought, even anxiety and tension over the match, can be controlled. Be prepared to experience frustration. When you fix your mind on a target subject, you will, at first, be bombarded with other thoughts. Business problems, vacation plans, your love life, any one of a hundred ideas can explode into a shower of irritating, distracting notions that shatter any attempt at concentration. This you must learn to overcome." He admonishes, "It is essential that you set yourself a series of graduated goals, the first of these within easy reach. At each level of proficiency, you will receive the reward of self-satisfaction and the incentive to progress on to the next level, until you reach your peak efficiency potential."

Brown, Barbara B., *Stress And The Art Of Biofeedback*, Bantam Books, Inc., 1977

On pages 34-5, Dr. Brown discusses muscle tension, even in sleep. On pages 53-5, I find too, that Jacobson's research justifies the processes and methods used in *Mental Training*'s **Selective Awareness Training** exercises. On page 90, Dr. Brown reports the Conner "relaxation effect is a cognitive effect manifest in change in autonomic reactivity...that relaxation training can affect autonomic reactivity with instruction and minimal training."

I recommend this book to any coach seeking background reading in mental training. I find it very readable.

Estabrooks, G. H., *Hypnotism*, E.P. Dutton & Co., New York, 1943

Hilgard, Ernest R., "Hypnosis And Consciousness," *Human Nature*, Jan. 1978, Vol. 1, No. 1, Page 42+.

Good for background about the conscious and the unconscious.

Jacobson, Edmund, *You Must Relax*, McGraw—Hill Company, Inc., New York, 1934
> This book should be placed on the required reading list of any future National Coaching School. A mental training program does require practice. Jacobson says, "The importance of daily practice cannot be too much emphasized to anyone who seriously intends to cultivate habits of relaxation whether lying down or during normal activities."

Jewell, Wanda R., (Report of the Korea 1978 World Championships), *The International Shooter*, Dec. 1978, Vol. I, No. 3, Page 11.
> Jewell gives us a good analysis of the problems she experienced in her first World Championships in 1974. At that time, she said she was "having the attitude of having to beat somebody, instead of trying to achieve my goal scores, were all prevalent in my preparation for the last World Championships (1974)." She identified the factors leading to her success in the 1978 World Championships in Korea, "Increased training time and range availability were major factors. Another factor leading to a better performance this time was increased mental training. After taking the EDGE Institute course this summer, I began using some of the techniques taught us. I coupled that with relaxation exercises."

Johnston, William, *Silent Music*, Harper & Row, New York, 1974.
> Good chapter: "Brainwave and Biofeedback."

Karlins, Marvin, and Lewis M. Andrews, *Biofeedback (Turning On The Power Of Your Mind)*,, J.B. Lippincott Company, New York, 1972.
> Worth obtaining for your library for its "Annotated List of Suggested Readings" and it's "Bibliography." Good hints, such as on page 29, "It is important to note that the patient is never told to "slow down his muscles" or "speed up his heart"--instead, he is asked to "keep the tone off" or "make the light dimmer."

Kreskin, *Kreskin's Mind Power Book*, McGraw—Hill Company, Inc., San Francisco, California, 1977.
> Take a look at this one. For a shooter, observe how simple is his formula for repetition, (page 134):
> Attention + interest + Repetition = Air
> Here are some chapter headings:
> Concentration
> Visual Imagery
> Unlocking the Secrets of the Inner Mind
> Memory
> Gaining Self—Confidence Through Mental Discipline

Laurie, Sanders G., and Melvin J. Tucker, *Centering: Your Guide To Inner*

© Bob Hickey

Growth, Warner Books, Inc., New York, 1978.

LeCron, Leslie M., *The Complete Guide To Hypnosis*, Harper & Row, New York, 1971.
> Part of my investigation into mind training. Note chapter titled, "Your Subconscious Mind."

Masters, Robert, and Jean Houston, *Umind Games*, Dell Publishing Co., 1972

"Mind Power: Alpha," (National Mento Corp.) *Radio—Electronics*, July 1976, Page 36+.
> Describes a device which can be built for use in monitoring alpha brain wave patterns "and converts these into signals that control an audio "beeper" and a video display created by a symbol generator." We are told "Devised by scientists, rather than yogis, alpha—wave biofeedback is a technique of mental training, through which the brain and the body are made to linkup more closely, so that the physiologic sources of stress come under the control of the mind."

Norvell, *The Miracle Power Of Transcendental Meditation*, Harper & Row, San Francisco, California, 1972.

Pratt, Robin Whitlock and Robert M. Nideffer, *Taking Care of Business*, Enhanced Performance Associates, California, 1981
> Subtitled "A Manual to Guide the Refinement of ATTENTION CONTROL TRAINING (A.C.T.) To be used in conjunction with the Test of Attentional & Interpersonal Style (TAIS)," is a more adequate title. This is one of the most comprehensive treatments of mental training currently available. Pratt points out "The key goes beyond concentration as it is typically oversimplified. **One must be able to demonstrate the different kinds of concentration at the right time.**" For those of you who have not yet done any serious mental training, Pratt has this advise, "**it is generally valuable to think through your actions, i.e., mentally** *look before you leap.*"

Pullum, Bill, and Frank T. Hanenkrat, Ph.D., *Position Rifle Shooting: A How—To Text For Shooters And Coaches*, Winchester Press, New York, 1973.
> If you are interested in serious training for world class competition, acquire this book read it, study it and adopt its principles.

"Test Anxiety" *Human Behavior*, Apr. 1978, Vol. 7, No. 4, Page 50+.
> Reports techniques of self—coaching strategies."

Walter, W. Grey, "The Electrical Activity of the Brain," *Altered*

Mental Training　　　　　　　　　　　　　　　　　　　　　　　　　　Chapter 9

States Of Awareness, June 1954, Page 4+.
　　Historical background about the discovery of brain waves. Helps in providing a base for understanding what is alpha state.

COACH'S CORNER

Alkire, Marie L., (Director, Schiessportschule I), *Schiessportschule Dialogues I*, United States Women's International Rifle Organization, Reliable Reproductions, Inc., Tempe, Arizona, 1977.
　　These are the printed transcripts of guided question and answer sessions with a Who's Who of American World Class Shooters, coaches and gunsmiths. It is a valuable reference book for all competitive shooters.

Anderson, Gary L., "Aiming Equipment," *Precision Shooting*, Apr. 1971, Vol. 15, No. 12, Page 101+.
　　This is good article which is about sights and the ways to utilize the sights for optimum results.

Anderson, Gary L., "Aiming Techniques," *Precision Shooting*, May 1971, Vol. 16, No. 1, Page 16+.
　　Here Anderson tells us, "The shooter who aims only to get a perfect sight picture so he can pull the trigger, is overlooking the fundamental principle of shooting that calls for maximum concentration on the hold as opposed to concentration on pulling the trigger when there is a perfect sight picture." He does a good job of comparing ring insert and post sight pictures. This is a very good article for highpower shooter. For example, Anderson points out, "Another valid question is where to focus, on the front sight or the bull. Actually, the best place to focus is on the sight picture. The shooter should think of the target and front sight as being on the same plane. The point of sharpest focus will be someplace in between...The accuracy of a sight picture depends a lot on what the shooter looks at. For example, he should not aim with a right by flicking his concentration from one side of the ring to the other. He should try, instead, to see the whole sight picture as a single awareness. The mind should learn to respond to the whole sight picture."

Anderson, Gary L., "Air Rifle Techniques," *Precision Shooting*, May 1970, Page 9+.
　　Coaches or shooters getting ready to "get into" air rifle shooting, should mark this article as a "must read" first! There

© Bob Hickey

are a multitude of hints such as, "The long barrel time and the movements created by the forward motion of the piston give the shooter plenty of opportunity to influence the strike of the bullet on the target by changing the pressure of the right hand or cheek. The air rifle must be held with much more consistent pressure than any other competition rifle."

Anderson, Gary L., "Basic Accuracy," *Precision Shooting*, Jan. 1973, Vol. 17, No. 9, Page 13+.
Ways a novice can help his rifle shoot better. Includes Rules of Basic Target Accuracy:
1. **Keep the rifle in good condition**-- tells how to do this.
2. **Keep the barrel clean**-- tells why and how.
3. **Application of fundamental bedding techniques**--tricks to keeping factory bedding jobs right...ways to handle rifles bedded in wood.
4. **Correct ammunition selection**-- simple checks for ammunition selection.

Anderson, Gary L., "Hook Butt Platt May Be Problem to Shooters," *Gun Week*, Sep. 1969.

Anderson, Gary L., "How Important Is Natural Ability," *Precision Shooting*, June 1971, Vol. 16, No. 2, Page 12+.
Anderson observes, "There seems to be no characteristic physical build that has greater potential for shooting success...A person who gets excited very easily or who knows extremes of happiness or sadness would find it difficult to keep his nervous expressions under sufficient control for shooting success...motivation is far more important in the development of a shooting champion than natural ability...Natural factors which we do feel affect the development of a winning shooter include muscle quality as opposed to strength, heart rate and the ability to process oxygen, nervous and emotional control, and mental and psychological capacity."

Anderson, Gary L., "The Importance of Proper Stock Fit," *Precision Shooting*, Nov. 1972, Vol. 17, No. 7, Page 18+.
"Match pressure," Anderson notes, "has a way of not only changing things, but also of making the shooter much more sensitive to minor deficiencies he was unable to see in the relaxed setting of practice." Unless a shooter's training includes special training matches, his training program has to be considered inadequate.

Anderson, Gary L., "Is Prone Really Unique?," *Precision Shooting*,

Mental Training Chapter 9

Nov. 1971, Vol. 16, No. 7, Page 18+.

Anderson, Gary L., "The Kneeling Position," *Precision Shooting*, Sep. 1971, Vol. 16, No. 5, Page 14+. A MUST for coaches! Good hints! For example, "If a kneeling roll is used...Sawdust is probably is probably the best filler since it is light and does not compress. A V is generally formed in the center of the kneeling roll to give greater support to the foot. The height of this V from the ground is one way of adjusting the relationships of the position, but for a starting thickness, two inches is about right...Fixing the location of the torso is next and and most critical step in kneeling. this must be done in such a way that the torso becomes rigid, that muscular effort in the back is minimized and that weight of the body remains balanced above the support surfaces."

Anderson, Gary L., *Marksmanship*, Simon and Schuster, New York, 1972. A book every beginner should be given when he or she starts to shoot. It is at once, very basic and very complete in its treatment of target competition shooting. For the flavor of this book, take a look at the table of contents.

> Shooting as a Sport
> Target–Rifle Competitions
> Equipment
> The Secrets of Shooting
>   1. Aiming Correctly
>   2. Trigger Control
>   3. Breath Control
>   4. Using the Sling
>   5. Bone Support
>   6. Balance
>   7. Relaxation
>   8. Head Position
>   9. Holding and Firing
>   10. Hitting Where You Aim
> Adapting the Shooting Secrets to the Four Positions
> On to Victory

Anderson, Gary L., "New Knowledge About Aiming," *Precision Shooting*, Oct. 1970, Page 13+ Anderson comments on the findings reported in an article by Nikolai Kalinichenko, a U.S.S.R. rapid fire pistol shooter and a 1954 World Champion, as translated by Richard J. Danik, title "How Soviets View Aiming Problems" and appearing in the September, 1970 issue of *The American Rifleman*. Anderson notes, for example, Kalinichenko reports his research indicates, "Precision of aim was best at 1.25mm." Anderson comments, "These tests seem to indicate that a slightly wider opening may be advantageous."

Anderson, Gary L., "Some Notes On Instructing New Shooters," *Precision Shooting*, Jan. 1972, Vol. 16, No. 9, Page 12+.

"If there is a starting point for new shooter instruction," Anderson states, "it is that the instructor must have thorough knowledge of shooting before he can teach anyone else about shooting. No matter how good a teacher he is, his ability to teach rifle marksmanship is going to be severely limited if he doesn't have an understanding of shooting and its problems that has been gleaned from actual experience. The instructor doesn't have to be a champion shooter, but he should have enough experience to have reached at least an NRA Expert or Master classification in the kind of shooting he is teaching."

Anderson, Gary L., "The Standard Rifle," *Precision Shooting*, Nov. 1969, Page 11+.

Overview of the concepts behind shooting the ISU Standard Rifle. As valid today as when the article was first published.

Antal, Laslo, Dr., (Great Britain), "The Effects Of The Changes of the Circadian Body Rhythm of the Sportshooter," THE RIFLEMAN, Spring 1975, Vol. LXXXII, No. 495, Page 24+.

This article is of value for all shooters who travel rapidly across several time zones to reach a tournament site. Antal notes, "Studies of circadian rhythms of the human body showed the existence of such variations in temperature, endocrine secretions, kidney functions, cardiac output and in the respiratory rate...It was found during performance tests that there exists a circadian rhythm in relation to applied mental and motor functions...The disturbances of the time zone shift manifested themselves as far as shooting performance was concerned in inability to concentrate, lack of coordination, muscular weakness and tremor, loss of reaction speed, loss of visual acuity, lassitude and early fatigue; in that order."

Dr. Antal conducted this study during the Commonwealth Games held in New Zealand. He had the cooperation "of shooters not only in the English team, but in the Welsh, Scottish, and Northern Irish contingent."

Dr. Antal's conclusions, "From the foregoing it may be established that rapid traversing of time zones has a considerable and lasting effect on the performance of sportshooters. Unless a sufficient period of acclimatisation is allowed to take place (minimum of 14 days in my opinion) the competitor may not be able to achieve his full potential...I strongly believe, as the evidence of my study show, that training during the first week of arrival should be avoided, since the disturbing effects are so great that they may have a profound psychological effect on the sportshooter's performance, even after full acclimatisation. Confidence lost during this period may not be fully recovered, impairing seriously the match performance."

Antal, Laslo, Dr., (Great Britain), "Social Habits and the Sportshooter,"
The Rifleman, Winter 1975, Vol. LXXXII, No. 498, Page 39.

Dr. Antal discusses eating habits, drinks, smoking and medications. For example, "Alcohol is a narcotic (and NOT a stimulant as many believe), it has effects upon the central nervous system, on gastric secretion and on circulation. Thus, the action of alcohol on the central nervous system includes reduction of our ability to concentrate, to carry out acquired skills, to do accurate work...Its action on the digestive system includes stimulation of the secretion of gastric juices, and thus can cause dyspepsia and gastritis...Its circulartory effects include dilation of the skin vessels, increasing of the diastolic volume of the heart, impairing of the heart's efficiency."

Antal, Laslo, Dr., (Great Britain), "Some Physiological and
Psychological Aspects of Pistol Shooting," *The Rifleman*, Spring 1977, Vol. LXXXIII, No. 505, Page 7+.

This article resulted from a lecture given to the Physical Education Faculty of the Liverpool Polytechnic. It should be required reading in every NRA Instructor Training Course. And it should be studied by aspiring coaches and instructors as a model of a way our shooting sport can be presented to non-shooters. Good, clear and concise examples. Dr. Antal identifies the essence of *Mental Training*'s effort, "However, the shot must be released by subconscious effort. If the shot is not released during the diminishing of the movement of the sights, and then an attempt is made to fire the shot during the complete standstill, the shots is fired consciously and the resulting "snatch" will result in a poor scoring shot...The shot is released as an automatic process when the sight picture is correct. This automatic process involves a nerve pathway from the visual analyzer in the cortex, to the motor centres controlling the muscles of the trigger finger."

Dr. Antal also discusses the roots of competition stress, "The psychological stresses of competition will interfere with this particular conditioned reflex...Physical manifestations of mental stress are well known:"

1. **raised blood pressure**
2. **raised pulse rate**
3. **hyper-ventilation**
4. **sweating**
5. **sensation of unnatural pressures in the stomach**

6. **bladder:**
   increased bowel action
   muscle tremor

These effects will result in unsteady aiming--consequently there is a block from the visual analyzer to the release of the shot...In difficult light conditions the visual analyzer might not be able to decide if a correct sight-picture is achieved, therefore there is hesitation and the shot is not released during optimum conditions...This inhibition is called in the trade the "frozen trigger finger."

Arnold, Siefried, (Germany), "Psychological Questions in Connection With Training," INTERNATIONAL SHOOTING SPORT, Apr. 1969, Page 41+.

Arnold points out, "The shooter should know that training for too long without a break will often cause a marked deterioration of his performances. This deterioration is quite often caused by a strain on the nervous system as a result of too frequent training and lack of relaxation. We can consequently establish that it is not the number of repetitions, but the way the exercises are repeated that is so important." He also informs us, "It is characteristic that shooters often manage to achieve very high scores during practice, but fail in a competition. One of the reasons for this discrepancy is no doubt that the shooter during practice can direct his whole attention to a clean, technical execution and thus avoid bad mistakes. In competition, however, he is in a completely different situation. A great part of his power is used to suppress his nervousness, and the slightest technical defect will therefore most certainly appear in a competition." It is important for the novice shooter to realize that he must schedule score practice into his training effort. Pre-planned duel matches with teammates should be a must on his agenda of training practice. The duel match must contain an element of risk. It is necessary that both duelists feel this element of risk and are quite aware of the other's concern for it. "Unfortunately," Arnold admonishes, "it has quite often been observed that many shooters do not understand this problem and consequently fail to carry out their practice correctly...The shooter does not understand why he fails in a competition, when his results during training have been satisfactory. Consequently he starts looking for the reasons for his failure. He changes his technique, his positions, his sights, etc. The reasons for his failure may seem unlimited to him."

According to Arnold, "the expressions, "technical practice" and "score practice" should once more be explained thoroughly...By <u>technical practice</u>, we understand the practice that aims at improving and autmatizing separate elements and the total process only...By <u>score practice</u>, we understand a training that is very close to the real competition. Score practice is also a score control and a check on the skill acquired...Each shooter must be able to perceive a clear definition between technical practice and score practice. Only when this definition is perfectly clear, will the shooter be able to concentrate all his attention on the improvement and the automation of his technical skill. The pre-planned score control (score practice) will, on the other hand, bring him close to the conditions of a competition. Unfortunately this point is very often neglected in shooting sport as well as in other sports...On the other hand, systematically divided score controls (score practice) might be of great psychological importance to the shooter. The shooter becomes self-confident and gets the feeling I CAN."

Auer, Leland, (Ph.d) "Letter to the Editor: Ref: "Clean That Barrel," *Precision Shooting*, Aug. 1972, Vol. 17, No. 4, Page 17 (Reprinted from June 1968, *Precision Shooting*).

Well worth the reading! "Didn't you ever observe the cloud of junk that comes out of a barrel when the wire brush emerges from the muzzle? And didn't you realize that this same junk (carbon, etc.) comes out at the breech when you reverse the direction of the brush through the barrel? And no rod guide will completely seal the action and trigger.

Bauer, Walter, Dr. (Germany), "Circulation, Breathing, Fitness and Shooting Results," INTERNATIONAL SHOOTING SPORT, July 1976, Page 22+.

Dr. Bauer established by scientific research, "that there is no direct relationship between the pulse rate and the level of scoring. In other words, good or bad shots can be made equally well with either a calm pulse rate or a fast erratic one." An experiment was also conducted which "indicates that there is little practical difference between the blood circulation levels of the top shooters (National "A" Squad), and those of any group of shooters selected at random...Thus the results of our experiments show that the answer does not lie in muscular strength, nor in the physical condition or circulatory system. The vegetative state and breathing do not appear to be of major importance, so where does the answer lie?...Shooting differs from other types of sport as the energy collected during a competition cannot be released in an explosive manner, but must be channeled by mental discipline into calmness, physical control and concentration."

Therefore, Dr. Bauer points out, "The importance of serious, regular and consistent training cannot be stressed enough. The anticipation method should produce new reflexes which enable the process of aiming and shot release to be made with consistent accuracy in any given circumstance. Autogenic training would appear to offer new dimensions, as an addition, not a replacement, in this area.

Bruce, Bob, (Great Britain), "Coaching...Or Teaching?", *The Rifleman*,
April 1977, Vol. LXXXIII, No. 504, Page 7+.
> The essence of the shooting sports, Bruce observe, "it must not be overlooked that ours is not a spectator sport, there is little to be seen as it happens. There is little to be seen in its execution except that the expert makes it look easy and no newcomer can be expected to know, by seeing, how he does it." Bruce points out an example of a diver and the spectator's affinity with him as he executes his routine. The shooting sport spectator does not have the same large body muscle movements to observe during the execution of a bullseye.
>
> With respect to coaches, Bruce points out, "They endeavor to base their recommendations on personal experience and always give reasons for so doing. Their endeavor is always to promote in the shooters the desire to think for themselves and to be self analytical at all times and not merely to assume infallibility."

Calderaro, Giuseppe, Dr. (Italy), "Psychologists and Psychotherapists
Are of Advantage to Shooters," INTERNATIONAL SHOOTING SPORT,
June 1975, Page 5+.
> With respect to cross-discipline sports involvement, Calderaro advises, "a good trainer must first establish what degree of adaptability the sportsman possesses before he includes an exercise from another discipline in his training program...stimulation is only of value when the particular movements involved are practiced repeatedly, away from the range, a fact which makes "dry firing" so valuable." He notes, "By psychoanalysis we can discover the reasons why he prefers shooting to other sports, what he expects of himself and what he requires from shooting. Having established these factors, one is then better placed to assess his fears and resistance to frustration, than would be the case using other subjective deliberations." Calderaro suggests, "Character development, in order to achieve a complete and harmonious personality." He points out that the "Usefulness of "dry-firing" and mental training which after relaxing with an autogenic training exercise, enables a training or match situation to be mentally envisaged and overcome...Putting an athlete into his optimum psychic state on the evening prior to a competition, (possible strengthening of his self confidence, using sematic or other stimuli, if necessary, to induce the requisite hypnotic state)."

Chapman, John, "An Easy Way To Pic Up a Point...Check Those Iron
Sights," *Competitive Marksman*, July/Aug 1974, Issue 1-1, Page 10.
> Chapman advises, "The simplest and most accurate method of checking the metallic sights is with a dial indicator and a magnetic base." He describes how to use this devise and show a good, clear picture of it in use.

Chapman, John, "Facts on Loading Technique and What It Means To You," *Competitive Marksman*, Nov/Dec 1974, Issue 1–3, Page 8.
    Chapman lets us in on the secret, "What most people don't know, although some have suspected it, is the way you put the .22 round into the chamber can greatly effect the performance of your rifle...the best groups were obtained by inserting the round into the chamber with the thumb until it contacts the land. If you lay the round on the loading platform and close the bolt, letting the loading ramp feed the round into the chamber, the groups will almost double in size. Also, not closing the bolt uniformly can effect the group size. A dirty bolt face, especially fouling in the recess where the cartridge head fits into the bolt face will effect groups."

Clark, A.J., (Great Britain), "XXI Olympic Games...Team Manager's Report...", *The Rifleman*, Autumn 1976, Vol. LXXXII, No. 501, Page 28.
    Good reading for the shooter aspiring to the international game. Shows problems do beset other national teams besides the U.S.A. Should be required reading for any first time National Squad Member. This type of report will serve to prepare shooters for what to "really" expect when they shoot in an international match..."The range was of simple construction, with none of the lavish frills of Munich——one serious drawback was the absence of running water, and chemical toilets without washing facilities were most unsanitary." It would be an asset to future American teams, if the team managers of the respective American teams, were to file similar reports for publication in the *InSights*, the junior NRA newsletter, and the NRA's *American Marksman*, after each international competition in which the U.S. teams participate.

Coleman, Jean, (Senior Clinical Psychologist), (Great Britain), "Psychology And Shooting", *The Rifleman*, June 1977, Vol. LXXXIII, No. 505, Page 13+.
    This article is intended to give "shooters an idea of the kind of work and research which is being done with the National Squads and also to pass on information which may help them to understand and work on some of their own problems." For example, "Relaxation techniques. Effective relaxation can help the shooter in several different ways. Daily relaxation as part of a training programme can help to reduce the general level of tension, and during an actual match can also be used to help combat match tension and fatigue." She points out that it is necessary to establish "Node points. Working out the critical points in the course of a shoot so that the shooter can pace himself effectively and produce maximum physical and mental effort where required...The first shot to count is obviously a node point of maximum anxiety and concentration." This was where the idea for *Mental Training*'s one shot matches came from. Since the shooter

is aware that the results and relative rankings of the shooters participating in the one shot match will be announce immediately, this is an effort to artificially reproduce, in training the maximum anxiety and concentration produced in a competition match. Back to Coleman, she points out, in addition, "The psychologist can also help shooters by teaching them to make use of mental rehearsal...it is believe to be an effective way of increasing skills in sport, and it can be used to desensitize specific problems such as trigger shyness."

Cooper, Malcolm, (Great Britain), "Britain Finds a New PSK Prospect
 ...Soviet International Match--Sukhumi, May 1975", *The Rifleman*, Autumn 1975, Vol. LXXXII, No. 497, Page 22+.
 A good background article for beginning shooters to read if they are interested in international competition. Makes international shooting seem more human and less formidable. Cooper won the 1984 Olympic Small-Bore 3-position shooting title in Los Angeles.

Cooper, Malcolm, (Great Britain), "Coaching and the National Squad",
 The Rifleman, Oct. 1977, Vol. LXXXIII, No. 507, Page 29+.
 About coaching, Cooper observes, "Few people choose this thankless task as a way of give back to the sport." In this article, the man who would later go on to win the gold medal in the 1984 Olympics, listed the duties of coaches as a part of a tribute to coaches on his National Squad. I believe it is a good delineation of the duties of a coach. If you are a coach, take a look at this list.

> 1) **Increasing knowledge on up-to-date techniques** 2) **The actual practice of putting over ideas and suggestions for improvement** 3) **Methods of motivation of individuals** 4) **Training Plans of Individuals** 5) **Physical training** 6) **Psychological ideas and training mentally** 7) **Planning and organizing group training** 8) **The organizing and setting up of ranges** 9) **The organizing and setting up of competitions** 10) **The organizing and setting up of schedules** 11) **The organizing and setting up of newsletters**

Delnord, Yves (France), "In Defense of Free Weapons," *International
 Shooting Sport*, June 1974, Page 20.
 Discussion of the free rifle versus the ISU Standard Rife and the concepts involved in their uses.

Dicara, Leo V., "Learning in the Autonomic Nervous System," *Altered
 States Of Awareness*, Jan. 1970, Page 74+.
 Before you work with biofeedback instruments, do read Dicara's article. It will take you from the visceral responses of rats

to speculation of human cures. "The evidence for instrumental learning of visceral responses suggests that psychosomatic symptoms may be learned...John I. Lacey of the Fels Research Institute has shown that there is a tendency for each individual to respond to stress with his own rather consistent sequence of such visceral responses as headache, queasy stomach, palpitation or faintness." Coaches can easily perceive how this can be used to assist them in training their shooters.

Frierson, David E. "Speed, the Essence of Rapid—Fire Pistol," *International Shooting Sport*, Feb. 1964, Page 22+.
    Good introduction to the technique of international rapid—fire. Gives this check—list he uses for his mental preparation:

1. Practice 3 or 4 dry lifts and runs.
2. Rest while putting solution in eyes.
3. Go through one "dry" drop, lift, and run, concentration on body movement.
4. Align sights, stiffen muscles, drop arm to correct angle.
5. Say "Ready" just before gun reaches lowest point.
6. Use practice string to get used to noise and recoil.
7. At sound of button, if audible, start fast lift, slowing up.
8. Concentrate on sights, blink eyes between shots.
9. Refocus eyes on sights.
10. Apply straight, determined pressure with point of finger.
11. Break contact between finger and trigger.
12. Swing body to next target.
13. Try to make all 10's in 8 seconds.
14. Six seconds: Rest, put solution in eyes, resin on hand; same as 1 – 13, except for fewer dry lifts and runs.
15. Four seconds: Same as for 6 seconds, except concentrate exclusively on sights and keep elbow and wrist stiffer.

    I also trace the idea for *Mental Training*'s one—shot matches to Frierson, "Here's a trick to make practicing the first shot competitive: Two shooters fire simultaneously on the turn of the targets, one on target No. 1, the other on target No. 5. Record the score each makes, but give 2 extra points to the one who gets his shot off first. This puts a premium on fast starting without neglecting accuracy. After 10 shots, add up the scores. This competition is a powerful stimulus and a wonderful teacher; you will find that it is no great trick to get off a good shot in one second or a bit less."

If you use glasses, Frierson has a suggestion for you, "I stick a piece of gummed paper smaller than a postage stamp in the middle of the left lens of my eyeglasses. This effectively blots out the target area but permits about the same amount of light to hit each eye. To cover the left eye with a heavy patch, as some shooters do, causes the pupil to dilate while the other remains contracted. This results in eye fatigue."

Again, speaking of problems with the eyes, Frierson, points out, "Probably every pistol shooter has noticed he can clear up momentarily a fuzzy sight picture by batting his eye several times. This spreads tears uniformly on the cornea and does away with casual aberrations. On a hot, dry day, and in the case of older eyes, this condition can persist and seriously affect one's scores. A simple remedy, though only a partial one, is to keep a bottle of Murine, Eyegene, or similar eyewash in your shooting box. I use it at the beginning and several additional times during a 60—shot match."

Gilmour, Neil, (Great Britain), "As Seen on TV...", *The Rifleman*,
Autumn 1974, Vol. LXXXI, No. 493, Page 33.
> Report of how the Hallamshire Rifle Club installed a TV monitor of their targets. Describes how it was accomplished, including how they solved the problem of trailing power co—axial cables.

Gonzalez, Jose, (Mexico), "Mental Aspects for Shooting With Small—bore Rifle", *International Shooting Sport*, August 1971, Page 10+.
> Gonzalez identifies, "The best thing during training is to give each shot the maximum attention, as if it were the only shot."

Gormley, John T., (Australia), (Lecturer in Physical Education, Adelaide College), "Achievement of Functional Objective in Pistol Shooting Through Repetitive Practices", *International Shooting Sport*, April 1977, Page 25.
> I think this article should be required reading for all advanced coaching schools. Gromley identifies such an important factor as what makes up a successful coach, "Coaches who are successful in a wide variety of sports are consistently found to demonstrate three behaviour characteristics that appear to be critically related to their success:
>
> 1. **are very knowledgeable and enthusiastic about their particular sport;**
> 2. **have analyzed their sport or event and identified its key features in terms of the components of skills and the strategies of play involved;**
> 3. **communicate effectively, recognize and cater for individual differences in the capacities and stages of learning of their pupils.**

Each of these factors indicates that the successful coach has acquired a

Mental Training   Chapter 9

wide variety of sub-skills that contribute to his/her overall successful performance. By implication, these skills can be learned."

Gromley observes and lists, "three aspects of coaching behavior in relation to the process of learning and practice:

1. **Motivation of the Learner (AROUSAL)**;
2. **Provision of a gross-framework of the skills to be planned (PLAN STRATEGY)**;
3. **Control of the conditions of learning and practice to obtain optimum performance (Display--Feedback/Knowledge Of Results)**."

With respect to practice, Gormley points out, "practice itself is no guarantee of improvement in performance. The amount and rate of learning is highly dependent upon the intent to improve:

1. **all practices should have clearly defined goals;**
2. **all practices should be repeated in meaningful ways so that correct responses can become automatic.**"

Also, Gormley observes, that "Learning results from three broadly defined processes:

1. **detection of progress by information sampling;**
2. **diagnosis of goal attainment;**
3. **modification of responses or goals;**"

Gormley's discussion of "Effective Use of Feedback," is clearly very important to a coach. It is in an attempt to show the shooter how to use feedback effectively that the <u>information gathering forms</u> of *Mental Training* were designed. "As coaches," Gormley says, "we should not add to the learners difficulties by bombarding him with words in the form of lengthy verbal instructions or direct his attention to feedback cues that are irrelevant to his particular stage in learn... Coaches can reduce verbalization and increase the use of visual material."

Gormley reports that, "Russian research on the formation of a skill points out that learning of a skill does not begin with actual practice but starts <u>before</u> with the "creation of the idea of mastering the specific skill." The learner must be able to mentally fulfill the "idea of the movement," before he can produce it." *Mental Training*'s <u>Initial Observation Form</u> was developed from this concept.

Gozalo, Angel Leon, (Spain), "Psychological Aspects of Shooting",
    International Shooting Sport, 1969, (Quoted from the journal *El Tiro Con Bala*).

                    Gozalo points out that shooters are subject "to the law about the gradation of values. This means that the shooter achieves his top form between 35 and 45, at an age when he has reached the highest degree of emotional balance...In this analysis we must assume that every shooter is a creature of moods, whose emotions and personalities change from day to day. Due to this perception I have often asserted that leaders and coaches should know the minds of their proteges." Gozalo also discusses how the shooter is influenced by vanity, need for freedom, self—discipline, personal sacrifices, self—confidence and the task of the coach in dealing with his shooter."

Guerin, Tom, "Fundamentals of Wind Doping," *Precision Shooting*,
Mar. 1974, Vol. 18, No. 11, Page 14 (Reprinted from May 1972, *Precision Shooting*).

Guerin's article on beginning wind doping techniques is geared to American prone shooting. He notes, "it is quite often necessary to use two or more of your senses to determine both velocity and angle of the wind."

Hart, Bob, "Clean That Barrel," *Precision Shooting*, Mar. 1974,
Vol. 18, No. 11, Page 21 (Reprinted from May 1972, *Precision Shooting*).

Hart tells us, "To get continued and maximum accuracy from a barrel it must be kept clean...When a barrel is new or in good condition it should be cleaned every 15 shots or oftener." For a mental training program to work, equipment must not be neglected."

Hassell, Bob, (Great Britain), "Rumanian Championships, Bucharest,
19—22 June", *The Rifleman*, Autumn 1975, Vol. LXXXII, No. 497, Page 23+.

Shooters starting to think seriously about participating international competition need to begin reading frank reports such as this "after—action" report of the Manager of the Great Britain team. Imagine it is your first international match and the team has been booked into two separate hotel, neither on the host shooting association's approved list. Thus no arrangements have been made to provide transportation to the range from these hotels. At least reading about this situation may help to prepare you to anticipate and accept problems so that you are not overwhelmed by them and throw up your hands, give up, and go home without shooting. You see, your preparation for international shooting has to go beyond your practice and match preparations. You need to devote some consideration to working on your tolerance level.

Kudrnovsky, Jaroslav, Dr. (Poland), "Regarding the Effect of Various
Internal Factors on Sighting", *International Shooting Sport*, Jan. 1969, Page 18+.

Identifying the basis of marksmanship triumph, Dr. Kudrnovsky says, "In target shooting the basis of success is the ability to aim correctly. Several factors, which can be divided into two sections, have an effect upon the act of shooting. These are, firstly, the external factors (light conditions, temperature, quality of the weapons and ammunition, etc.) and, secondly, the internal factors (tiredness, effects of alcohol, smoking, medications, diet, etc.) which are bound up with the individual characteristics of the shooter...the act of shooting also depends upon the full co—ordination of the mental and physical abilities which every shooter must possess."

Dr. Kudrnovsky's test results showed "muscular activity produced a slightly beneficial effect on the ability to sight...The cause of the poor performances achieved after consuming alcohol lies primarily in the poor muscular co—ordination which results and also, to a greater or lessor degree, on the disruption of mental stability which is so vital to the concentration necessary of top class performances...The taking of various preparations both of a nerve strengthening or a tranquillizing nature are shown to be completely unsuitable by virtue of the clearly negative effect that they have upon the eyes' visual capabilities."

LaFortune, F., Jr.,Dr., M.D., Dr. (Belgium), "Should the Standing Position Be Suppressed?," *International Shooting Sport*, Aug. 1975, Page 14+.

Dr. LaFortune warns, "In rifle shooting, the standing position may, in the long run, be the cause of some troubles of the osseous system and more particularly of the spinal column...When the shooter is in the standing position, he will draw advantage from bringing his rifle horizontally over the center of gravity of his body. In other words, he will put his pelvis "under" his weapon. He will thus increase the curvature of thelumbal part of his spine (hyperlordosis) and, at the same time, force a twist which extends into the dorsal segment. In order to keep the head in a natural vertical position, the upper dorsal and the cervical segments will increase their curvature in the opposite direction (kyphosis). In the frontal plane, we notice an S—shaped deviation (scoliosis) of the whole spine...When a shooter does not use a palm—rest <u>all those curvatures would be accenturated</u> in order to enable the hand to reach the rifle...For those who practice three, four times, or even more often a week, the possibility of spine—malformation is not imaginary at all and, if the intervertebral ligaments are relatively weak, an accelerated evolution towards discal hernia is to be feared."

Pease, Bob, "The Pros and Cons of Cleaning Rods," *Precision Shooting*, Jan. 1973, Vol. 17, No. 9, Page 17+.

This article reports on a cleaning rod survey. Pease reports on the opinions of those using the particular types of cleaning rods, with a chart for box score and results summarized. What makes this survey unique, is that Pease polled a number of top notch shooters, tool makers, gunsmiths and barrel makers to get their opions "on just what should and should not be used in a good match rifle barrel." Of those surveyed, 6 out of 13 favored a one—piece steel rod. 4 out of 13 surveyed favored a plastic coated rod, and 3 out of 13 felt there was no difference between a steel or a plastic rod. Good hints on how to clean. This should be on every shooter's must read list. One of the people surveyed was Ferris Pendell, "shooter, bullet die maker and formerly a die maker and bullet tester for Sierra bullets" and he offered this suggestion:

> A patch wet with Hoppe's passed through the barrel <u>before</u> brushing will serve to push most of the dirt and grit out of the barrel and prevent the brush from picking it up. He feels that nothing will beat music wire polished free of nicks for a cleaning rod and states that softer materials will pick up and hold abrasive materials which can damage a fine barrel. He cites the fact that in lapping a barrel a soft material is used that will hold the lapping compound which is in itself an abrasive. Pindell recommends a split wood dowel for wiping out the chamber after cleaning.

Porsch, Harald ,Dr.,and Dr. Wolfgang Sovinz, (Austria), "Telemetric Tests On Shooters," *International Shooting Sport*, Sep. 1974, Page 18+.
    Drs. Porsch and Sovinz report on the results of telemetric tests carried out during the Austrian National Air Pistol Championships in Graz, Austria, in 1974, on two shooters and on four shooters during the Regional Air Pistol Championships, also in Graz in 1974. Their findings demonstrate that a shooter obtains the best results when he reduces "his pulse rate by a least 10% — 15%." And that, "He must know when he has achieved this and release the shot only when he has done so." They feel, "shooting is a sport which demands self—discipline and self—observation." They question "whether or not it is adviseable to test a shooter before he attempts to become a top class shot." They assert, "Shooters who are not naturally prone to excitement (raised pulse rates), are better suited to competitive shooting and, with the proper guidance, will quickly climb to the top."

Pullum, Bill ,Col.,USA, "Anxiety," *The American Rifleman*, Mar. 1979, Page 36+.
    Pullem defines and discusses causes of anxiety, and suggests some ways to attempt to control it.

Pullum, Bill ,Col.,USA, "Coaches Corner: After a Poor Performance..,"

Competitive Marksman, July/Aug 1974, Issue 1-1, Page 3.
  Colonel Pullum describes concentration and its importance inthe shooter's performance. He gives training methods to be used in learning to direct your concentration. "When you have reached a state of awareness that permits you to accurately describe what your thoughts were at the moment you released the shot and further describe, in detail, where the rifle recoiled and exactly where the shot went, you have begun to learn to concentrate."

Pullum, Bill, and Dr. Frank T. Hanenkrat, Ph.D., *Position Rifle Shooting: A How-To-Text For Shooters And Coaches,* Winchester Press, New York, 1973.
  This is, without qualification, the best book on position rifle shooting which has yet been published. It is still available in most reputable book stores. If not, then have the clerk check for its availability in their copy of *Books In Print.* The ISBN of this book is: 0-87691-097-5. To give you an idea of why you nee this book, take a look at the table of contents:

  I — **Psychology: The Champion's Secret Weapon**
   1 — Concentration
   2 — Mental Discipline
   3 — Match Pressure
   4 — Confidence and the Will to Win

  II — **Training**
   5 — The Training Program: A Schedule of Progress
   6 — Mental and Physical Conditioning

  III — **Special Problems**
   7 — The Eye and the Sight System
   8 — Recoil, Muzzle Jump, and Zero Sight Setting
   9 — Adverse Weather Conditions

  IV — **Equipment and Positions**
   10 — Equipment
   11 — Positions

  V — **Coaching**
   12 — Coaching a Team
   13 — Coaching the Individual

Robinson, Derek, (Great Britain), "Team Manager's Report, (41st World Shooting Championships)," *The Rifleman,* Winter 1974, Vol. LXXXI, No. 494, Page 10+.
  Robinson gives an overview of the problems encountered by teams in the home of competitive shooting, Switzerland. "The

organization left much to be desired. Each manager was given a book, which contained all the information he could have possibly needed. It must have taken many weeks to compile, bu unfortunately when any problem arose that was not covered by this book, the officials were lost...The closing ceremony was a washout, both officially and weather wise; it poured with rain, we were all given plastic macs and made to march around a muddy arena, stand and listen to speeches and after these were over we all marched to the "banquet." Each of us had two tickets, one for a squsage roll, the other for a glass of beer, and these were served from the back of a lorry, in the rain of course."

Roth, J.A., Dr., (Great Britain), "Vision for Pistol Shooting,"
    The Rifleman, Autumn 1976, Vol. LXXXII, No. 501, Page 43+.
          Dr. Roth discusses the eyes and visual requirements for shooting. Several good hints: "People in the 40—45 year old age group should try using reading glasses for shooting -- they will either be just right, or fractionally too strong. Very slightly shortsighted people in any age group should try shooting without glasses -- if the error is very small the sight picture should be clear without effort. "Normal" eyes should try the effect of very weak positive lenses. These should make a prolonged shoot less tiring...Polarising glasses present no particular advantage to the shooter, as they are designed to reduce glare reflected from horizontal surfaces rather than vertical ones."

Stefan, Ion, Dr., (Romania), "The Relationship Between Medicine and
    Top—Level Shooting," *International Shooting Sport*, July 1976, Page 12+.
          Dr. Stefan declared that, "The biological foundation of a top class shot is based on the following important factors: Excellent functioning of the central and vegetative nervous systems, together with the analytical and inhibitive senses, servo—mechanisms, etc.; Excellent functioning of the visual faculties; Excellent blood circulation; The ability to contain nervous excitation (occasionally a natural talent which can be improved through training); The dynamic balance between the excitability process and inhibition; Excellent function of the internal organs.
          Dr. Stefan indicated that, "The functioning of thenervous systems and their related elements...can be improved by reaction exercises and simulated weapon training...Psychological tests on nervous excitability are important...A further step in the selection of first class marksmen could be the carrying out of tests in circumstances which closely correspond to the conditions which prevail during the shooting of an actual competition."

Sullivan, Brian, (AP Science Writer), "Hundreds Now Practicing Mind Over
    Matter," *The Anchorage Times*, Sunday, Nov. 1978, Page D—7.
          Sullivan focuses on the uses of biofeedback instruments at the

Menninger Foundation of Topeka, Kansas. "Two biofeedback instruments are used -- the hand temperature trainer, which helps individuals raise their hand temperature to increase overall blood flow and lower overall blood pressure, and the electromyograph, or EMG, for measuring muscle tension, and the ability to relax...If the person can warm his hand to 90 degrees, the resulting relaxation should lead to increased blood flow through blood vessel dilation activity, usually of the forehead muscles. It the person can reduce muscle tension to the point where the EMG records five microvolts or below, he shows he has learned relaxation. Three microvolts signifies deep muscle relaxation."

Umarov, Makhmoud, (U.S.S.R.), "Must Master Shots Have 'Nerves Like Steel Cables'?," *International Shooting Sport*, Aug. 1963, Page 97+ (Abstracted from Umarov's book titled: *The Psychological Training Of A Shooter*, published in Russian about 1959).

Umarov discusses the "differences inperformance during training and actual competition." He declared, "The chief cause of the drop in performance under actual competitive conditions in relation to the scores reached during training lies in negative influence brought on by the excitement of the start." He stated, "The results of most shooters will, however, fall as soon as the mind becomes aware of the fact that these results will be important, i.e., as soon as the sense of responsibility begins to assert itself." He notes, "In a competition, the shooter is in a state of increased nervous tension and reacts more readily to extraneous influences. This increased sensitivity is brought about by the awareness of one's responsibility and by the impressions made by the more or less festive atmosphere attendant upon a competition."

Umarov feels, "If a shooter who is not used to the presence of spectators gets an idea that these spectators are particularly interested in his very own performance, his excitement becomes even stronger." He advises, "Getting used to the presence of spectators is a very gradual process and is part and parcel of competitive experience. One could accelerate the process by admitting spectators to practice and trial shoots during training." What happens then, he notes is that, "Once the shooter has become firmly accustomed to the proximity of spectators, their presence becomes a quite positive factor to him."

When an unwanted rumination occurs, Umarov suggests what to do, "One must not be in a hurry to fire a shot so long as there are thoughts of secondary importance on one's mind."

Umarov felt that the beginning shots of a competitor required special prepartation: "Uncertainty is also caused by bad shots right at the beginning of a competition. Such bad shots are mostly due to unnecessary haste and insufficient practical adjustment. They can, moreover, be attributed to a discordance in the shooter's co-ordination of movements due to the occurrence of inhibitions in the central nerve system. The discordance usually manifests itself in delaying the moment of let-off, i.e., in tarrying over the instant in which the "presssure point" should be overcome, thus causing the latter to fall too late. At the onset of this phenomenon, when the weapon is held absolutely still and points well at the aiming mark, the weapon does not go off, the finger does not "pull through," and the shot is fired only after the weapon has already swayed out of the correct line of sight and away from the point of aim. The shooter's reaction to this occurrence is uncertainty. Overcoming the trigger resistance prematurely (caused by excessive excitement and perplexity on the part of the shooter) will produce the same effect." Umarov admonishes the shooter that "one must acquire the ability to "feel" a good shot before pressing the trigger."

Wigger, Lones ,W., Jr., Major.,USA (now LTC), "What Makes A Champion Shooter," *Competitive Marksman*, July/Aug 1974, Issue 1-1, Page 11.

Wigger lists these criteria as being necessary, "if a person has aspirations of becoming a shooting champion:

1. better than average intelligence;
2. learning to shoot at an early age;
3. complete dedication to the shooting sport withdefinite goals;
4. an ideal environment which provides the opportunity and necessities needed for an individual to learn, progress, and achieve his goals;
5. the development and training of the mental aspects needed;
6. possibly the most important aspect, the development of competitiveness and desire."

Wigger stated that he believes he reached the level of performance necessary to compete on a world level due mostly to the influence of the International Rifle Team in 1960. Pullum, the team coach, according to Wigger, "stressed that shooting was 90% mental; and thinking, psychology, and mental discipline is what really produces champions." Then too, "Associating with champions makes you think like a champion...For the aspiring international shooting champion it is not only imperative he compete in all the local matches; but whenever possible, he must compete with shooters from foreign countries as well."

Wood, Jan, (Great Britain), "Women's World," *The Rifleman*, Spring 1975, Vol. LXXXII, No. 495, Page 37.

A good insight into good international manners. How your hosts will view you and how to show appreciation in return, "At

Mental Training   Chapter 9

the N.S.R.A Prize Giving, the Swedish visitors were welcomed by the N.S.R.A. Chairman, and they in return presented the N.S.R.A. with a miniature banner, to commenorate the occasion."

I believe this is a fitting way to conclude this book. It demonstrates to you, the beginning shooter, that you are entering into an international comradeship with persons who share your enthusiasm for the sports of marksmanship. You will be received with open arms wherever your sports shooting interests take you. *Mental Training* will help you achieve that level of shooting proficiency which will suit you.

I believe the "Roots of Mental Training" form a substantive source for *Mental Training*. And, on behalf of the shooters yet to come, I thank those sources fo *Mental Training* for contributing to the tree of shooting knowledge. These are my roots of *Mental Training*. Many of the articles have much else of substance in them. I only showed you how they contributed to my program of *Mental Training*.

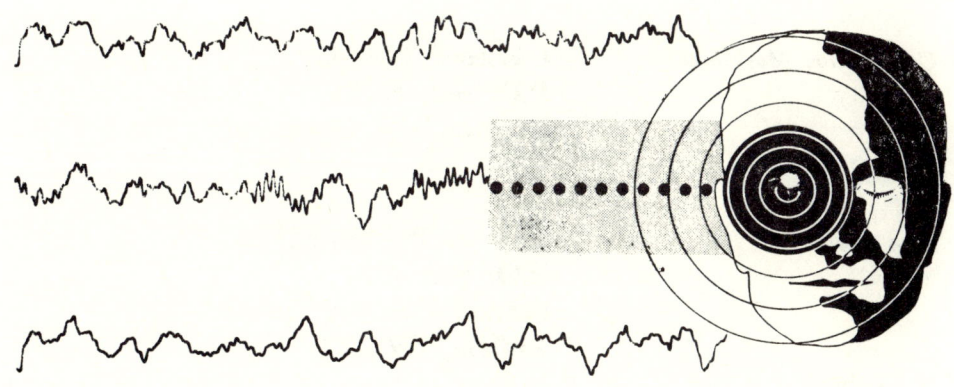

© Bob Hickey

APPENDIX: A

SOURCES OF WORKS CITED
(Limited To Marksmanship Specific Article Sources)

The American Marksman 1600 Rhode Island Avenue, N.W.
Washington, D.C. 20036
U.S.A.

The American Rifleman 1600 Rhode Island Avenue, N.W.
Washington, D.C. 20036
U.S.A.

Competitive Marksman (Ceased Publishing)
P.O. Box 55971
Houston, TX 77055
U.S.A.

Gun Week Haweye Publishing, Inc.
P.O. Box 411
Station C
Buffalo, NY 14209
U.S.A.

The International Shooter (Ceased Publishing)
U.S.W.I.R.O.
P.O. Box 865
Mesa, AZ 85201
U.S.A.

Appendix A: Sources

Precision Shooting
    8 Cline Street
    Dolgeville, NY 13329
    U.S.A.

The Rifleman
    National Small-Bore Rifle Association
    Lord Roberts House
    Bisley Camp
    Brookwood, Woking
    Surrey GU24 ONP
    ENGLAND

Shooting Sport
    Union internationale Tir (UIT)
    D-62 Wiesbaden-Klarenthal
    WEST GERMANY

Commanding Officer
United States Marksmanship Training Unit
Fort Benning, GA 31905
U.S.A.

International Rifle Marksmanship Guide

International Running Target Guide

Pistol Marksmanship Guide

Rifle Instructors And Coaches Guide

International Skeet & Trap Guide

APPENDIX: B
COACHING METHOD: GUN HOLDING

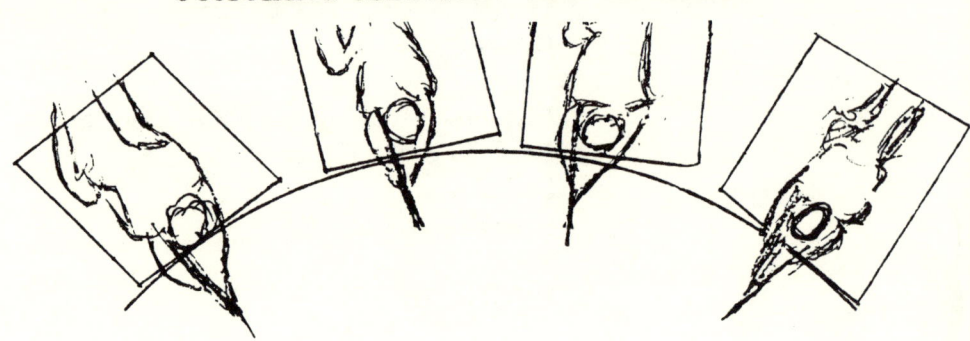

1. Remove all bolts from guns.
2. Have the team members assume the shooting position.
3. Put aiming circles on the wall.
4. Have a helper or shooter's partner adjust the aiming circles so the circle is inside the natural point of aim of the shooter.
5. Allow 30 minutes for the **Gun Holding Practice**.
6. Have the shooters record the sight pattern movement on the **Sight Pattern Chart**, figure 2-9, page 38. The focus of the shooter's effort should be to identify the sight pattern which occurs just as the shooter **mentally** fires the shot, see pages 16 and 17.
7. The coach uses the Position Inventory form, figure 7-3, page 187, and make notes of the improvements shooters should consider making in their positions.

© Bob Hickey

APPENDIX: C
MIKE'S DIARY

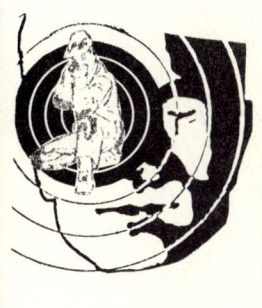

My thanks to Mike Spangler, of Chugiak, Alaska, for permission to use parts of his shooting diary to illustrate how a shooting diary works. I've used Mike's diary because we adults often forget how difficult writing can be for high school students.

At the time these diary entries were written, Mike was 17, and a junior at Chugiak High School. His rifle team had never won a high school rifle league match in the Anchorage School District Rifle League Program. Chugiak team members had a losing tradition with which to view their participation in the shooting sports. A few of Mike's teammates joined him in my mental training sessions.

In March of 1978, just a few months after these shooter started working with the mental training program, Chugiak High School placed second in the Anchorage NRA 3−Position Junior Rifle Sectional. When the results were determined nationally, the team had placed ninth in the National Scholastic Team Championships. A couple of weeks after the 3−Position sectional, Chugiak High School won tha Anchorage NRA 4−Position Junior Rifle Sectional. They placed fourth in the nation when the national championships had been determined. The power of *Mental Training!* It turned this team completely around.

Start your own diary about your shooting today. The step you take in beginning your diary may make the difference between being just another recreational shooter or being an Olympic Champion.

DATE: 1-10-78 Tuesday

TIME: 4th hour

PLAN: <u>kneeling - position</u>
3 shots each outside bull

GOAL: I want <u>5-ring</u> hold (shots)

ORDER OF SHOOTING:

order
1◉ 5◉ 7◉
2◉   8◉
3◉   9◉
4◉ 6◉ 10◉

EVALUATION OF GOALS MET:

<u>HOW MANY GOOD</u>
1 - 2   5 - all
2 - 2   6 - 1   9 - 2
3 - 2   7 - all   10 - 2
4 - 1   8 - 2

score = 20

DATE: 1-11-78

TIME:
After school

COURSE OF FIRE:
shot 10 prone; 10 standing

PURPOSE OF SHOOTING:
for qualification for fridays match

EVALUATION OF PERFORMANCE:
prone - head position was screwing me up. — shot - 93

standing - couldn't steady down shot - 58

EXTRA PRACTICE:
→ Then shot 55 standing shots.

EVALUATION OF PERFORMANCE:
was very hot and I also could not steady the gun down onto the target most of the time.

PROBLEM ANALYSIS:

I had on an extra T-shirt and this may have caused the heat.

FUTURE PRACTICE PLAN:

I need to go over my standing position soon and see if I am am doing anything wrong

TARGET FEEDBACK ANALYSIS:

there was one good 10 on this target out of 55 shots

POSITIVE POINTS:

$\frac{530}{243}$
$\overline{307}$
out of 550

NEGATIVE POINTS:

29
24
22
18
12
31
17
21
34
21
14

243

NUMBER OF SHOTS → MEETING INDIVIDUAL SHOT GOAL:

40 shots inside 4-ring.

Mental Training   **Appendix C: Mike's Diary**

DATE: 1-12-78

EVALUATION OF PERFORMANCE:

The whole day has been bad and I am getting a head-ache.
I just finished a MT cards for prone and couldn't concentrate on what I was doing.

MISCELLANEOUS OBSERVATION:

Head cleared up at about 8:45 and I got caught up on selective awarness goals.

© Bob Hickey

DATE: 1-13-78
Friday

MATCH GOAL ACHIEVEMENT EVALUATION:

<u>After Match</u> total - 245
　　Prone - 91
　　Standing - 71
　　Kneeling - 83

Overall I felt very good - (X - a fellow team member) took my target on standing and got me mad. I lost 12 points on my first 3 shots. Prone was Bad and I couldn't get comfortable. The shots kept going all over the place. When I changed my position in kneeling it helped quite a bit. I need a lot of practice in standing.

DATE: 1-14-78

LOCATION: Bartlett

EQUIPMENT PROBLEMS:

No (Spotting) scope — I can't see what I am shooting. The bolt keeps sticking about every other time. I have to force it down.

POSITION DESCRIPTION:

<u>Standing position</u> —
Left foot — Most of weight on ball of foot. Some weight on heel

Right foot is the same except a little more weight on the ball of foot

DATE: 1-16-78

LOCATION:
Chugiak
4th Hour ROTC

PLAN:
Prone - Am going to sight in - Last saturday Mr. Hickey tightened up forward screw

PROBLEM:
I think my head position is screwing me up.

SOLUTION TO TRY:

Arm / Gun

Try to increase angle between Arm & Gun.

INDEX

A

"A New Way To Make Pain Disappear", 226
"A Psychotechnical Portrait of the Sport Shooter", 218
A—36 indoor International 50—foot target, 118, 129
ache in the foot, 72
"Achievement of Functional Objective in Pistol Shooting Through Repetitive Practices", 242
Act of Shooting, 37, 38, 41, 58, 58, 60, 60, 66, 138, 152, 179
action of alcohol, 235
adrenaline, 25, 127
aggressive attitude, 129
Aggressive Trigger Release Chart, 192
aggressive trigger—release, 192
aiming circles, 16
"Aiming Equipment", 231
"Aiming Techniques", 231
"Air Rifle Techniques", 231
Alaska, 156
Alkire, Marie L., 146, 148, 165, 224, 231
alpha, 19
alpha production, 227
"Alpha Rhythms: Back to Baselines, 227
Alpha State, 11, 50, 144, 145, 148, 149, 153, 154, 158, 163, 164
   Relaxation Technique, 158
   Training, 12, 144, 149
   waves, 12
"Alpha Waves and Anxiety: No Link?", 227

Altered States Of Awareness, 203, 230, 240
Alton, Illinois, 10
Ammo Expenditure History, 194
ammunition, 125, 126, 133
"An Easy Way To Pick Up a Point", 238
"Anatomy of Firing a Shot – Part II", 217
Anderson, Gary L., 15, 202, 210, 211, 212, 213, 217, 224, 225, 231, 232, 233, 234
Anderson, George B, 226
Andrews, Lewis M., 229
ankle, 147
Antal, Dr. Laslo, 234, 235, 235
anxiety, 12, 158, 227, 228
"Anxiety", 246
arm, 58
Arnold, Siefried, 236
Art Student's Anatomy", 219
"As Seen on TV", 242
ASCII, 197
At Home Gun Holding Practice Time, 101
At Home Mental Training Cards Practice, 102
At Home Selective Awareness Practice Time, 101
at—home—practice, 182
attention, 12, 19, 24, 50, 50, 51, 54, 62, 66, 74, 76, 88, 189
attitude, 144, 165, 166, 179, 192
Auer, Leland, 237
Auer, Victor, 213, 214
Autogenic training, 237
"Awareness: Exploring, Experimenting And Experiencing", 223

B

Backes, Clarus J., 203
backside of the hand, 58
Barlow, J.A. (Brigadier), 203
"Basic Accuracy", 232
Bassham, Lanny R., 26, 117, 226
Bauer, Dr. Walter, 237
Berger, Hans, 158
Beta State, 11
Beta waves, 163
"Bill Rigby, Biography & Interview", 215
biofeedback, 158, 229, 230, 240, 248, 249
Birmingham, England, 125
Bisley, England, 32
bladder, 236
Blair, Wes, 228
bowel action, 236
Brain waves, 150
"Brain-Compatible Teaching", 205
breath control, 152
breathing process, 131, 177
"Britain Finds a New PSK Prospect", 240
British juniors, 182
Brown, Dr. Barbara B., 12, 228
Bruce, Bob, 218, 238
buttplate, 147, 148
Buys, Donna, 226

C

Calderaro, Dr. Giuseppe, 218, 238
calf muscle, 68
cameras, 157
Camp Perry, Ohio, 10
Canada, 158
cardio-vascular system, 209
Carson, Gavin, 214
Centering: Your Guide To Inner Growth, 229
cerebrum, 27;Delnord, Yves, 240
challenge, 142
Chapman, John, 238, 239
check sheets, 40
"Circulation, Breathing, Fitness and Shooting Results", 237

circulatory system, 42
Clark, A.J, 239
"Clean That Barrel", 244
coaching, 9
   "Coaching & the National Squad", 240
   Coach's Corner, 19, 246
   files, 182
   method, 166
   schools, 181
   "Coaching...Or Teaching?", 238
Coke match, 216
Cole, Dr. William, 11, 28, 165
Coleman, Jean, 239
Commonwealth Games, 234
Competitive Marksman, 214, 215, 226, 238, 239, 247, 250
computerized servo system, 204
computers, 108, 148, 182, 196, 197
concentration, 11, 47, 155, 210, 212, 213, 214, 217, 228, 229, 230, 231, 237, 239, 240, 241, 245, 246, 247
conceptual units for mental exercising, 40
conditioned reflex, 27
confidence, 182
conscious, 11, 27, 28
consistent, 97
Cooper, Malcolm, 240, 240
Cordell, Franklin D., 226
cortex, 51, 52, 209
creative subconscious, 28, 29
Csaba, Dr. & Dofa, Dr. Jozsef, 218

D

Dahl, Winston A. (LTC, USA), 207, 209
Danik, Richard J., 233
Davis, Roy Eugene, 214
day-dreaming, 17

diaphragm, 223
diary, 15, 105, 106, 107, 109, 110, 111, 130, 134, 135, 137, 148
   entry, 146
   Diary Form, 140
Dicara, Leo V., 240

Digestive Spasms, 221
discal hernia, 245
"Dropping Points", 218
dry firing, 23, 24, 214, 219, 223, 238
   Chart, 39
   "Dry-firing As the Foundation of the Training, 215
   Dry-Firing Practice, 151
duel match, 142, 216, 216, 216, 216, 221, 223, 236
   Duel Match Contract, 142, 143
dyspepsia, 235

E

Eccles, John C., 203
EDGE Institute, Inc., 11, 28, 165
effects of alcohol, 245
8080 assembly language, 197
electromyograph, 249
Eley Ten-X, 125
Emotional Tension, 222
Emptaz, Gilbert, 219
England, 182
enhanced sense of responsibility, 216
equilibrium, 80
equipment, 133, 147
Estabrooks, G. H, 228
experiments, conducting, 25
Eyegene, 242
eyewash, 242

F

"Facts on Loading Technique and What It Means To You", 239
Family Weekly, 226
Farris, Edmond J., 219
fatigue, 220
feedback, 13, 14, 97, 106, 108, 109, 114, 116, 117, 121, 123, 124, 127, 227
Fels Research Institute, 241
Fitz-Randolph, Kurt, 203
Fixx, James F., 220
Freeman, Dr. P.C., 204

Frierson, David E., 241
"Fundamentals of Wind Doping", 244

G

Gallwey, Timothy W., 226
Garcia, Jose Gonzalez, 220
gastritis, 235
Gatty, Ronald, Ph.D, 226
Giebler, Gale R., 226
Gilmour, Neil, 242
goal, 97, 109, 115
   for Day, 146, 147
   oriented, 107
   statement, 99
Gonzalez, Jose, 215, 215, 242
Gormley, John T., 242
Gozalo, Angel Leon, 243
Gray, Henry, 224
Guerin, Tom, 204, 244
gun holding, 23
   homework, 22
   practice, 16
   Gun Holding Practice, 151
   Practice Program, 144
   Program, 53
Gun Week, 202, 225, 232

H

Haidurov, Vladimir, 214
Hallamshire Rifle Club, 242
hand temperature trainer, 249
Hanenkrat, Dr. Frank T., Ph.D, 230, 247
Hart, Leslie A., 205
Hart, Bob, 244
Hassell, Bob, 244
Hickey, Bob, 156
Hilgard, Ernest R, 228
Hinds, Sidney R., Jr. (Colonel, USA), 208
hold control, 21
"Holding, Aiming, Firing", 223
Home Time Schedule Plan, 12, 99, 195
"Hook Butt Platt May Be Problem to Shooters", 232
Houston, Jean, 230

"*How Children Postpone Pleasure*", 226
"*How Important Is Natural Ability*", 232
Human Behavior, 230
Human Nature, 226, 228
"*Hundreds Now Practicing Mind Over Matter*", 248
hyper—ventilation, 235
hyperlordosis, 245
Hypertension, 221
"*Hypnosis And Consciousness*", 228
Hypnotism, 228

I

"*I Attempt To Run 1 To 2 Miles Daily*", 202
IBM compatibility, 196
Illinois All—State Junior Rifle Team, 10
Illinois State Rifle Association, 10
"*In Defense of a Sport*", 213
"*In Defense of Free Weapons*", 240
inconsistency, 97
individual shot goal, 97, 107, 112, 113, 114, 116, 117, 121, 128, 132, 152, 153, 164
individual shot performance, 127
information tracking, 196
Initial Observation Form, 169 168, 173
inner awareness, 12
inner humiliation, 14, 142
Inner Tennis Playing The Game, 226
Institute of the Pennsylvania Hospital, 227
internal stimuli, 19
internalizing, 19
International Rifle Marksmanship Guide, 209
International Running Target Guide, 207, 207
International Shooting Sport, 210, 211, 215, 216, 218, 219, 220, 221, 223, 224, 236, 237, 238, 240, 241, 242, 243, 244, 245, 246, 248, 249

International Skeet & Trap Guide, 209
intervertebral ligaments, 245
involuntary reflexes, 214
"*Is Prone Really Unique?*", 232

J

Jacobson, Edmund, 229
Jacobson Method, 219
Jaramillo, Jesus M., 210
"*Jerking Trigger Most Dramatic Error For Competitive Rifle Shooter*", 225
Jewell, Wanda R., 229
Johnson, Pamela J., 226
Johnston, William, 229

K

Kalinichenko, Nikolai, 233
Kansas State University, 146
Kansas State University Turkey Shoot, 10
Karlins, Marvin, 229
Kaypro, 182, 200
Kennedy, John F., 107
Kern, Steven R., 215
Key, Wilson Bryan, 210
Klingner, Armin, 15
"*Klingner's Fleeing East Germany Results In Gold Medals For West*", 202
kneeling, 42, 44, 46, 57, 57, 57, 58, 68, 68, 68, 70, 70, 72, 72, 129, 146, 147, 158
Koestenbaum, Peter, 226
Korea, 229
Kreskin, 229
Kreskin's Mind Power Book, 229
Kudrnovsky, Dr. Jaroslav, 244
kyphosis, 245

L

Lacey, John I., 241
lack of coordination, 222
LaFortune, Dr. F., Jr., M.D., 245
"*Learning in the Autonomic Nervous System*", 240

LeCron, Leslie M., 230
left foot, 68
left knee, 147
Leonardo DaVinci Anatomical Drawings, 220
"*Letter to the Editor: Ref: Clean That Barrel*", 237
Lincoln, Illinois, 10
Lincoln Sportsmen's Club, 10
Little Guy Inside, 12, 14, 18, 19, 21, 26, 42, 53, 53, 53, 53, 99, 107, 109, 110, 114, 122, 124, 127, 128, 135, 137, 145, 146, 149, 151, 153, 154
Loesel, Dr. Heinz, 220
loss of attention, 222
loss of concentration, 222
lower back, 88

M

Macrae, David, 220
magnesium carbonate, 222
managing anxiety, 226
marksmanship, 183, 233
    training, 116
Masters, Robert, 230
match expenses, 141
Match Schedule Form, 141
Mathe, Dr. Jean, 220
Media Sexploitation, 210
Medical Sports Institute, 218
"*Medications – No Help In Improving Performances*", 220
Meik, Mirosvikov, 221
Mellish, Bob, iv, 32
Menninger Foundation, 249
mental approach, 97
"*Mental Aspects for Shooting With Small–bore Rifle*", 242
mental
    attitude, 98
    competitive edge, 189
    condition, 147
    discipline, 18
    inventory, 40
    practice, 10
    preparation, 7

    preparation, 182
    program, 117
    rehearsal, 10
    Shot Rehearsal, 129
    training, 182
"*Mental Training – Another View*", 204
Mental Training Cards, 18, 29, 30, 111, 151
Mental Training Cards Feedback Chart, 37
"*Mental Training Most Important Element In Making Good Shooter*", 202
"*Mental Training––an important aspect*", 218
Mexico City, 155
mirage, 19, 181
mirror, 41, 44, 154, 154
    use, 43
Mischel, Walter, 226
Montes, Dr. Jose Ignacio Valesco, 221
Motivational techniques, 20
motor exercise, 26
motor muscle mechanisms, 26
motor muscles, 25
Murdock, Margaret, 26
Murine, 242
muscle memory groups, 25
muscle relaxant effort, 153
muscular tension, 218, 219, 228
Muscular Trembles, 222
Mutke, Peter H.E, 223
muzzle jump, 176
Mydriasis, 222

N

N.S.R.A, 251
National Rifle Association, 118, 181
natural point of aim, 131, 175
nervous system, 209, 214, 220, 235, 236, 248
nervousness, 211, 212, 221, 236
New Coaching Program Outline, 167

"*New Developments In The Standing Position*", 217
"*New Knowledge About Aiming*", 233
New Zealand, 234
Nideffer, Robert M., 230
Norvell, 230
novice shooter, 30
NRA, 117, 128, 129, 130
    Basic Marksmanship Course, 9
    Basic Marksmanship Program, 7
    Class C school, 181
    coaching schools, 181

O

Oerter, Al, 212
Ohio State Indoor Team Matches, 10
Olympic Games, 10, 155, 156, 157
On The Firing Range Practice Time, 102
One Shot Matches, 188, 189, 191
organize, 95
Orne, Martin T., 227

P

pain—in—the—back, 86
Parish, David, 215
Parmentier, Stanley J. (Colonel, USA), 207, 209
Paskewitz, David A., 227
Pease, Bob, 245
Peot, Joseph J. (Colonel, USA), 210
"*Perfect Shooting*", 210
performance level, 117
perspiration, 222
Phoenix, Arizona, 18, 156
physical condition, 147
Physical Fitness Digest, 226
"*Physiological and Psychological Aspects of Pistol Shooting*", 235
"*Physiology of Imagination*", 203
Pistol Marksmanship Guide, 208
pistol shooting, 42
point—of—aim, 147
    shifts, 131
  new shifts, 131
    natural, 175

polarising glasses, 248
Polikanian, Max, 214
polyuria, 222
Porsch, Dr. Harald, 246
Position Inventory, 185, 187
Position Rifle Shooting, 230, 247
position shooting, 25
Pratt, Robin Whitlock, 230
Precision Shooting, 202, 204, 210, 211, 212, 213, 217, 223, 224, 225, 231, 232, 233, 234, 237, 244, 245
problem analysis, 135
Prokop, Dave, 227
prone position, 134, 135, 147
"*Prone vs. Position — Tempest in a Teapot*", 204
psychic state, 238
"*Psychological Aspects of Shooting*", 243
"*Psychological Preparation of the Shooter*", 221
"*Psychological Questions in Connection With Training*", 236
Psychological War On Fat, 226
"*Psychologists and Psychotherapists Are of Advantage to Shooters*", 238
"*Psychology And Shooting*", 239
"*Psychology of the Match Competitor*", 228
Pullum, Bill (Colonel), 11, 25, 94, 98, 212, 230, 246, 246, 247
pulse, 147, 220, 220, 221, 224, 235, 237, 246
purpose of preparation, 217

R

raised blood pressure, 235
range plan file, 182
reading file, 183
recoil, 138
Recoil Chart Form, 139
recorder, 186
recreational club shooter, 19
Recreational Shooting Formula, 141

reflex conditioning, 27
reflexive
    analysis, 18
    reaction, 144
    reactions, 11
"Regarding the Effect of Various Internal Factors on Sighting", 244
rehearsal, mental, 24
    non-verbalized, 24
rehearse, 18, 29, 30, 31
relaxation techniques, 239
Reticular Activating System, 20, 51, 52, 53
"Rifle Captain's Report", 215
Rifle Instructors And Coaches Guide, 210
Rifle Range Observation Form, 182, 184
"Rifle Shooters Training", 219
Rigby, William R.(Bill), 223
Robinson, Derek, 247
Roots of Mental Training, 105, 165
Rotaru, Nicolae, 216
Roth, Dr. J.A., 248
"Rumanian Championships, Bucharest", 244
rumination, 150, 151, 152, 153, 155, 157
Rumination Control Training, 151
Russian shooting coaches, 214
"Russian Success Formula Made Easy?", 214

S

Safety Line, 173
safety precaution, 174
Sanders, Laurie G., 229
Schiessportschule Dialogues I, 11, 25, 29, 94, 231, 156
Schiessportschule II, 11, 98
Schultz Method, 219
Science News, 227, 227
"Science of Athletics's", 203
scientific method, 138
    research, 149
scoliosis, 245

secret of the champions, 30
Secrets Of Inner Power, 214
Selective Awareness, 223
    Session, 56
    Training, 20, 40, 40, 42, 45, 50, 51, 137, 145
self-awareness, 18
sense of responsibility, 142, 249
sensory pathways, 28
Shooter Observation Form, 179, 180
shooter's database, 196
Shooter's Database Log Program, 196, 197
shooting analysis, 127
shooting diary, 122, 185
"Shooting in the Wind", 211
shooting preparation time, 8
"Shooting Records Systems", 225
shooting tactics, 29
"Should the Standing Position Be Suppressed?", 245
Sight Pattern Chart, 16, 24, 38
sight pattern, 16, 39, 53
Silent Music, 229
"Social Habits and the Sportshooter", 235
"Some Aspects of the Shooter's Tactical and Psychological Preparation", 216
"Some Notes On Instructing New Shooters", 210, 234
South African Marksman, 214
Sovinz, Dr. Wolfgang, 246
"Speed, the Essence of Rapid-Fire Pistol", 241
spine-malformation, 245
"Sport Shooting Psychology", 212
spotting scope, 24, 108, 118, 123, 124, 125, 132, 133, 188
standing, 31, 42, 64, 109, 129, 137, 155, 173
Stefan, Dr. Ion, 248
Stevens, John O., 223
stimulation of muscle cells, 150
stream-of-conscious, 149, 151
Stress And The Art Of Biofeedback, 12, 228

© Bob Hickey

subconscious, 11, 24, 25, 26, 27, 29, 107, 114, 115, 116, 122, 123, 135, 149, 150, 154, 185
subcortex, 209
Sullivan, Brian, 248
super master, 20
sweating, 235

T

Tabor Head, Marion, Maryland, 147
tachpsychiae, 222
tachycardia, 221
tachypnoea, 221
tactical situations, 179
tactical thinking, 216
"Tactics in Shooting", 211
Taking Care of Business, 230
Target Analysis Chart, 119, 120 113, 117, 121, 122, 123, 124, 128, 129
Target Analysis Record, 200
target numbering system, 130
"Team Manager's Report, (41st World Shooting Championships)", 247
"Telemetric Tests On Shooters, 246
tension control deterioration, 80
terminal coding, 200
"Test Anxiety", 230
"The 1972 Olympics in Munich: A Critique", 214
"The Acclimatization of a Shooter to a Competitive Atmosphere", 221
The American Rifleman, 228, 246
"The Anatomy Of Firing A Shot — Part I", 202
The Anchorage Times, 248
The Body Clock Diet Book, 226
The Complete Book Of Running, 220
The Complete Guide To Hypnosis, 230
The Dart Book, 227
"The Dynamics of Score Improvement", 224
"The Effects Of The Changes of the Circadian Body Rhythm of the Sportshooter", 234

"The Electrical Activity of the Brain", 230
The Elements of Rifle Shooting, 203
"The End of the Season...or the Beginning?", 225
"The Importance of Proper Stock Fit", 232
The International Shooter, 203, 209
"The Kneeling Position", 233
The Miracle Power Of Transcendental Meditation, 230
"The Olympic Shooter and His State of Mind", 215
"The Physical Aspects of Shooting with the Smallbore Rifle", 220
"The Pros and Cons of Cleaning Rods", 245
"The Realities of Shooting Standing", 223
"The Relationship Between Medicine and Top-Level Shooting", 248
The Rifleman, 214, 215, 218, 204, 234, 235, 238, 239, 240, 242, 244, 247, 248, 250
"The Training Effect", 213
"The Training Plan", 224
"The World Class Shooter", 226
thigh, 68
thought control, 155
Thought Technology, 158
thumb, 49
Today's Education, 205
toes, 78
Topeka, Kansas, 249
torso, 233
torso, 68, 78
torso swing, 78
training
   method, 29
   plan, 95, 100, 103, 104
   Training Plans Program, 145
   schedule, 18, 100
   techniques, 20

trigger
    control, 148, 214, 233
    "*Trigger Control*", 213
    finger, 27, 58, 66, 144, 163
    puller, 30, 105, 116
    release, 24, 151
    squeeze, 66
    squeeze methods, 213
Tucker, Melvin J., 229
TV match, 157
TWA Ambassador, 203

U

U.S. Olympic Rifle Team, 18
Umarov, Makhmoud, 212, 249
Umind Games, 230
United States Advanced Marksmanship Unit International Shooting Clinics, 10
United States Smallbore Rifle Championships, 10
United States Women's International Rifle Organization, 11, 25, 94, 98, 146, 156, 165
University of Pennsylvania, 227
upper back, 86
USWIRO, 11

V

Vasoconstriction, 222
video camera, 182
Videomotor Phenomenon, 218
Vinci, da Leonardo, 7
"*Vision for Pistol Shooting*", 248
visualization, 29
vocalizing, 145

W

Grey, Walter W., 230
Webster's Third New International Dictionary, 13
Weinstein, Lew, 223
"*What Makes A Champion Shooter*", 250
Wigger, Lones W., Jr. (LTC USA), 98, 99, 250

Wilson, Stuart K., 227
wind patterns, 32
windage, 181
wobble area, 117, 210, 213, 225
"*Women's World*", 250
Wood, Jan, 250
Writer, Jack, 10, 155, 156, 157

X

"*XXI Olympic Games...Team Manager's Report*", 239

Y

YMCA, 175
You Must Relax, 229

CHALLENGE

When you acknowledge the wish–dream of someday representing your country in the Olympics of tomorrow, you need a way to meet that challenge.

Mental Training is a way. *Mental Training* provides you a framework to meet the goals you set for yourself in striving for your wish–dream of tomorrow's Olympics.

You have the challenge of becoming the *now generation!* With *Mental Training,* you have a program which provides you with the tools to win tomorrow's Olympics, which are the birthright of your generation. Only you, of the *now generation,* can decide whether to allow the older generations to step up to receive the Gold Medals cast for your generation.

> The torch running
> passing to you,
> generation of now.
> Will it fire your pride?
> Will it be reflecting
> off medals golden
> in tomorrow's
> Olympiad?
>
> — Bob Hickey